GW01458829

THE DISPERSAL AND SOCIAL EXCLUSION OF ASYLUM SEEKERS

Between liminality and belonging

Patricia Hynes

First published in Great Britain in 2011 by

The Policy Press
University of Bristol
Fourth Floor
Beacon House
Queen's Road
Bristol BS8 1QU
UK

t: +44 (0)117 331 4054
f: +44 (0)117 331 4093
tpp-info@bristol.ac.uk
www.policypress.co.uk

North American office:
The Policy Press
c/o International Specialized Books Services
920 NE 58th Avenue, Suite 300
Portland, OR 97213-3786, USA
t: +1 503 287 3093
f: +1 503 280 8832
info@isbs.com

British Library Cataloguing in Publication Data
A catalogue record for this book is available from the British Library.

Library of Congress Cataloging-in-Publication Data
A catalog record for this book has been requested.

ISBN 978 1 84742 326 9 hardcover

Cover design by The Policy Press.
Front cover: image kindly supplied by wwwistock.com
Printed and bound in Great Britain by TJ International, Padstow.
The Policy Press uses environmentally responsible print partners.

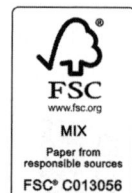

FSC
www.fsc.org
MIX
Paper from
responsible sources
FSC® C013056

To Robbie, my gorgeous boy

'We have our roots in our hands. We carry them
from place to place. Then we put them down and have to
pull them out again. You are waiting for life
for years. You have no rights to define what you do.'

(refugee, dispersal location, July 2003)

Contents

List of boxes, figures and tables

Boxes

Figures

Tables

List of abbreviations

AO	accommodation only
AP	accommodation provider
ARC	Application Registration Card
ASA	Asylum Support Adjudicator
CUKC	Citizens of the United Kingdom and Colonies
DL	Discretionary Leave
EA	emergency accommodation
EEC	European Economic Community
ELR	Exceptional Leave to Remain
EMCASS	East Midlands Consortium for Asylum Seeker Support
ERF	European Refugee Fund
ESOL	English for speakers of other languages
ESRC	Economic and Social Research Council
EU	European Union
GP	general practitioner
HP	Humanitarian Protection
IAP	inter-agency partnership
IC	induction centre
ICAR	Information Centre about Asylum and Refugees
ICT	Inter-Agency Coordination Team
ILR	Indefinite Leave to Remain
ILPA	Immigration Law Practitioners' Association
IND	Immigration and Nationality Directorate
IPPR	Institute for Public Policy Research
JWG	Joint Working Group for Refugees from Chile
LGA	Local Government Association
LLR	Limited Leave to Remain
MUD	moral underclass discourse
NAM	New Asylum Model
NAO	National Audit Office
NASS	National Asylum Support Service
NGO	non-governmental organisation
NHS	National Health Service
NRU	Neighbourhood Renewal Unit
ODPM	Office of the Deputy Prime Minister
PAP	private accommodation provider
PAT	Policy Action Team
PSE	Poverty and Social Exclusion Survey
RANS	Restricted Access to NASS Support
RCO	refugee community organisation
RED	redistributionist discourse

RHA	Refugee Housing Association
RSD	refugee status determination
RSL	registered social landlord
RSP	refugee service provider
SAL	Standard Acknowledgement Letter
SEU	Social Exclusion Unit
SID	social integrationist discourse
SO	subsistence only
SUNRISE	Strategic Upgrade of National Refugee Integration Services
SWARF	South West Asylum and Refugee Forum
UK	United Kingdom
UKBA	UK Border Agency
UNHCR	United Nations High Commissioner for Refugees
UNRWA	United Nations Relief and Works Agency
US	United States

Glossary

1951 Refugee Convention	1951 United Nations Convention Relating to the Status of Refugees
AO support	Accepting accommodation-only support means that the asylum seeker is expected to be able to support themselves using their own savings
Application Registration Card	A credit card sized card that proves the identity of the asylum seeker. Details on the card include name, date of birth, work permit status, nationality, fingerprint, Home Office reference number and support entitlements
Asylum seeker	A person who has left their country and has applied for asylum and is awaiting refugee status determination
Asylum Support Adjudicator	Considers appeals by asylum seekers against refusal or termination of support
Dispersal	Compulsory dispersal of asylum seekers. Commenced April 2000
Failed asylum seeker	Term used by the Home Office to describe an asylum seeker who has been refused status
Gender-related persecution	Refers to the experiences of women who are persecuted because they are women
Gender-specific form of harm	Refers to gender-specific forms of abuse such as sexual violence, 'honour' crimes and female genital mutilation
Group dispersal scheme	Dispersal of a group of asylum seekers
Hard cases	Term used by the Home Office to describe section 4 of the Asylum and Immigration (Treatment of Claimants, etc.) Act 2004
Inter-Agency Coordination Team	Team in the Refugee Council that administered the inter-agency partnership (IAP) and liaised between IAP and NASS
Inter-agency partnership	Of six refugee agencies (Migrant Helpline, Refugee Action, Refugee Arrivals Project, Refugee Council, Scottish Refugee Council and Welsh Refugee Council)
Immigration and Nationality Directorate	The part of the Home Office that dealt with immigration, nationality and asylum issues (now the UK Border Agency)
Informal dispersal	Term often used by practitioners to describe the informal arrangements between local authorities in London and local authorities around the country where asylum seekers were dispersed prior to the commencement of the system of compulsory dispersal

Interim Support Scheme	Support provided by local authorities because of their duty of care under the National Assistance Act 1948. Introduced on 6 December 1999 and initially expected to continue for two years but continued until 5 April 2004
Refugee	A person who has been recognised as a refugee as defined by the 1951 Refugee Convention
Refugee status	The award of 'refugee' status following refugee status determination
Restricted Access to NASS Support (RANS)	Term used by NASS in official documents to describe Section 55 of the Nationality, Immigration and Asylum Act 2002
Section 55	Section 55 of the Nationality, Immigration and Asylum Act 2002. 'In-country' applicants ineligible for any form of NASS support unless a claim is made 'as soon as reasonably practicable'. Commenced 8 January 2003. Some exemptions
Self-write dispersal scheme	Dispersal of individual asylum seeker
SO support	Accepting subsistence-only support means that the asylum seeker is not expected to live in designated accommodation or undergo dispersal

Acknowledgements

First, my appreciation goes to the Economic and Social Research Council (ESRC) for funding the initial research and to the NSPCC for allowing me the time to write it. Without the assistance and help of many people, this book would not have been possible, and noteworthy thanks go to Rosemary Sales and Karen Duke at Middlesex University who supported my initial study and to Vaughan Robinson for his extremely useful comments. Since then, my colleagues at the National Society for the Prevention of Cruelty to Children (NSPCC) have been a continuous support and source of encouragement so thanks go to Jane Ellis, Alison Jobe, Susana Corral, Debbie Allnock, Pam Miller and Lorraine Radford. I would also like to thank Alison Harvey from the Immigration Law Practitioners' Association and Nadine Finch from the Garden Court Chambers for their invaluable training and insights into immigration and asylum law. Special thanks also go to Hannah Lewis and Fraser Murray for their invaluable comments on this book and encouragement throughout and to Alessio D'Angelo for his GIS expertise.

Particular thanks go to both Silvie Bovarnick from the NSPCC and Jenny Pearce at the University of Bedfordshire who have been an incredible and continuous source of inspiration and support throughout the work for this book.

Although they must remain nameless, my thanks also go to the staff of refugee service providers in London and the three dispersal locations where this research was conducted for their suggestions, cooperation and agreement to take part in interviews and focus groups during their busy working schedules. Also, my thanks go to my interviewees at the Home Office, the one and only private accommodation provider willing to speak to me and the other representatives of regional consortia, local authorities, registered social landlords, solicitors, doctors and refugee community organisations. Special thanks go to two interviewees, Maria and Mujgan, for the most interesting and challenging interviews conducted for this study.

I will always be grateful to the staff at RWA, particularly Feride Baycan who challenged my thinking about refugees and asylum seekers, provided me with new perspectives about gender relations and also provided me with valuable contacts. The experience of putting together the *Refugee Women's News* will never be forgotten and I thank RWA for the friendships that I would otherwise not have made.

There are many other people who have, over the years, influenced my thinking about refugees. These include Bel Angeles, Georgia Dona, Barbara Harrell-Bond, Wolfgang Herdt, Liz Hilton, Eve Lester, Sean Loughna, Lynn Lynn, Mustafa Ongan, Jackie Pollack, Ashley South, Effie Voutira and many others who must remain anonymous. I am especially grateful for the time spent with refugees and asylum seekers who imparted their experiences to me and allowed me into their homes.

The biggest thanks go to my son, Robbie, for keeping me going and allowing me just enough sleep and energy to be able to complete the book. Thanks go too to Mark Powell for being there for me when it mattered most.

Preface

My interest in the subject of this book – the social exclusion of refugees and asylum seekers – has developed over many years. During the 1990s, working as a practitioner within refugee camps in South East Asia, I became aware of how Burmese, Khmer, Laotian and Vietnamese refugees were subjected to policies by host governments that did not match with their experiences or meet their needs. I saw firsthand how the so-called 'humane deterrence' policies that emerged during the Comprehensive Plan of Action for Indo-Chinese refugees involved making Vietnamese refugees move their personal belongings from their temporary accommodation to different accommodation every few weeks. These policies also prescribed how hilltribe refugees from Laos were contained within camps over decades, pending some form of 'durable solution'; how Khmer refugees lived in insecure camps close to the border, one of which gained the honour of housing the largest population in South East Asia with no electricity; and how Burmese refugees were controlled at the mercy of border guards who oversaw whole camps being relocated at short notice, maintained strict control and sometimes forcibly repatriated populations of these camps to Burma into the hands of one of the cruellest military regimes and abusers of human rights the contemporary world knows. Thus, after escaping persecution in countries of origin, human rights abuses against refugees continued to occur over long periods of time.

Returning to the United Kingdom (UK) from the Thailand–Burma border in 2000, I found that the asylum system was itself in flux, with a new Asylum and Immigration Act that set up a system wherein asylum seekers were dispersed across the country. Asylum seekers fleeing persecution were also subject to a raft of other policy mechanisms designed to deter their entry, including deportation, detention and destitution. Dispersal, pending the outcome of a refugee status determination process, was not receiving the same attention from refugee advocates as the more urgent and pressing needs of campaigning against deportations, getting adults and children out of detention centres or supporting people who had not been granted any legal status to remain in the UK. At the same time, media reports of fatalities, hostility and racism were emanating rapidly from dispersal cities. Asylum seekers were being moved around the country while waiting for decisions that would affect the rest of their lives. Some investigation was necessary.

The bulk of this book is based on a study funded by the ESRC on the dispersal of asylum seekers in England. This financial support is gratefully acknowledged, without which this book would never have been written.

This research into contemporary dispersal was designed reflexively, incorporating what has come to be known as 'user' involvement, in an attempt, in the words of one of my interviewees, 'not to miss the point'. Fully aware that my background and experiences working with refugees in camps overseas and within the UK informed my methodological choices and arguments made herein, this book is overtly qualitative and based on the voices and beautiful contradictions inherent in any human, refugee or not.

Research for the book necessarily involved a methodology capable of conveying complexity. This led to a multi-method approach being adopted so that a comprehensive and multidimensional account of dispersal could be produced. Prior to fieldwork, a period of overt ethnography through employment with a refugee community organisation (RCO) highlighted a tense relationship between state structures of control against the capacity, agency and resilience of individuals within the system. Subsequent interviews and focus groups with asylum seekers, refugees, voluntary and statutory agency staff were conducted in three lesser publicised dispersal locations as well as in London. An emphasis on conducting the research ethically, reflexively and empathetically allowed for the principle of 'avoiding harm' – an essential component of any research strategy – to be interpreted more structurally beyond the immediate circumstances of individual asylum seekers. This meant that the dignity of individuals became a consideration, and trust, between researcher and researched, was taken seriously. The heterogeneity of interviewees was also an essential consideration throughout. Access to participants was through multiple and alternative gatekeepers, often in contexts where asylum seekers were actively rebuilding their lives and/ or voluntarily educating themselves. Attempts to balance the gender ratio of participants were continuous and ultimately led to a 50:50 split of refugees and asylum seekers in these locations. Statistics and maps of multiple deprivation and dispersal are also provided for contextual purposes.

Overall, this book seeks to understand how asylum seekers experience the dispersal system and processes of social exclusion inherent in the system. Linking the global social exclusion of refugees to the circumstances of asylum seekers in the UK, it argues that asylum policies devised under an overarching framework of deterrence increases the sense of liminality – or limbo – and mistrust experienced by asylum seekers. While the two concepts of liminality and mistrust have previously been used to describe refugees living in refugee camps in their regions of origin, it quickly became clear that the policy of dispersal also placed people within liminal spaces and deepened mistrust of asylum seekers as a group through their increased visibility. These practices are now deeply entrenched in asylum policies in traditional resettlement countries, including the UK. This book therefore seeks to provide empirical material to challenge such negative assumptions inherent in asylum policies, exploring ways in which asylum seekers are socially excluded as a result of the dispersal and asylum systems and illustrate how asylum seekers resist policy-imposed liminality and create their own sense of 'belonging' in the absence of official recognition.

Patricia Hynes
October 2010

ONE

Social exclusion and refugees

Introduction

Refugees flee persecution to avoid death or torture and represent a small proportion of the total number of migrants in the world. Most flee into neighbouring countries where they may live in makeshift camps for several decades at a time, rarely commanding the attention of the international media. Alternatively, some attempt often arduous journeys in search of asylum in traditional resettlement recipient countries of North America, Europe and Australia.

Proportionately, the number of refugees reaching these countries is low. Asylum policies from these countries continue to emphasise containment in regions of origin and by drawing up legislation, regulations and policies to exclude new arrivals, the definition of who qualifies as a refugee has constricted over time. Over 70% of the world's refugees are therefore hosted in developing countries (Buscher et al, 2005). Of the 9.6 million refugees known to the United Nations High Commissioner for Refugees (UNHCR)[1] in 2003, two thirds (6.2 million) were in 'protracted refugee situations'[2] in 38 locations around the world – 22 of which were in sub-Saharan Africa (2.3 million). Most refugees, therefore, never leave their regions of origin and this lack of responsibility sharing for refugees undoubtedly contributes to the arrival of asylum seekers from across the world into the United Kingdom (UK).

In the same year in the UK, of those applying for asylum, only around 6% were granted refugee status at the initial decision stage (Lewis, M., 2005). Numerically, therefore, the numbers of refugees who reach the UK are insignificant in global terms. Policy and media attention on asylum seekers, however, invariably portrays a contrary picture and people seeking asylum currently encounter a whole range of legislative measures and policy mechanisms designed within an overarching policy framework of deterrence. In recent years, these measures have included detention, deportation (now known as 'administrative removal'), destitution and compulsory dispersal to urban centres outside London and the South East of England.

---

[1] UNHCR figures do not include Palestinians as they are covered by a separate mandated agency, the United Nations Relief and Works Agency (UNRWA).
[2] The UNHCR definition of a protracted refugee situation is based on the criteria of a refugee population of 25,000 or more persons who have been in exile for five or more years.

The bulk of this book is about one of these policy mechanisms – the compulsory dispersal of asylum seekers following the Immigration and Asylum Act 1999. Many commentators have suggested that dispersal in the UK is voluntary because asylum seekers can opt out of obtaining accommodation by being supported by family and friends (see, for example, Boswell, 2003). However, if an asylum seeker is destitute and wishes to obtain accommodation, dispersal is the only means of obtaining accommodation. If an asylum seeker is destitute and does not have family and friends to support and accommodate them, dispersal on a no–choice basis is their only option. In this book, this limited or complete lack of choice is denoted by calling the contemporary dispersal system compulsory, particularly as asylum seekers interviewed did not themselves view the system as voluntary (see also Lewis, 2010). The main focus throughout the book is on formal and informal social exclusion of asylum seekers during dispersal and the impact this policy has on the ability of individuals to access services, maintain or establish social networks and feel a sense of 'belonging', which, in UK policy terms, is often referred to as 'integration' or 'social inclusion'.

The UK is not alone in utilising dispersal as a policy mechanism. Several other European countries, including Sweden and Germany, have had forms of dispersal for several years. In Sweden, dispersal of refugees began in 1985 and developed into a 'Sweden–wide strategy' of compulsory dispersal a few years later (Hammar, 1993, p 110). In Germany, a system for 'inter-Lander burden-sharing' began in 1974 (Boswell, 2001, p 5), with legislation in 1982 containing measures to 'lower the social conditions' of asylum seekers, which were, as argued by Boswell (2001, p 7), as much about 'deterrence and control' as they were about spreading costs.

Asylum seekers in the UK inhabit a state of ambiguity in regard to their status. Despite being legally in the UK, they are very quickly placed in contexts wherein proving their legality takes a dominant role in their lives and within the refugee status determination process. Practitioners involved in the day-to-day lives of refugees often refer to people being 'in limbo', something that has been termed by anthropologists as 'liminality'. Liminality is considered a particular state experienced by people as they pass over the threshold of one phase of their life to another. This has been applied to refugees who occupy a 'liminal' space in refugee camps situated in developing countries. It is the state of being between statuses, be these fixed cultural classifications or more formalised legal statuses (Kunz, 1973; Bousquet, 1987; Malkki, 1995b; Turton, 2004). As Lewis (2007) has suggested:

> The condition of being an asylum seeker legally denotes limbo status: someone who has recently left 'there', but who is not yet allowed to be fully 'here', betwixt and between (Turner, 1969). In the prolonged ritual process of claiming asylum, the liminal period is legally finalized if refugee status (or another form of protection) is granted.

This state of being 'betwixt and between' (Turner, 1967, quoted in Malkki, 1995b, p 7) – temporarily a marginalised 'outsider' – is used in this book to bridge the existing literature on forced migration and social exclusion.

Liminality can no longer only be used to describe refugees living in camps in their regions of origin. It is now an increasingly important concept in understanding how policy on asylum is made in the traditional resettlement countries. An historical analysis of past dispersal of refugees and immigration and asylum legislation within the UK illustrates this. Linked to this is the issue of trust, which is central to any study on refugees (Daniel and Knudsen, 1995; Voutira and Harrell-Bond, 1995; Colson, 2003; Hynes, 2003a). Trust is also a key element in debates around 'social capital', 'social cohesion', 'community cohesion', 'social networks' and 'social exclusion' (Marx, 1990; Putnam, 1993; Cantle, 2001; Lupton and Power, 2002; Griffiths et al, 2005; Korac, 2005; Sen, 2006; Zetter et al, 2006; Beirens et al, 2007).

It is suggested herein that the current environment within which asylum policy is made is based on the flawed assumption that asylum seekers are a group to be mistrusted, disbelieved and therefore deterred from arriving. It is also suggested that this assumption runs directly counter to other policy initiatives that seek to promote 'social cohesion', 'social inclusion', community engagement and initiatives to combat trafficking, forced marriage and 'honour'-based violence.

This chapter will continue by outlining what is meant by the social exclusion of refugees – globally, in terms of Europe's asylum policies, and domestically. Asylum and immigration legislation as well as past instances of refugees fleeing persecution over the past century are explored. Continuities and differences with past cases of dispersal are examined to show how the creation of a qualitatively new environment for people seeking asylum in the UK has occurred since the mid-1990s.

The policy context and social exclusion

Social exclusion and refugees: a regional and global issue

Social exclusion as it relates specifically to refugees has been examined at a global level (Richmond, 2002) but there is a paucity of literature on the concept specifically in relation to refugees or asylum seekers in the UK.

Usage of the term 'social exclusion' seems to have originated in France where it referred to those who were excluded by the state from formal social protection in the 1970s (Burchardt et al, 2002b; Pierson, 2002). '*Les exclus*' (the excluded) included disabled people, lone parents, the uninsured unemployed and, particularly, young adults (Burchardt et al, 2002a). Other European countries picked up on the concern with unemployment and ultimately established the European Observatory on social exclusion, adopting 'social inclusion' resolutions that now appear at European Union (EU) level (Burchardt et al, 2002a). The originating concept at regional level did not include refugees, asylum seekers or migrants in mind although issues about their 'inclusion' do now appear. The term cannot be used uncritically. As Richmond (2002, p 43) suggests, the usual definition of social exclusion does not recognise that countries such as the UK, or regions such as Europe, are themselves an 'affluent part of a world system'.

The shorthand term 'Fortress Europe' emerged during the 1990s to describe how the adoption of common EU standards and policy harmonisation would exclude asylum seekers and legitimise a 'lowest common denominator' approach to standards of protection for refugees (Geddes, 2000; Refugee Council, 2004a). Member states of the EU agreed to draw up minimum standards to reduce the disparities on procedures granting refugee status. The establishment of a common European asylum system is ongoing with a Qualification Directive,[3] which agreed a common interpretation of the 1951 United Nations Convention Relating to the Status of Refugees (hereafter the '1951 Refugee Convention'). The other main instrument is the Reception Directive,[4] which sets out conditions to support asylum seekers. The objective is to reach a common European asylum system by 2010. Considered by many to be an exercise in lowering protection standards across the EU, the very exercise of harmonisation implicitly excludes non-EU agendas.

The initial focus of EU migration policy was controls on entry, particularly for asylum seekers (Sales, 2007). Freedom of movement and the abolition of internal borders occurred simultaneously with a strengthening of the EU's external borders and 'Fortress Europe' described the array of controls put in place to exclude people seeking asylum from non-EU countries. Policy developments originating in the Schengen Group, in which ministers from major EU states meet to develop policies on border control and security, have been incorporated into EU law (Hynes and Sales, 2010).

Other 'deterrent' measures adopted over the past few decades have included an increase in detention of asylum seekers, the restriction of social assistance and restricted access to employment as well as restrictions on family reunification (UNHCR, 2000, p 162). Harmonisation of such policies essentially formalises social exclusion that has occurred within individual states.

At a global level, Castles and Loughna (2004, p 182) have argued that globalisation is a process of differential inclusion and exclusion with different levels of income and human rights being obvious causes for migration. For refugees – or forced migrants – the process of becoming a refugee is itself a result of political processes that involve restructuring the social order of nation states, meaning that particular groups will be excluded, often forcibly (Zolberg, 1983; Zolberg et al, 1989). This exclusion of particular groups, or 'persecution', is a fundamental aspect of being a refugee according to the 1951 Refugee Convention, which provides the international legal definition of a refugee as someone who:

---

[3] EU Council Directive 2004/83/EC.
[4] EU Council Directive 2003/9/EC.

... owing to a well-founded fear of being persecuted for reasons of race, religion, nationality, membership of a particular social group or political opinion, is outside the country of his nationality and is unable or, owing to such fear, is unwilling to avail himself of the protection of that country; or who, not having a nationality and being outside the country of his former habitual residence ... is unable or, owing to such fear, is unwilling to return to it.

This definition was made universally applicable following the 1967 Bellagio Protocol Relating to the Status of Refugees (the '1967 Bellagio Protocol'), which removed all geographical and temporal limits of the 1951 Refugee Convention. Refugees falling within this definition benefit from certain rights – in particular the principle of *non-refoulement*, which prescribes that refugees cannot be returned to a country where they are likely to face persecution or torture (Goodwin-Gill, 1996). Causes of persecution relate closely to civil and political human rights violations in the countries of origin of refugees and, to a lesser extent, social and economic human rights violations.

Connections and continuing links between countries of origin and asylum, covered in the literature on transnationalism,[5] create 'multiple affiliations which question the dominance of the nation-state as the focus of social belonging' (Castles, 2003, p 20). Exclusion from citizenship in the country of origin leads to forced migration and once a refugee has faced this exclusion, the journey to a country of asylum is necessarily often based on finding some form of 'belonging', or space to form multiple affiliations, elsewhere. For refugees, social exclusion often translates into political powerlessness and, subsequently, a lack of citizenship or statelessness. The route to some form of 'belonging' is therefore fraught and being contained within refugee camps, often in protracted situations, is the end result for most refugees in the world today. Beyond this, migration may well be 'one of the unexpected and unplanned ways in which the South and North reconnect' (Castles, 2004, p 212), even if policy and legislative barriers are constructed to deny these connections. Historical legacies of empire, technologies that connect the 'South' to the 'North' and social networks that connect people across the globe are all aspects requiring attention if social exclusion as it relates to refugees or asylum seekers is to be understood.

Social exclusion and asylum seekers: a UK issue

Social exclusion includes both formal exclusion from certain rights and informal exclusionary practices as a result of, for example, the structure of service provision or discrimination on the part of service providers. It has been defined as when individuals or groups suffer multiple types of disadvantage in various social sectors

---

[5] 'Transnationalism' refers to multiple ties and interactions linking people or institutions across the borders of nation states (Vertovec, 1999).

such as education, employment, housing and health (Castles, 2002, p 18). Castles (2002, p 18) also provides a definition of 'cumulative exclusion' for those people who are largely outside mainstream economic, social and political relations, and who lack the ability to participate, which is crucial to full citizenship. Levitas (2000, p 358) suggests that the socially excluded are understood to be a group 'outside mainstream society', sometimes being considered to be 'outside society' itself.

In the UK, the term 'social exclusion' became established in policy discussions during the 1990s (Anderson and Sim, 2000). It is considered to be a problematic and contested concept that has different meanings according to different ideologies (Levitas, 1998; Anderson, 2000; Burchardt et al, 2002b). The shift from a focus on poverty to social exclusion and the lack of emphasis on inequality as the dominant structural dynamic in society have each been subject to debate (Levitas, 2000). Levitas (2000) identified three discourses that use the idea in different ways. First, there is a redistributionist discourse (RED), which emphasises poverty as a prime cause of social exclusion. Under this framework, the way in which poverty inhibits social participation and excludes people from ordinary living patterns (Townsend, 1979, quoted in Levitas, 2000, p 359) is highlighted. Social exclusion in the RED framework is complex, dynamic, multidimensional and accepts that discrimination and exclusionary practices cause poverty (Levitas, 2000, p 359). Second, there is a moral underclass discourse (MUD), which presents the socially excluded as culturally distinct, focuses on the behaviour of the individual and is concerned with the issue of 'dependency'. Responsibility for the 'underclass' is placed on the individuals themselves and their perceived antisocial behaviour and unwillingness to seek employment (Burchardt et al, 2002b). Under MUD, there is a focus on the consequences of social exclusion for social order and emphasis on particular groups. Third, there is a social integrationist discourse (SID), which emphasises paid employment as the main way in which integration into society is achieved (Levitas, 1998, pp 2, 7-28). The socially excluded are the 'workless' or those at risk of this (Levitas, 2000, p 359). A central tenet of New Labour's thinking on social exclusion relates to getting people into paid employment as this is seen as a vital link to mainstream society (Sales, 2002).

For dispersed asylum seekers, RED provides a broader concept than poverty and allows for investigation of processes rather than static measurements as well as capturing the multidimensional character of social disadvantage. Crucially, it also allows for discrimination and exclusionary practices that cause poverty and hardship to be incorporated into the analysis. Traces of MUD are evident in official discourse about asylum seekers with the threat of asylum seekers also emphasised in sections of the media. The 'myth of dependency' in forced migration studies has long since been debunked in the literature describing refugee camps (Waldron, 1987). As asylum seekers are excluded from paid employment until a less temporary status is granted, they are effectively excluded from any analysis under the SID framework.

After New Labour took power in 1997, social exclusion became a central concept with the formation of the Social Exclusion Unit (SEU),[6] which defined it as occurring when 'people or places suffer from a series of problems such as unemployment, discrimination, poor skills, low incomes, poor housing, high crime, ill health and family breakdown'.[7]

Burchardt (2004, p 219) argues that the SEU's approach of targeting specific groups – young people,[8] rough sleepers and ex-prisoners – had the 'drawback' of the 'inevitable omission' of other vulnerable groups. This emphasis on particular groups and the 'rhetoric' surrounding the launch of the SEU was rooted in the MUD framework (Levitas, 2000, p 360). Levitas (2000, p 380) also argues that social exclusion for the SEU that revolved around specific groups had three disadvantages – a danger of stigmatising the already 'excluded' groups; not looking at the reasons why these groups experience social exclusion in the first instance; and the numbers of those socially excluded according to the SEU focus being much lower than those affected by poverty.

The link between social exclusion and multiple deprivation is difficult to separate analytically with the two terms used interchangeably in the literature and no agreed set of indicators to describe social exclusion (Levitas, 2000, p 365; Zetter et al, 2003). The SEU worked with the-then Neighbourhood Renewal Unit (NRU) (now Communities and Local Government) in order to tackle deprivation and commissioned the Indices of Deprivation 2000 and 2004 in order to measure deprivation for each ward and local authority district in England. These indices combined indicators from a range of domains such as income, employment, educational attainment and housing into a single deprivation score.[9] Funding for the 88 most deprived local authority districts identified by the SEU in 2001 was managed by the NRU, which was set up to ensure that the neighbourhood renewal agenda was implemented effectively.

Lupton and Power (2002, p 136) also suggest that the negative acquired characteristics of deprived areas are associated with a process of diminishing social capital because of smaller social networks and mistrust. Mistrust of neighbours, service providers and authority figures is a broader feature of social exclusion beyond dispersal of asylum seekers and provides a link between social exclusion and forced migration.

Asylum seekers were not included in the work of the SEU as they come under the remit of the Home Office. Hills and Stewart (2004) have argued that the

---

[6] Initially based in the Cabinet Office and from May 2002 in the Office of the Deputy Prime Minister (ODPM). The SEU closed in 2006.

[7] www.socialexclusionunit.gov.uk/page.asp?id=213

[8] Pupils excluded from school or truanting; teenage parents; 16- to 18-year-olds not in education, employment or training; young runaways; and children in care.

[9] The Indices of Deprivation 2000 were constructed by the Index Team at Oxford University for the Department of the Environment, Transport and the Regions. The Indices of Deprivation 2000 were utilised as the boundaries complied with data provided with asylum statistics and census data.

UK remains an unequal society with a number of gaps in the strategy of the government. One of the gaps and omissions identified is government policies for asylum seekers of whom 'the risks of exclusion are acute' due to legislation and policy interventions that have actively increased social exclusion in relation to employment, income and housing (Burchardt, 2004, p 209). Invoking a RED framework, it is highlighted how the restrictive welfare entitlements of asylum seekers create social exclusion, with Burchardt (2004, p 226) commenting that even those eligible for support only receive 'one third of that required to be on the poverty line'[10] and asserting that asylum policy has not been an example of joined-up government.

The element of being outside mainstream society was examined by Robinson (2003a, p 108) who suggested that asylum seekers needed to be represented as 'outsiders' before the 'manipulation of their settlement patterns [could] be even considered'. This relates directly to the social exclusion of asylum seekers with no other group in the UK having their settlement patterns so tightly controlled or managed. When asylum seekers are perceived as a group 'outside' society this means that they become 'more visible as a group' (Sales, 2002, p 457), denying any strategies of invisibility they may wish to adopt as individuals.

For refugees, the process of social exclusion commences prior to arrival in the UK (Zolberg, 1983; Zolberg et al, 1989; Richmond, 2002; Castles and Loughna, 2004). Burchardt et al (2002b, p 8) suggest that for social exclusion generally, 'bygones are not bygones but represent the starting point for the present'. For refugees and asylum seekers, bygones and individual past histories inform the processes of social exclusion encountered in the UK and this consideration of 'bygones' is important. Understanding processes of exclusion and persecution already encountered in countries of origin and during the journey to the UK requires conceptualisation beyond Scholte's (2004, p 20) 'methodological territorialism' where social relations are investigated through the lens of territorial geography. Asylum seekers in the UK are often viewed in purely national terms, resonating with what Castles (2005) refers to as 'the tyranny of the national' in research and the danger of framing research and any subsequent attempt to influence policy on refugees in only national terms rather than as a transnational issue (see also Castles, 2004). Castles (2004) considers that this is a key explanation as to why migration policies in industrialised countries so often fail to achieve their aims.

The incorporation of refugees and asylum seekers into nationally or regionally based definitions is a challenge that requires extending and expanding the definition of social exclusion beyond geographical borders. This adoption of a transnational lens for inquiry means that the social exclusion of refugees and asylum seekers needs to be understood in a global context.

---

[10] While the UK has no official poverty line, Burchardt et al (2004) use 60% median equivalised income after housing costs for the whole population.

Although social exclusion in the UK was conceived without migrants in mind, it is a useful concept in its multidimensional form, in understanding the experiences of dispersed asylum seekers. It does, however, require encompassing not only their present circumstances but also 'bygones' and spatial expansion beyond the borders of the UK to explore and include the human rights situation and different levels of income in their countries of origin.

Legislative and historical framework

UK immigration and asylum legislation

Deterrence in the UK is not new and has been an overarching feature of immigration and asylum legislation and policy in the UK with the exclusion of migrants being legitimised by legislation for over one hundred years (Holmes, 1988, 1991; Cohen, 1994; Kushner and Knox, 1999; JCWI, 2002; Schuster, 2003; Solomos, 2003; Bloch and Schuster, 2005). What *is* new in recent years is the intensity of the debate surrounding the asylum 'crisis' and how policies to detain, deport, make destitute and disperse asylum seekers now occur simultaneously as components of an overall approach (Crisp, 2004b; Schuster, 2005b; Van Hear, 2005, pp 10-12).

Table 1.1 provides a non-comprehensive chronology of British legislation relating to immigration and asylum since 1905. As can be seen, the Commonwealth Immigration Acts in the 1960s began restrictions for citizens from Commonwealth countries, culminating, in 1971, with the Immigration Act 1971, which ended major, permanent, primary migration from Africa, the Indian subcontinent and the African-Caribbean. The Act came into force on 1 January 1973, the same day the UK joined the Common Market, so migration within Europe was opened at precisely the same time legislation excluded those from outside Europe (JCWI, 2002). This was an important day – claiming asylum necessarily became a significant form of migration, with the number of 'spontaneous' arrivals of asylum seekers to Europe beginning to rise in the 1970s (UNHCR, 2000, p 156) and becoming an increasingly significant issue in the 1980s (Duke, 1996).

The UK signed and adopted the 1951 Refugee Convention in 1954 but it was not until the Asylum and Immigration Appeals Act 1993 that this Convention was incorporated into domestic law.

Table 1.1: Annotated chronology of British legislation relating to immigration and asylum

Year	Legislation	Annotation
1905	Aliens Act	Set up a new system of immigration control and registration and placed responsibility for all matters of immigration and nationality with the Home Secretary who had the power to deport immigrants considered to be criminals or paupers; refugees excluded from restrictive measures
1914	Aliens' Registration Act	Mandatory registration of all aliens over the age of 16 with the police; main target of legislation was Germans in the UK
1919	Aliens Restriction Act	Renewed the requirement for aliens to register with the police
1947	Polish Resettlement Act	Created National Assistance Board in charge of the resettlement of Poles; allowed Poles to access employment and unemployment assistance
1948	Nationalities Act	Permitted entry of 'Citizens of the United Kingdom and Colonies' (CUKC) and the right to live in the UK
1962	Commonwealth Immigrants Act	Breaking of colonial ties began; restricted entry of Commonwealth citizens; distinction between 'Old' and 'New' Commonwealth
1968	Commonwealth Immigrants Act	Removed right of entry from those without 'patriality'; denied entry to East Africans settled in Kenya, Uganda and Tanganyika
1969	Immigration Appeals Act	Created Immigration Appeals Tribunal
1971	Immigration Act	Subjected citizens of the New Commonwealth to further restrictions; ended major, permanent, primary migration to the UK from Africa, the Indian subcontinent and the African-Caribbean; renewed the requirement for aliens to register with the police
1973	Immigration Rules	Eased entry for European Economic Community (EEC) nationals
1981	British Nationality Act	Restricted British citizenship further
1984	Immigration Procedure Rules	Provided for appeals to be heard by a single adjudicator
1985	Change to immigration procedure rules	Introduction of visas for Tamils
1987	Carriers' Liability Act	Airlines fined for carrying passengers without correct documentation
1988	Immigration Act	Repeal of right of men settled in UK pre 1973 to be joined by their families

Year	Legislation	Annotation
1993	Asylum and Immigration Appeals Act	Incorporated the 1951 Refugee Convention into domestic law; embedded the 'safe third country' removal process; restrictions on those who could apply for asylum in the UK
1996	Asylum and Immigration Act	Introduced sanctions on employers who gave work to unauthorised asylum seekers; imposed severe restrictions on welfare entitlements; reduced access to social services for certain asylum seekers
1999	Immigration and Asylum Act	Creation of the National Asylum Support Service (NASS) and implementation of dispersal for 'destitute' asylum seekers; introduced voucher system; imposed duties on registrars to report 'suspicious' marriages; strengthened powers of immigration officers; one-stop appeals; replaced Immigration (Carriers' Liability) Act 1987 and extended liability to the carriage of clandestine entrants in any vehicle, ship or aircraft
2002	Nationality, Immigration and Asylum Act	Withdrawal of 'in-country' support; plans for induction, accommodation, reporting and 'removal' (previously 'detention') centres; introduced Gateway Resettlement programme for quota refugees; introduced Application Registration Card (ARC) with photograph, details and fingerprint of individual; repealed provision for automatic bail hearings; extended statutory provision for voluntary assisted returns programme; required employers to ensure that employees are entitled to work. Criminalised those who arranged or facilitated trafficking into the UK for prostitution
2004	Asylum and Immigration (Treatment of Claimants, etc) Act	Arrival in the UK without a passport or valid identity document made a criminal offence; tightening of credibility boundaries; withdrawal of basic support for families if voluntary return to country of origin not undertaken; community activities for 'hard cases'; 'local connection' to local authority area required if housing required; withdrawal of backdating of benefits and replaced by integration loan; unification of the appeal system; 'safe third countries' list expanded; criminal offence not to cooperate with deportation procedures; electronic monitoring
2006	Immigration, Asylum and Nationality Act	Replaced the Asylum and Immigration Act 1996; ended granting Indefinite Leave to Remain (ILR) to recognised refugees; strengthened border controls; introduced an integration loan to replace integration grants for recognised refugees

Year	Legislation	Annotation
2007	UK Borders Act	Extended powers to the UK Border Agency (UKBA). Included provisions on powers of immigration officers; immigration offences; biometric identify cards; conditions on Limited Leave to Remain (LLR); exchange of information between UKBA and other agencies. Amended laws on trafficking to extend the extraterritorial reach so that acts outside the UK could be criminalised regardless of original nationality
2009	Borders, Citizenship and Immigration Act	Original intention was to simplify immigration law. Strengthened border controls; extended time to gain citizenship in the UK; full access to social housing and benefits reserved for citizens and permanent residents; concept of 'earned citizenship' introduced; integration of customs functions with the UKBA; new UKBA duty to ensure safeguarding and promotion of the welfare of children in immigration, asylum, nationality and customs functions

Sources: Kushner and Knox (1999), JCWI (2002), Bloch and Schuster (2005), Kerrigan (2005), Schuster (2005b), Migrants Rights Network updates (various dates). See also Moving Here at www. movinghere.org.uk/default.htm; Immigration Law Practitioners' Association information sheets at www.ilpa.org.uk

A new Bill to simplify immigration and asylum law is currently being drafted with the intention that all existing immigration laws since the 1971 Immigration Act will be replaced. A draft of the Bill was released in July 2008 for consultation, attracting criticism that rather than being a project of simplification, the Bill was a fundamental re-haul of the concepts and terminology of UK immigration and asylum law (Migrant Rights Network, December 2009). The major proposals in this Bill included the introduction of a single, streamlined power of 'expulsion' and limits on the grounds of appeal.

Contemporary deterrence of asylum seekers

Since the mid-1990s, the manifestation of the deterrence environment towards asylum seekers has been through Acts of Parliament in 1993, 1996, 1999, 2002, 2004, 2006, 2007 and 2009. This legislation has gradually eroded the rights of asylum seekers, leading to what Carter and El-Hassan (2003, pp 10-11) term 'institutionalised exclusion'. Detention, destitution, dispersal and deportation have been key 'normalised and essential' facets of this erosion of rights (Schuster and Bloch, 2005; also see Lewis et al, 2008, for an in-depth account of destitution in one region of the UK). Access to services such as housing has been restructured several times, with each restructuring incrementally excluding asylum seekers from formal rights and entitlements further.

The 1996 Asylum and Immigration Act introduced severe restrictions on welfare entitlements and placed a requirement on employers to check the immigration status of potential employees, introducing other internal immigration controls such as immigration checks at the point of accessing services and other benefits. This represented a 'major shift' from a 'culture of service' to a 'culture of suspicion' by service providers, benefits agencies, social services, employers and other agencies (JCWI et al, 1998, pp 1-4). It was at this time that the phrase a 'culture of disbelief' became shorthand to describe the relationship between the Home Office and refugees.

Until the mid-1990s, 'quota refugees' and 'spontaneous refugees', also called 'non-quota refugees', were the two distinct groups of refugees identified (Duke, 1996, p 2; Carey-Wood et al, 1995). The new social category of 'asylum seeker' from the mid-1990s was the summation of 20th-century legislation, with recent subcategories of 'deserving' or 'genuine' refugees versus 'undeserving', 'bogus' asylum seekers or 'economic migrants' (Sales, 2002) a continuation of a process of recasting the image of refugees. Zetter (2007, pp 174-81) has outlined how such bureaucratic 'fractioning' of the refugee label allows the management of 'new' migration. The New Asylum Model (NAM) introduced to deal with all applications for asylum made after April 2007 means that asylum seekers are segmented into seven different categories, each with their own assessment criteria, which predetermine the outcome of claims (Zetter, 2007), and the model speeds up the process officially referred to as 'administrative removal' but more commonly called deportation. As Squire (2009, pp 5-10) has suggested, the 'contemporary articulation of asylum as a "problem" or "threat"' is evident not only in the UK but also more widely across Europe.

Zetter et al (2003, p 91) has argued that the 1993 and 1996 Acts were formulated during 'peak' years of asylum applications, suggesting an essentially reactive approach to asylum applications with the legislation introduced at times when applications rates were comparatively low. The 1999 Act and the dispersal policy were also formulated at a time when the number of applications for asylum was rising.

Figure 1.1 illustrates how compulsory dispersal began when applications had already peaked in the second quarter of 2000 (Q2 2000) and remained relatively constant until the end of 2002. Thus, in numerical terms there was no reduction in the number of new arrivals, with numbers remaining relatively constant for some two years after its introduction. If any causal link between policy change and application figures can be made – and it is doubtful that this link can be made (see below) – it was section 55[11] of the subsequent 2002 Act that coincided

---

[11] The Nationality, Immigration and Asylum Act received royal assent on 7 November 2002. Section 55 of the Act means that, as from 8 January 2003, social support for 'in-country' applicants has been difficult to obtain. The Home Office refers to section 55 as Restricted Access to NASS Support (RANS). A sustained national campaign by the voluntary sector to repeal section 55 led first, on 17 December 2003, to 'as soon as reasonably practicable' being defined as 72 hours and, second, from June 2004, to the relaxation of this controversial policy.

Figure 1.1: Asylum applications, October 1997–December 2004

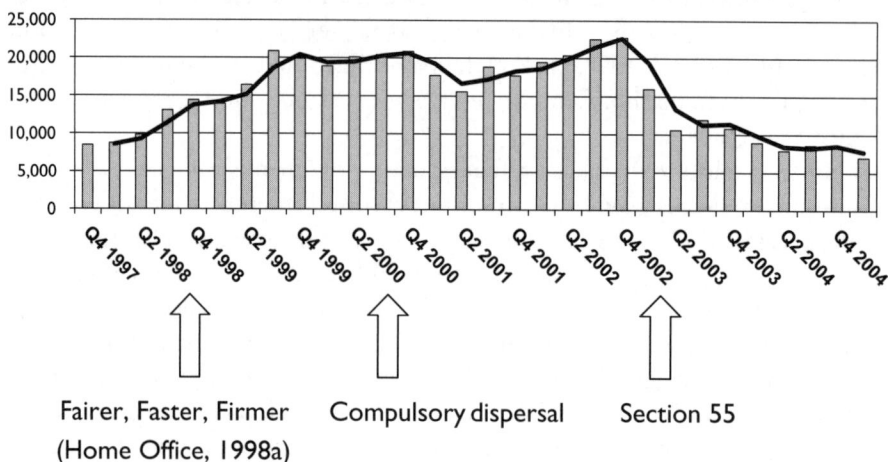

Source: Home Office asylum statistics (www.homeoffice.gov.uk/rds/immigration1sub.html)

with the numbers of asylum applications dropping during the first and second quarters of 2003 (Q2 2003).

The controversial nature of dispersal has since been surpassed – in the eyes of campaigning groups and sections of the media – by measures to deter and reduce the number of asylum seekers. These measures included denying permission to work, a concession that once withdrawn impacted on the social exclusion of asylum seekers.[12] The withdrawal of 'in-country' support for those who did not apply 'as soon as reasonably practicable' for financial support (section 55), proposals to take the children of 'destitute' failed asylum seekers into care if they do not 'voluntarily' return to their country of origin (section 9) and proposals to introduce compulsory voluntary work in return for support for people refused asylum (section 10) were successfully contested by the voluntary sector. These regulations were introduced while the voluntary sector was implementing dispersal on behalf of the government and could be seen as acting as 'decoy policies'[13] as campaigns from the voluntary sector focus on the most controversial aspects of new legislation, thus allowing other aspects to pass unchallenged. For example, the Home Office publication, *Controlling our Borders: Making Migration Work for Britain – Five Year Strategy for Asylum and Immigration*, provided an illustrated timeline of such 'reduction measures' (Home Office, 2005, p 18).

While there is a commonsense perception that there is a relationship between deterrence measures and numbers of new arrivals, there is little evidence that

---

[12] The Home Office withdrew permission to work from asylum seekers on 23 July 2002.
[13] Informal conversation with former Immigration and Nationality Directorate (IND) policy advisor, May 2005.

this is the case (Zetter et al, 2003; Schuster, 2005a, pp 163-5). The alternative argument, that generous social support acts as a 'pull' factor, is also unsupported by evidence. The assertion of direct links between asylum policy and its impact is something that requires extreme caution as causal links are difficult to establish (Zetter et al, 2003; Middleton, 2005). Many authors have also shown that choice of destination countries is dependent on other factors such as social networks (see, for example, Koser and Pinkerton, 2002).

The model of 'reduction measures' provided in the Home Office timeline showed a link between policy and impact, with the most dramatic drop being due to Restricted Access to NASS Support (RANS) – commonly known as section 55 from January 2003. The impact of section 55 has been documented by refugee agencies (Refugee Council, 2002d; Refugee Action, 2003; GLA, 2004) and, as one representative of a refugee network commented, 'A large number of asylum seekers who arrive in Liverpool are not being included in the figures because they miss a 72-hour deadline in which to register their claim' (Hookham, 2004). Thus, the number of registered claimants would not necessarily reflect the number of asylum seekers. While it is impossible to disaggregate the statistics accurately, any discussion on the period from January 2003 needs to consider 'reduction measures' in this context as well as indicators of conflict in countries of origin. Conflict in source countries and other contextual factors such as social networks, diaspora communities, colonial links, common language, historical legacy and geographical location each need to be factored in when considering the impact of policies (Castles et al, 2003, pp 28-32; Zetter et al, 2003, p 118; Middleton, 2005).

Both 9/11 in New York and 7/7 in London have placed asylum seekers firmly onto national security agendas and more control of asylum seekers is considered to be a 'commonsense' or pragmatic approach among policy makers. Gibney (2001, p 7) argued that the rise in numbers by the 1980s led to the democratisation of asylum policy in Western countries. It was argued that a shift from 'high politics (matters of national security)' to 'low politics (matters of day to day electoral politics, including employment, national identity and the welfare state)' were characteristics of this democratisation (Gibney, 2001, p 7). Gibney went on to argue that this shift meant that political elites believed that controlling asylum was key to electoral victory and that the 'roots of restrictive asylum policies' lay in this perception (Gibney, 2001, p 7). Since 9/11 and 7/7, matters of national security have meant that asylum has again become a matter for 'high politics' but has continued, it is suggested, to remain a permanent fixture of 'low politics'. Now the issue is simultaneously one of low and high politics and the issue of asylum has become more visible overall.

Past dispersal of refugees in the UK

There have been several dispersal programmes for refugees across the UK and the differing motivations and rationales for dispersal illustrate much about the national context into which refugees arrive.

Before 1967, when the Bellagio Protocol made the refugee definition international, dispersal of refugees in the UK included Belgian, Polish and Hungarian refugees. Approximately 250,000 Belgians arrived between 1914 and 1918; from the 1940s to the early 1950s, there were some 300,000 Polish displaced persons; and around 20,000 Hungarian refugees fleeing communism post-1956 (Kushner and Knox, 1999; Black, 2001; Robinson, 2003a, 2003b). The voluntary sector had a role in the implementation of each of these, with government funding matched with charitable donations from the public. The expectation for the Belgians was, ultimately, that most would repatriate as their migration was seen as temporary (Kushner and Knox, 1999; Black, 2001).

A key goal behind the Polish dispersal was employment (Robinson, 2003b), with the requirement for post-war labour meaning that schemes were put in place for European Volunteer Workers who were 'more "racially" desirable' than Afro-Caribbean workers (Kushner and Knox, 1999, p 218). This was combined with a parallel policy of encouraging the repatriation or onward migration of Polish 'displaced persons' and, in order to encourage repatriation, uncomfortable reception facilities were provided in 265 camps across the UK (Robinson, 2003a). The avoidance of so-called 'Polish ghettoes' to prevent a security threat was a Foreign Office rationale for dispersal (Kushner and Knox, 1999, p 228; Robinson, 2003a, p 109).

The Hungarians arrived during a time of labour shortages and when post-war housing shortages were less acute (Kushner and Knox, 1999, p 241). Their distribution across the UK was, therefore, led more by the availability of employment than accommodation. Barracks were used prior to relocation to hostels across the UK and permanent resettlement was based on assimilation.

Between 1967 and 1989,[14] Ugandan Asian, Chilean and Vietnamese 'quota refugees' were dispersed across the UK under agreed resettlement schemes. Some 29,000 Ugandan Asians expelled by Idi Amin in 1972 were voluntarily dispersed (Robinson, 1986; Marett, 1993; Robinson, 1993b; Kushner and Knox, 1999; Martin and Singh, 2002; Robinson, 2003b). Over half held British passports with rights of entry and abode (Kushner and Knox, 1999, p 269) and lacked any 'myth of return' (Robinson, 1986). In locations such as Leicester, where there was a growth of the National Front, the city council took out adverts in the Ugandan press discouraging refugees from settling in the city (Martin and Singh, 2002, p 11). Leicester gained a reputation as the 'most unwelcoming of all places' to these refugees (Marett, 1993, p 248). This was in marked contrast to the perception of Ugandan Asians in the city at the end of the century, when they were described as 'central' to revitalising the city and the rest of the Midlands, creating at least 30,000 jobs (Kushner and Knox, 1999, p 287).

---

[14] 1989 was the year of the fall of the Berlin Wall and considered by some theorists and refugee agencies to be the reason for the rise in 'spontaneous' arrivals of refugees to Europe (UNHCR, 2000, p 158).

The government relied on the voluntary sector to implement resettlement, distancing itself from the work through the Uganda Resettlement Board and military camps were again utilised to facilitate dispersal (Kushner and Knox, 1999; Robinson, 2003b). A dispersal policy was incorporated into refugee resettlement with 'red' areas where refugees were not sent due to high minority populations and 'green' areas with low minority populations where they could be sent (Kushner and Knox, 1999; Bloch and Schuster, 2005). These areas were chosen on the basis of the size of the pre-existing minority ethnic population in an attempt to 'avoid ghettoisation' (Robinson, 2003b). Finding work for refugees was no longer a main objective, with acquisition of mainstream housing being a key aim (Robinson, 2003b). This dispersal was voluntary and resulted in only 38% being housed in the designated 'green' areas (Kushner and Knox, 1999, p 275).

Between 1974 and 1979, approximately 3,000 Chilean 'quota refugees' arrived in the UK (Kay, 1987; Kushner and Knox, 1999; Robinson, 2003b). There was broad public support for this group and solidarity campaigns, leading one participant of this research to describe the perception of the Chileans as being "The last of the romantics ... because of the romance of revolution and change that people identified with then".[15]

This identification by trades union of socialist ideals and political views, plus the ability to have their previous employment experience recognised through accreditation schemes, assisted the process of resettlement for many Chileans.

Although not a formal programme of dispersal, availability of accommodation – based on the political biases of the local authorities involved – was the main rationale for the *de facto* distribution of Chileans across the country, with employment opportunities secondary (Kushner and Knox, 1999, p 300). Implemented by the Joint Working Group for Refugees from Chile (JWG), funded by the Home Office, this 'dispersal policy by default' (Robinson, 2003b, p 114) led to disempowerment (Kay, 1987, cited in Robinson 2003b), difficulties with language, isolation and inadequate provision of services for those who had experienced torture (Robinson, 2003b).

Media representation of the Vietnam war and the Vietnamese 'boat people' setting out on precarious journeys across the South China sea, plus the deterrence policies of South East Asian countries, ultimately led to a recognition that a large-scale resettlement programme was necessary to distribute the so-called 'burden' of Indo-Chinese refugees. These programmes were set up through processing and transit centres in the region of origin. Largely perceived as refugees fleeing communism, some 11,500 people of this diverse population – only 1.1% of all South East Asian refugees – arrived in the UK between 1979 and 1981 (Kushner and Knox, 1999, pp 307-12; Refugee Action, 1993, p 10). Cases of family reunification then occurred between 1983 and 1993 (Duke, 1996). These arrivals

---

[15] Interview with a female representative of a refugee community organisation (RCO), London, November 2002.

were through highly visible resettlement programmes (Jones, 1982; Hitchcox, 1987; Gold, 1992; Duke and Marshall, 1995; Joly, 1996; Robinson, 2003b).

Hale (1993) argued that this resettlement policy had four main principles. First, refugees were to be prevented from becoming dependent on external assistance and encouraged to enter into mainstream British life. Second, they were to be made job ready as soon as possible to regain independence. Third, they were to use existing welfare mechanisms. Fourth, they were to be dispersed throughout the country in clusters of four to 10 families. This fourth principle, and most common reason given in support of dispersal, was based on the 'need to avoid ghettoes' (Jones, 1982, p 40). A plan for clustering Vietnamese refugees fell apart during dispersal with the geography of resettlement being governed by the pattern of housing offers (Refugee Council, 1992; Tomlins et al, 2002). The voluntary sector was relied on heavily with their own 'zones of responsibility'[16] (Hitchcox, 1987, p 13) across the UK, with the Home Office again distancing itself from implementation. As Hitchcox (1987, p 5) argued, this role for the voluntary sector had disadvantages because agencies did not have control over allocation of funds, little influence over the policy and because they were partially funded by the government their function as pressure groups was constrained.

This ad-hoc policy was described in a 1985 report by Parliament's Select Committee on Refugee Resettlement and Immigration, which concluded that dispersal policies were 'almost universally regarded as mistaken' (quoted in Robinson, 1998, p 150) in that the refugees put their energies and efforts into 'secondary migration', that is, relocating to communities with family and ethnic linkages rather than to settling in the localities where they were dispersed. The report stated: 'It is hard to think of any problem facing the Vietnamese which would not have been less severe or difficult to resolve if the disastrous policy of dispersal had not been adopted' (House of Commons Affairs Select Committee, 1985), p xxii). As Jones (1982, p 41) suggested, the diversity of the population was a factor in this because refugee families were separated by ethnicity, class and religion and that it was unlikely that relationships would develop due only to close proximity to each other. Uncritical notions of 'community' support could not, therefore, be assumed.

Even though internationally there were disproportionately high numbers of recognised refugees arriving in less developed countries and low numbers seeking asylum in industrialised countries, no further dispersal programmes of 'quota refugees' were arranged until 1992 when Bosnian 'quota refugees' were offered temporary asylum in the UK (Robinson and Coleman, 2000; Robinson, 2003b).

Between 1992 and 1995, a further dispersal of 2,585 Bosnian 'quota refugees' occurred. Robinson (2003b) argued that the Bosnian resettlement programme

---

[16] The Refugee Council covered the South of England and South Wales. Ockenden Venture covered North Wales, the Northwest and the Midlands northwards. Refugee Action, which emerged out of the Save the Children Fund involvement, had operations in Scotland, Northern Ireland, the East and Northeast of England.

was far more successful than previous programmes for 'quota refugees' because it incorporated lessons learned from past failures and lessons from this programme could be considered in future policy. While the Home Office wanted resettlement to occur in local authority, housing association and private accommodation, the Refugee Council (2000b) urged that private sector housing was inappropriate for vulnerable persons. The Refugee Council refused to implement dispersal and forced the government to amend its policy so that 'clustering' took place (Robinson, 2003a, p 119). While no 'critical mass' of the number of refugees to each cluster area was agreed on, suggestions of 150 to 300 individuals were outlined in discussions. The voluntary organisations involved also stated that they were unwilling to become involved if no choice was given to the refugees over the resettlement destinations and housing, although choice was ultimately varied and largely driven by housing supply.

From 1999, approximately 24,000 Kosovan refugees were offered temporary protection in the UK. Considerable media coverage and the expectation that residence would be short term and temporary characterised this offer (Robinson, 2003b). Boswell (2001) suggests that the relative success of the approach of the Bosnia Project led to a more systematic dispersal system for the reception of refugees from Kosovo. Generous funding by the Home Office, active participation of local authorities (Boswell, 2001, p 10) as well as clustering 'led to more successful settlement' (Audit Commission, 2000a, p 16). Leicester was one of the first cities to accept Kosovan refugees arriving as a part of this evacuation programme and now hosts a 'substantial Kosovan Albanian refugee community'[17] (ICAR, 2003).

Nevertheless, the evidence base from past dispersals did not lead to shaping the contemporary policy of compulsory dispersal for asylum seekers. Critical reflection on past cases of dispersal was important because, as Black (2001, p 70) argues, 'work on the negative impacts of forced geographical dispersal of refugees in the United Kingdom in the late 1970s and 1980s helped to move UK policy away from dispersal for at least a decade. By the late 1990s, the failures of past dispersal policies were not 'fully mobilized in attempts to resist the new UK government policy of dispersal encapsulated in the National Asylum Support System (NASS)' (Black, 2001, p 70). Given that the idea of evidence-based policy has been 'in vogue' (Young, 2003) since 1997 when New Labour took power (Sanderson, 2002; Wyatt, 2002), this lack of critical reflection on past experiences of dispersal was surprising.

The creation of a qualitatively new environment for asylum seekers

There are several key differences between the past dispersal of refugees and contemporary dispersal of asylum seekers. While there are clearly some continuities with the past, the overtly hostile political environment directed towards asylum

---

[17] www.icar.org.uk/res/map/regions/eng_emid/leice/over.html

seekers in recent years has affected the policy response as well as the experiences of asylum seekers.

In the past, ad-hoc dispersal arrangements were implemented for 'quota refugees' who arrived *en masse*, following highly publicised emergency situations such as the Vietnamese 'boat people'. The arrival of these 'quota refugees', therefore, was often seen as an 'event' that occurred between particular dates and the number of arrivals was subject to negotiation by the government. These programmes involved recognised refugees, whose legal status was not in doubt, and access to mainstream financial support was a key principle. Following the 1999 Act, for the first time, all nationalities of what Duke and Carey-Wood referred to as 'non-quota refugees' (Carey-Wood et al, 1995; Duke, 1996, p 2), who did not hold refugee status or any temporary protection status, were dispersed to cities and large towns across the UK.

The countries of origin are now more diverse and, with exceptions[18] (Castles et al, 2003; see also Zetter et al, 2003, p 120), the arrival of these individuals or families has seldom been related by the media to any 'emergency' in countries of origin. The ad-hoc dispersal arrangements of the past explicitly recognised refugee situations as individual historical occurrences, each with their distinct character, and policies – misguided or otherwise – were created around this. Contemporary dispersal is based around a much more 'macro' or 'one-size-fits-all' approach that homogenises all nationalities into one category of 'asylum seeker'. This does not recognise ongoing debates about the root causes of refugee-generating processes (Zolberg, 1983; Zolberg et al, 1989; Castles, 2003, p 106) or the suggestion that restrictive measures are ultimately ineffectual in global terms (Castles and Loughna, 2004).

Asylum seekers are now separated from mainstream benefits support, provision of accommodation, employment and other entitlements that would promote 'inclusion'. Whereas previous dispersal programmes were not, with the exception of the Polish Resettlement Act 1947, backed by legislation, contemporary dispersal is firmly established in law. Again with the exception of the Polish dispersal, the UK government has distanced itself from the implementation of these policies by utilising the voluntary sector. The strong stance taken by the voluntary sector in influencing the Bosnian programme cluster policy, and in demanding choice over destination and housing, is of note. Although the voluntary sector has also implemented dispersal on behalf of the government in the past, its role in implementation of contemporary dispersal is on a contractual basis. This places the voluntary sector in the pressured frontline role of implementing negative and

---

[18] For example, a link has recently been made in the media between the human rights situation in Zimbabwe and anti-deportation campaigns. It is not always the case that media reports link the arrival of asylum seekers with reports about the country of origin. However, a report by the Institute for Public Policy Research did explicitly recognise the direct link between refugees and situations of conflict (Castles et al, 2003).

punitive legislation, regulations and policies that run counter to their historic role of advocates of refugee rights.

The policy introduced by the 1999 Act is an accommodation-led one and asylum seekers do not have any choice as to where or what type of accommodation they will be dispersed to. Whereas the political biases of local authorities influenced the de facto dispersal of Chileans (Kay, 1987), contemporary dispersal has been structured around regional consortia established in England, Wales, Scotland and Northern Ireland to organise support for dispersed asylum seekers. These were local-authority led, but involved 'partners' including refugee agencies in an Inter-Agency Partnership (IAP), registered social landlords (RSLs) and a limited number of refugee community organisations (RCOs). The role of these consortia was, however, strictly determined by central government policy and the 'key characteristic of these regional bodies is that they have "responsibility without ownership"' (Harrison, 2006). Local authorities are no longer required to provide 100% of necessary accommodation; there is now a substantial role for the private sector housing market. Contemporary dispersal enables a role for private bus companies to transport asylum seekers to dispersal areas and private accommodation providers and their subcontractors to accommodate them. The privatisation of services to asylum seekers and refugees is something that has been considered in the past to be insensitive to the needs of a vulnerable population.

The divergence of thinking on how dispersal locations were chosen could not be more clearly illustrated than by comparing the response to Ugandan Asian arrivals and present arrivals. In the space of just 30 years, areas considered 'red' (too many minority ethnic people) and 'green' (small numbers of minority ethnic people) for Ugandan Asian arrivals are now inversed with a focus on dispersal to areas with a pre-existing multicultural presence. Although contemporary dispersal is, in principle, to areas with a pre-existing multicultural presence, in practice, dispersal to monocultural cities such as Glasgow and Hull has also been an outcome. One of the aims of dispersal was to avoid racial tensions and, with this in mind, the pre-existence of multiethnic populations was initially considered optimum when dispersal was being designed.

The principles surrounding the Vietnamese dispersal were very much based around rapid assimilation. None of the first three principles identified by Hale (1993) of prevention from becoming dependent on external assistance, being made job ready as soon as possible and using existing welfare mechanisms would result in 'social exclusion' – it was only the fourth principle of dispersal of between four and 10 families that ultimately led to isolation and resulting secondary migration. Dispersal policies in the 1970s and 1980s for Ugandan Asians and the Vietnamese have resulted in sizeable secondary migration to cities with ethnically, class or religiously linked communities. Robinson and Hale (1989) charted the secondary migration of Vietnamese households within Britain and while there is evidence about 'secondary migration' in previous cases of dispersal (Robinson, 2003, p 154), the existing knowledge about 'secondary migration' in contemporary dispersal is fragmented. A new policy to maintain the 'local connection' of newly recognised refugees in dispersal areas is effectively a barrier to any 'secondary migration' (Lukes and Hynes, 2008).

Bloch and Schuster argue that dispersal is now one of the 'normalised essential instruments' of control along with deportation and detention of asylum seekers (Schuster, 2004; Bloch and Schuster, 2005, pp 491–512). Control is maintained through requirements for asylum seekers to report to 'reporting centres', which are a mix of police stations and UKBA offices, on a regular basis in dispersal locations. It is also a contractual obligation for accommodation providers to notify the authorities if an asylum seeker is absent from their allocated property.

Hitchcox (1987, p 6) argued in relation to the compulsory dispersal of Vietnamese refugees that changes in policy from employment-led to housing-led dispersal reflected the state of the British economy at the time, which 'moved from full employment in the 1950s, to nearly, four million unemployed in the 1980s' (1987, p 6). Whereas the resettlement of Hungarian refugees in the 1950s reflected the availability of employment, the Vietnamese dispersal in the 1980s reflected the availability of housing (1987, p 5). Contemporary dispersal that involves placing new arrivals in public or private accommodation does not reflect the British economy or the availability of employment – with the inverse a more accurate description. Contemporary dispersal is operating in a context wherein 'deregulation, market testing and privatisation has shrunk the state and reduced its tendency to intervene to ensure social justice' (Robinson, 2003a, p 22). Ironically, it is in this context that the creation of the dispersal system has increased the role of the state with social support now controlled separately for this population.

There has been a proliferation of agencies involved in contemporary dispersal. For 'quota refugees', needs have been met by statutory services in the same way as the general population. For contemporary asylum seekers accessing services, this involves identifying parallel private and public sector agencies, often signposted through refugee service providers.

It can be argued that the differences between past cases of dispersal and contemporary dispersal of asylum seekers outlined above combine to create a qualitatively different environment. It is also certainly the case that hostility towards asylum seekers has emerged over the past 15 years (Squire, 2009) and the plethora of policy mechanisms designed to deter asylum seekers is much greater now than in the past (Schuster, 2004; Bloch and Schuster, 2005). Contemporary compulsory dispersal also redistributes people in ways that deny choice of destination and type of accommodation, requiring people to either comply and adapt or resist systems imposed on them. This added dimension of lack of choice over basic needs such as housing and over where to live decreases the rights of asylum seekers.

Outline of the book

This chapter provided an outline of how social exclusion relates specifically to refugees at a global level and how it relates to dispersed asylum seekers. Set within an historical account of the previous dispersal of refugees, it has shown how the introduction of a centralised policy of dispersal has created a qualitatively different environment for asylum seekers.

In Chapter Two, key terms in the UK asylum debate and key concepts central to the arguments made throughout this book are explored, showing how the concepts of 'liminality' and 'trust' link existing literature on social exclusion and forced migration. These different concepts were chosen because they emerged from grounded data analysis (Glaser and Strauss, 1968). While 'social exclusion' was conceived without migrants in mind, it is suggested that it is a useful concept in understanding the experiences of asylum seekers in the UK. The suggestion throughout the rest of this book is that both liminality and (mis)trust provide essential lenses into understanding and conceptualising how asylum seekers interact with state agencies, including the now surpassed NASS system. It should be noted that while the administrators of dispersal are no longer called NASS, the dispersal system has not changed in any real sense and many practitioners involved in the system still refer to it as 'the NASS system'. Processes of social exclusion continue and analysis within this book therefore remains pertinent.

In Chapter Three, the official rationale, structure and implementation of compulsory dispersal are explored. Separating asylum seekers from the mainstream system of welfare provision has created a more visible group and entrenched the perception of asylum seekers as being somehow 'outside' society. It is argued that this institutionalised departure from equal access to state provision, separation and the provision of parallel services specifically for asylum seekers results in social exclusion.

Chapter Four outlines the geographic social exclusion of asylum seekers as a result of the dispersal policy. Figures are presented to provide a descriptive tool and to show how dispersal evolved geographically over time. It is argued that the geography of dispersal was a reflection of the exclusionary policy context and the availability of unpopular housing.

Chapter Five explores the process of social exclusion as a result of compulsory dispersal using qualitative data from asylum seekers and refugees. The earlier stages of the refugee experience and their global social exclusion are considered to show how the focus on an administrative process does not allow for an understanding of the prior experiences and subsequent needs of asylum seekers. It is argued that the asylum and dispersal systems are studies in liminality or, more precisely, legislative and policy-imposed liminality.

The power to define who can access welfare and other services is now based on legal status. Chapter Six elaborates on this formal exclusion from the rights expected by others. Dispersal away from London and the South East brought into question issues around accessing legal, translation, health, education and other services. These issues and the temporary character of services provided are explored. Gaps in services, particularly around gender-specific services and mental health, are identified.

Chapter Seven illustrates how asylum seekers gain information about services through the maintenance and creation of social networks. The chapter explores a range of experiences, from the total destruction to the persistence of social networks over space and time. It is argued that, for asylum seekers who are able to have recourse to social networks, this is the most important way in which they create a sense of 'belonging' in the absence of legal status.

Chapter 8 continues the argument that the asylum and dispersal systems create legislative and policy-imposed-liminality. Asylum seekers resist this liminality and different forms of belonging emerge that do not reflect official policy mechanisms designed to 'integrate' refugees and run counter to the government's social and community cohesion agenda. A theoretical continuum between liminality and belonging is used to show how there are ongoing and simultaneous processes of policy-imposed liminality and resistance to this imposed sense of liminality as a result of the design of dispersal and other asylum policies. It is argued that the trajectory of asylum policy in the UK has increased the chances of liminality and mistrust being experienced. Finally, the book concludes by bringing together the theoretical, empirical and conceptual concepts of the preceding chapters.

TWO

Key terms and concepts

Introduction

There are several key terms used in debates about asylum in the UK that need discussion as they are often ambiguous, contested and have different meanings dependent on who is using them. This chapter begins by outlining how these terms – 'integration', 'resettlement', 'belonging', 'social inclusion', 'social cohesion' and 'community cohesion' – are used throughout this book.

Thereafter, a number of key concepts that are central to the arguments, in particular the notion of 'burden-sharing', liminality and trust, are explored. The literature on forced migration already relates the concepts of 'liminality' and 'trust' to refugees in camps. Social exclusion of asylum seekers and the lack of the ability to re-establish normal routines, during what will be shown throughout this book to be a liminal period during dispersal, relates closely to the creation of a space for trust. Both concepts assist in our understanding of how asylum seekers experience compulsory dispersal. The transnational characteristics of social networks of refugee are then highlighted.

Perceptions of asylum seekers and refugees and the power to define who is portrayed positively or negatively are crucial. The question of whether there is a 'refugee experience' or whether all forced migrants are just 'ordinary people' is asked to discuss how refugees are currently perceived within the UK, with descriptions of refugees from the literature and past cases of dispersal provided to challenge contemporary labelling.

Key terms in contemporary UK asylum debates

There is no agreed definition of what **integration** means but it is popularly understood to connote a complex process that any newcomer to a country goes through in order to become a part of a new society (Castles et al, 2002). While popular attitudes often seem to be based on the assumption that integration is a one-way process, academics and experienced practitioners stress that it is a two-way process as it requires the host society to adapt in some way to accommodate the newcomer and allow access to employment and services (Castles et al, 2002). The latter view has been broadly accommodated by policies of multiculturalism wherein distinct group identities are considered legitimate and shared histories, cultures or languages are respected and diversity recognised in social policies (Finney and Simpson, 2009). In any democratic country, integration involves including newcomers in political processes and presupposes equality at every level of society. In 2004, Ager and Strang provided *Indicators of Integration* for the Home Office, a framework of what constitutes successful 'integration', which suggested 10 core domains reflecting normative understandings of integration. These domains were grouped under four themes of which the foundation of 'Citizenship and Rights' would include an explicit discussion about what this would mean for newcomers and to what extent refugees are allowed access to full and equal entitlements to participation (Ager and Strang, 2008, pp 173-7).

The term 'integration' has been adopted by the Home Office to describe the process that refugees go through once they have already received a positive status determination. In policy terms, the period before the receipt of legal status is not considered to be a period where integration occurs. In this book, the term '*resettlement*' is therefore favoured over 'integration'. 'Resettlement' acknowledges that refugees would already have been settled in their countries of origin and that displacement is the cause of their current circumstances. It also avoids some of the confusion and chaos (Robinson, 1998) that is connoted by the term 'integration'. The process of resettlement also allows for the entire cycle of displacement to be considered.

Belonging in this book refers to international, regional, national or local affiliations and thus incorporates international linkages or networks that allow the individual to connect in some way to their current locality. Whilst physical residence in a locality does not automatically translate into social belonging, (Dona, 2010), for refugees and other migrants, these transnational linkages enable a form of belonging. This relates closely to the creation and maintenance of trust that Colson (2003, p 5) notes: 'Trust depends upon continuing links with a home place, a profession, or membership in some other grouping that spans localities and time. Pantazis et al (2006) explore the absence of data on social relations in previous analyses of social exclusion when presenting findings on social exclusion in the 1999 Poverty and Social Exclusion (PSE) Survey.[1] The PSE treats exclusion from social relations as an aspect of social exclusion and Levitas (2006) stresses how the *social* aspects of social exclusion have not been at the centre of EU or UK debates. Key to this is the 'extent and quality of social networks and the extent to which individuals are socially isolated' (Levitas, 2006, p 138).

'Belonging' can also be temporally expansive, not only incorporating the present and future circumstances of individuals but also drawing on the past. It begins much earlier than arrival in the UK, incorporating circumstances in the country of origin and membership of particular groups prior to leaving. For asylum seekers and refugees, persecution may be based on such membership of particular social groups or political opinion. Any definition of belonging would necessarily be extremely broad, moving beyond nationally based modes of incorporation of *jus soli* (inclusion by birth) and *jus sanguinis* (bound by blood and the soil of the

---

[1] The PSE Survey is the only comprehensive source of information on the extent and nature of social exclusion and deprivation in contemporary Britain.

land with all others being 'alien'). It also includes transnational social networks, moving beyond any geographically determined interactions.

The main problem with the term 'belonging' is that within the UK it has become a controversial concept, often linked to right-wing political rhetoric. Theoretically too, Castles (2003, p 21) has suggested that caution should be used when using the notion of 'belonging', since it 'seems to put too much emphasis on the subjective and cultural aspects of forced migration and to neglect its structural dimensions'.

Based on his influential study of French lifestyles, Bourdieu (1984) argued that every aspect of consumer behaviour – from holidays and choice of wallpaper to food preferences and clothing styles – says important things about where individuals belong in society. 'Belonging' in this sense refers especially to class, education, ethnicity, religion, generation and the place lived in. Shared tastes also provide access to membership of desired groups. Thus, each subgroup expresses its own special 'habitus' (Cohen and Kennedy, 2000, p 238). For Bourdieu, 'habitus' refers to a set of cultural orientations of the members of a social group or subgroup. Through their life experiences they express and display preferences for distinctive tastes in consumption and lifestyles, which allows for new practices to be generated.

The question of **identity** has long been at the heart of historical and contemporary accounts of race, with Bloch and Solomos (2010, p 6) arguing that the current 'preoccupation with identity can be taken as one outcome of concerns about where minorities in contemporary societies actually belong'. They assert that identity is fundamentally about belonging, it is about 'personal location', 'social relationships' and 'involvement with others' with an infinite list of possible belongings in each person.

In this book, 'belonging' is used as it emerged from data generated by the research as a favoured term by respondents when thinking about their more 'subjective' or intangible experiences of becoming a part of UK society and feeling 'at home' in the country. The notion of 'home' has been invoked for many years in the international refugee regime to justify repatriation of refugees either voluntary or involuntary. As Demuth (2000) suggests, 'home' is a concept that often comprises diffuse 'feelings' of home based on where an individual lives and belongs, or wants to belong. The distinction must be made therefore between physical residence is an actual geographic location and where an individual believes they belong.

Social inclusion is also a broad and vague term with no agreed definition that has some connotation of people needing to somehow fit in to some pre-existing society. In policy terms, the promotion of social inclusion and social cohesion has been a central and strategic goal of the EU since the Lisbon Summit in 2000 and member states now have to produce biennial action plans for social inclusion (Levitas, 2006).

Within the UK, concerns about the 'parallel lives' (Cantle, 2001) of minority ethnic communities have led to a focus on **social cohesion** or **community cohesion** to overcome such separations and social fragmentation more generally.

These terms are much debated and not yet fully defined (Solomos, 2003). As Lewis (2010) suggests, the fear of a multicultural society 'highly fractured along lines of encapsulated, unified migrant populations' has been given momentum by the Cantle report and key figures such as Trevor Phillips.[2] Lewis (2010) also suggests that presumptions of culturally and racially distinct 'communities' separate from mainstream society are an outcome of this momentum as well as speeches made by Trevor Phillips around the UK in which he referred to the UK as 'sleepwalking into segregation' and other politicians (see Finney and Simpson, 2009, for a critique of such statements). The term 'social cohesion' itself draws heavily on Putnam's (1993, 2000) suggestions around the concept of 'social capital' in which considerable importance has been placed on trust and reciprocity. For example, the recently formed Commission on Integration and Cohesion defined a cohesive community as one that involved a 'strong sense of trust in institutions locally to act fairly' (COIC, 2007, p 42). Different constructs of the concept of 'social capital' that focus on the potential resources that can be maintained and reinforced through exchanges or consider how a sense of belonging within a community can firmly exclude those not considered to 'belong' (Bourdieu, 1986; Sen, 2006) are outlined later.

Empirical material provided within this book highlights how the rhetoric of social cohesion, based on the building of connections between people (bridging and bonding) contradicts the policy and practice of compulsory dispersal and an asylum system based on deterrence, which stigmatises, separates and excludes people from society.

Refugees and key concepts

The notion of 'burden-sharing'

The idea that the 'burden' of assistance to refugees can be shared has a long history and is well established in the global refugee regime (UNHCR, 2000; Thielemann, 2003b; Betts, 2004). 'Burden-sharing' can be about sharing or shifting financial and other costs. The 'prejudicial connotation' of the term 'burden-sharing' (Thielemann, 2003b, p 225) has been highlighted by a number of academics and campaigning organisations. Alternatives such as the 'equal balance of efforts' (Thielemann, 2003b, p 225), 'the political economy of North–South responsibility-sharing' (Betts, 2004), international obligations or 'international solidarity obligations'[3] have as yet failed to have any impact on the way in which refugees are debated. The term has been widely adopted by UNHCR,

---

[2] Chief Executive of the former Commission for Racial Equality (now merged into the new Equality and Human Rights Commission).

[3] The term used by a representative of Latin America UNHCR during speech at the 9th International Association for the Study of Forced Migration biennial conference, Sao Paulo, Brazil, 9-13 January 2005.

---

international non-governmental organisations (NGOs), EU members, national governments, UK-based service providers, the voluntary sector, academics and other agencies working with refugees globally, regionally, nationally or locally.

A special edition of the *Journal of Refugee Studies* in September 2003, examined 'burden-sharing' in a European context, referring to how refugee burden-sharing issues had increasingly risen to the top of the political agenda at the *regional* level (Thielemann, 2003b). Thielemann argued that the purpose of 'burden-sharing' was to 'institutionalise redistribution' in ways counter to how distribution would occur without intervention and he broke this down in three ways (2003b, p 228):

- the harmonising of refugee and asylum legislation he calls 'sharing policy';
- the redistribution of resources he calls 'sharing money';[4]
- the reallocation of asylum seekers or 'sharing people', which was considered to be the most effective but also the most controversial way to share the burden throughout the EU (2003b, p 232).

Proposals have, on occasions, been mooted for Europe-wide systems to disperse asylum seekers. UK proposals in early 2003 for extra-territorial processing of people to countries outside the UK again shifted this 'burden' and, as argued by Betts (2004), was a logical extension of the perception by policy makers that the asylum system in the UK still requires 'solving'. It was during the 1990s that the concept of burden-sharing was increasingly woven into national policy, with policies of containment designed at an international level to deter 'Third World refugees' (Robinson, 1996, quoted in Robinson, 2003a, p 5).

Following the Immigration and Asylum Act 1999 in Britain, this institutionalisation of redistribution of people occurred with the creation of a separate, centralised agency run by the Home Office to organise financial support for asylum seekers – the National Asylum Support Service (NASS). Boswell (2003) has argued that both the UK and Germany have attempted to manage the 'problem' of the 'burden' of asylum seekers through dispersal, although in many cases this has also exacerbated inter-ethnic tensions and racial violence in new receiving areas.

Liminality

Liminality, from the Latin word for 'threshold' (*limen*), connotes the position of being betwixt and between and was initially associated with the work of Arnold van Gennep (1960) and Victor Turner (1967). Many other authors have extended the original ideas of these authors, including Zygmunt Bauman, who used the concept of liminality and rights of passage to explain post-communist societies (1992), later proposing that the desire for community is about seeking safety in an

---

[4] The establishment of the European Refugee Fund in September 2000 is cited as a European example of how 'sharing money' is now occurring throughout the EU. It had a budget of €216 million over a period of five years (Boswell, 2003, p 331).

insecure world (2001, quoted in Lewis, 2010) and, in explaining the predicament of refugees in camps he used the expression 'to be in but not of' the societies that receive them (Bauman 2000 quoted in Dona, 2010) Edmund Leach also used 'liminality' (1976) in exploring the structures of communication.

Within the literature of forced migration, there is considerable reference to refugees living in 'limbo', particularly in relation to refugees in camps (Kunz, 1973; Bousquet, 1987; Reynell, 1989; Hitchcox, 1990; Malkki, 1995b; Turton, 2004). The term 'limbo' has also been used to describe the asylum and dispersal systems in the media and other refugee-specific publications in the UK.

Bousquet's (1987) study of Vietnamese refugees in closed camps in Hong Kong, 'Living in a State of Limbo', explored the 'intermediate state in which one has exited from the old but is not yet accepted elsewhere' (1987, p 34). It described how the government of Hong Kong opposed attempts to improve camp conditions to retain the perception of the camp as a temporary holding centre and how the lives of refugees revolved around waiting (1987, pp 43-7). Life in camp was considered by the refugees to be a continuation of the 'long process of alienation' in Vietnam and they considered themselves to be expelled from normal existence (1987, pp 49-52). Malkki (1995b, p 1), in her ethnography of Hutu refugees in Tanzania, also explored how refugees 'by virtue of their "refugeeness" occupy a problematic, liminal position', quoting Turner's analysis:

> [T]ransitional beings are particularly polluting, since they are neither one thing nor another; or may be both; or neither here nor there; or may even be nowhere ... and are at the very least 'betwixt and between' all the recognised fixed point in ... cultural classification. (Turner, 1967, quoted in Malkki, 1995b, p 7)

Thus, the position of individuals in the 'liminal stage', following a 'rite of separation' and prior to a 'rite of incorporation', was one of change for having crossed the threshold of one status while not yet having crossed into another. Because of this the individual was 'neither here nor there; beyond normal' making this liminal stage a 'zone of socio-cultural non-identity, non-existence' (Rapport and Overing, 2000, p 230). The treatment of individuals at this stage, as suggested by Rapport and Overing, was based around them being a threat to others:

> Individuals at this stage were often removed from everyday sight, or else treated as if invisible. They were often spoken about as dead or as dissolved into amorphous, unrecognizable matter ... [and] were often treated as unclean and polluting to those still going about their everyday lives; also as potentially dangerous.... Hence, initiates in the liminal stage were often the responsibility of certain ritual officers or experts who managed their lives until the rite of reincorporating them into socio-cultural space, time and identity was to be effected. (2000, p 230)

The theme of pollution was developed by Douglas in that 'what was liminal and neither here nor there was at once polluting, dangerous and powerful' (Douglas, 1966, quoted in Rapport and Overing, 2000, p 230). Kunz (1973, p 133) considered that refugees occupied such a liminal state:

> At this stage the refugee still does not look forward, but already knows that the doors are closed behind him. His main preoccupation is therefore the redefinition of his relation towards his country of birth, family and friends. He is taking the first step that will change him from a temporary refugee into exile. He has arrived at the spiritual, spatial, temporal and emotional equidistant of no man's land of midway-to-nowhere and the longer he remains there, the longer he becomes subject to its demoralizing effects.

The exclusion of asylum seekers from ordinary living patterns through exclusionary practices and the inability to restore normal routines during the dispersal process means that they also occupy a liminal space – they have left their country of origin but are not accepted in the UK. Lives revolve around waiting and their position is one of being 'betwixt and between' during the asylum and dispersal processes. Invisible as individuals, they are homogenised into one mass, which has become perceived as threatening and potentially dangerous. Asylum seekers are simultaneously everywhere and nowhere – imagined as a 'community' (Anderson, 1991) yet 'outside' mainstream society. Their positions within the social structure are liminal, yet the social system in which they remain does not change. They come under the responsibility of the Home Office and experts of different agencies involved in the dispersal system until refugee status determination (RSD) and the rite of 'integration' occurs. Liminality acts as a conceptual bridge between the socially excluded and those undergoing forced migration because both demonstrate similar characteristics of living beyond a normal existence and being considered to be 'outside' mainstream society in some way (Levitas, 2000, p 358).

Trust or mistrust

Trust, or mistrust, is central to any study on refugees (Colson, 2003) and the establishment of a locus of trust (Voutira and Harrell–Bond, 1995) will not always be straightforward once betrayal has been experienced. Daniel and Knudsen (1995, p 1) have argued that 'The refugee mistrusts and is mistrusted' and they suggest that the success of asylum and refugee policies invariably pivots on a fulcrum of trust (1995, p 4):

> In the best of all possible worlds, at the point of a refugee's reincorporation into a new culture and society, trust is reconstituted, if not restored. The real world, however, is not the best of all possible worlds.... Unlike life under 'ordinary' circumstances, or more correctly,

under circumstances over which one exercises a certain measure of control, in the life of a refugee, trust is overwhelmed by mistrust.... (1995, pp 1–2)

'Trust' is an ambiguous term; it is complex and multifaceted and, once lost, takes time to be restored. Spanning academic disciplines, the plurality of meanings of 'trust' are gendered, and relate to class, ethnicity, age and the situational identity of the individual concerned. It can be considered a universal notion although there will be personal, gendered and cultural differences in the concept (Muecke, 1999; Peteet, 1999). It can also relate to an intangible sense of confidence felt in political systems or institutions, something that the European Social Survey, for example, examines when discussing 'generalised trust' across European cultures (Reeskens and Hooghe, 2008). In research, trust is often treated as a variable in surveys – with the methodological difficulties of reliability and cross-cultural validity acknowledged – rather than as a process (Hardin, 2006; Khodyakov, 2007).

Herein, trust is divided into 'social trust' (Togeby, 2004, p 522), 'institutional trust' (Demos, 2003, p 6), 'political trust' (Newton, 2006) and 'restorative trust' (Voutira and Harrell-Bond, 1995, p 219; Daniel and Knudsen, 1995). **Social trust** is understood as an individual being able to have confidence in another person. **Institutional trust** (Demos, 2003) is understood as having confidence in political institutions such as the police, parliament and the courts. For asylum seekers this also applies to their belief in institutions set up to administer support and their claims for asylum. This is gendered as it encompasses the public/private dichotomy wherein, for women who may have less experience of dealing with institutions, trust will need to be established. **Political trust** (Newton, 2006) refers to satisfaction with democracy and confidence in the democratic process. For asylum seekers, their belief in the integrity and quality of the RSD process and the legal processes that envelop this are key. **Restorative trust** is understood to be a process an individual undertakes to regain social, political or institutional trust. In exile this issue is complex, relating to an individual's sense of liminality or belonging as well as the formal or informal social exclusion they have encountered.

For refugees, mistrust of political processes and the institutions involved is a feature of the wider processes involved in the 'asylum cycle' (Koser, 1997) or 'refugee experience' (Ager, 1999). Restructuring the social order of the nation state in countries of origin generates refugees, and social exclusion inherent in this process will have already been encountered and, potentially, left a legacy (Zolberg, 1983; Zolberg et al, 1989; Richmond, 2002). Mistrust that predominates in refugee 'communities' may be due to religious, ethnic, language or other lines of fragmentation that have occurred in a wider process of restructuring this social order.

Voutira and Harrell-Bond (1995) have challenged the notion that encounters between helpers within the structure of the international humanitarian regime and refugees have any potential for restoring trust. The political economy of aid structures and inherent tensions of a global structure to facilitate the containment of refugees requires questioning any possibility of there being a 'locus' for nurturing trust in such situations (Voutira and Harrell-Bond, 1995, p 219). However, some restoration of social trust can occur through trans-religion, trans-ethnic or trans-language groups in situations of conflict, albeit slowly through projects that bring people together to reconstruct groupings along lines of fragmentation (Hynes, 2009). For refugee agencies the ability to facilitate this depends on the approach of the organisation, fieldworker, track record of the organisation and, importantly, the recognition that power relations matter.

Colson (2003) relates this theme of trust to migration studies more broadly. Trust, she argues, rests on reciprocity, the expectation of a shared future – with trust and belonging inextricably linked and dependent on continuing links with a home, place, profession or membership in some other group that spans localities and time.

Trust and reciprocity are also key elements in debates around the concept of social capital, with some 'social capital' theorists placing importance on there being an empirical association between generalised 'social trust' and measures of 'political trust, such as confidence in political institutions and satisfaction with democracy' (Newton, 2006). Trust is also a central feature of the Putnam's (1993, 2000) writing on the concept of 'social capital', although Bourdieu (1986) does not explicitly address the issue of trust in his writings. When Sen (2006) explored 'social capital', he argued that a sense of shared identity between members of the same community has to be supplemented by the recognition that this can exclude those perceived to be 'outside' such communities. Asylum seekers are marginalised and alienated from local hosts (Zetter, 2007) and are perceived as 'outside'. For this reason, any association between social and political trust cannot be assumed for refugees or asylum seekers. The social networks of an asylum seeker are affected during displacement and therefore social capital, which relates closely to these networks, are also affected.

Trust is also an essential component of social policies around community engagement, participation and community development. When Zetter et al (2006) explored the links between immigration, social cohesion and social capital, they found that a much more nuanced vocabulary was needed if social cohesion was to be used as a policy instrument.

Trust cannot be assumed within particular 'communities'. The notion of 'community' is contested, with Griffiths et al (2005) suggesting that assumptions of unified communities have a disempowering effect on refugees overall. Anderson's (1991) seminal work on 'imagined communities' in constructing nationalisms – that nationalisms beyond face-to-face contact are imagined – also applies to 'communities'. 'Community' based on the notion of shared language or a particular nationality hides inequalities, its own hierarchies of discrimination and, importantly for refugees, internal factionalism and differences within groups that are a result of the particular 'vintage' of their migratory history (Kunz, 1973).

Debates surrounding social exclusion also cite trust as an essential component. Mistrust of neighbours, service providers and figures in authority is influential in thinking about the negative acquired characteristics of multiply deprived areas and 'cycles' on ongoing deprivation (Lupton and Power, 2002). Institutionally separated, mistrusted and dispersed without choice to cities already experiencing multiple deprivations has led to the presence of asylum seekers being resented.

Transnational social networks

The term 'social networks' is used in a metaphorical sense rather than in the highly technical and mathematical language of network analysis (Scott, 1991, pp 6-8). Such 'relationship webs' (Baker, 1990, p 64) and the 'social worlds' (the sum of all the migrants' relationships and the forces that impinge on them at a particular time) that Emmanuel Marx (1990) describes are often key to understanding the experience of migration. They are also often overlooked by policy makers.

Two decades ago, Marx (1990) pointed out the need to examine 'social networks' within studies of refugees and in doing so created an understanding of forced migrants being within 'transnational social spaces' (Castles, 2003, p 27; Boswell and Crisp, 2004, p 16). Marx drew on Thomas and Znaniecki's (1918) seminal work on Polish immigrants in Chicago to chart the stages of resettlement and the establishment of formal associations. This included how migrants tried to avoid formal institutions provided by the host community where they felt powerless to control outcomes (Colson, 2003). This more 'meso' perspective of social networks means that a middle-range perspective can be gleaned although research on the role of networks in the process of integration has been lacking (Marx, 1990; Castles, 2003, p 27; Boswell and Crisp, 2004, pp 10-17). Forced migration is a 'social process in which human agency and social networks play a major part' (Castles, 2003, p 13).

Marx (1990) combined 'network analysis' with the 'social worlds' of refugees, bearing in mind the whole of the social life of refugees because it embraced matters whose significance he could not appreciate and the network of social relationships of individuals. This idea around the social world of refugees is not confined to a particular geography or territory – these social worlds and social relations cross borders. This approach allowed for understanding the motivations and decision-making processes of migrants, simultaneously incorporating the social forces impinging on them.

In relation to the social networks of refugees, Marx (1990, p 196) placed 'total destruction', whereby the social world of a refugee collapses completely, at one end of a continuum and at the other end were those whose social worlds persisted as they moved. Refugee groups who arrived *en masse* were more likely to be at this latter end of the continuum as some links are maintained while some new networks are created. Towards the centre there were those whose social world had become 'more circumscribed' but who were able to maintain some links or establish new ones (Marx, 1990). Marx argued that when a refugee's social network was 'severely disrupted' they suffered a 'loss of social competence' similar to 'that of a newborn baby' (1990, p 197). Asylum seekers within the dispersal process are not a result of *en masse* migration and social networks are seldom taken into consideration throughout the dispersal process. Human agency, however, means that some social networks are maintained and others created. The policy of dispersal does not facilitate the maintenance of a refugee's social world but new social networks will of course be created. Secondary migration, which often revolves around creating, reformulating or maintaining social networks, is one way in which individuals resist the imposition of exclusionary practices. Secondary migration is not, therefore, necessarily the negative outcome considered by policy makers. It can be viewed as a positive outcome in that the individual involved has begun their own process of 'belonging' in the UK.

Social networks are based on dynamic and fluid relationships, be they strong, weak, positive or negative, that interconnect people globally, regionally, nationally and locally. Granovetter (1973, pp 1360–80) laid great emphasis on the 'strength of weak ties' in relation to possible 'mobility' opportunities in a largely mathematical study of networks. There is no single definition of social networks but Koser and Pinkerton (2002) proposed a definition that incorporates this idea of weak ties of global networks being utilised during forced migration of asylum seekers:

> Social networks comprise personal contacts with friends and family as well as commercial contacts with migration agents including labour recruiters, travel agents, smugglers and traffickers. Relations with networks can be voluntary and involuntary. Networks can facilitate migration in a range of ways, including by disseminating information. However, migration can take place in their absence. Networks exist and function across a range of countries, including origin, destination and also transit countries. (2002, p 36)

The incorporation of agents and other examples of weak – or remote until the point of need – ties illustrates how refugees are forced to trust in order to flee and survive persecution. In a study conducted for the Home Office on the social networks of asylum seekers and dissemination of information about countries of asylum, Koser and Pinkerton (2002, p 1) found that social networks were the most trusted method of obtaining information. These social networks may be weak, strong, temporary or permanent.

Perceptions of asylum seekers and refugees

Within the UK, prejudicial labels assigned to refugees and asylum seekers have framed debates within which policies are created. In order to understand this contemporary situation, a history of the 'refugee' is explored.

Is there a 'refugee experience'?

The 1951 Refugee Convention, plus the establishment in 1950 of an international agency set up to promote protection for refugees – the United Nations High Commissioner for Refugees (UNHCR) – provided for the first time a formal structure for responding to the needs of refugees and devised standards for the protection of refugees under international law (UNHCR, 2000, p 2). The ability to fit the definition laid out in the 1951 Refugee Convention determines how people are treated and, increasingly in countries of asylum, how they are able to access services.

The 1951 Refugee Convention and the setting up of UNHCR provided essential and formal standards for the protection of refugees from persecution. This also meant that refugees were essentially separated from other migrants and 'refugee studies', or the study of forced migration, has incorporated concepts and evidence about refugees that are based on this distinction (see Chimni, 2009, for an outline of how 'refugee studies' has moved to 'forced migration studies'). Defining the refugee is a complex task as there are legal, sociological, literary and various other definitions and understandings of what a refugee is. 'Refugee' is a label that conveys powerful and complex meanings (Zetter, 1988). Black (2001, p 63) argues that legal definitions cannot be utilised uncritically by social scientists in that displaced populations do not necessarily fall easily within the labels devised by policy makers. In broader sociological terms, the 'refugee experience' (Baker, 1990) or 'asylum cycle' (Koser, 1997) is a process that begins even before a refugee moves across a border and takes on the legal labels of the international refugee regime. This longer-term social process has its own dynamics (Castles, 2004) and adoption of the categories and concepts of policy makers can be unhelpful 'in the pursuit of scientific understanding' (Turton, 2003, p 1). The distinction between the legal and wider sociological understandings of refugees and 'asylum seekers' is therefore necessary. Policies are, however, exclusively designed for 'refugees' and 'asylum seekers' in the UK and refugee studies is rooted in the distinction between refugees and other migrants.

A debate about migration 'nominalist' versus 'realist' perspectives explores this distinction further (Hein, 1993; Koser, 1997). The 'nominalist' perspective stresses the more structural position of refugees in relation to other migrants, with the label 'refugee' being no more than a social construct with considerable similarities between refugees and other labour migrants. The 'realist' perspective seeks to understand the motivations and decisions of refugees at an individual level, viewing violence, flight and exile as definitive factors of the 'refugee experience', with the subsequent focus on trauma and 'victimhood' distinguishing refugees from other migrants. Koser (1997, p 6) considers the 'nominalist' and 'realist' perspectives to be extremes of a single conceptual continuum and argues that any approach that adopts just one perspective exclusively can be considered 'analytically invalid'. He also argues that the category of 'so-called spontaneous asylum seekers' embodies this debate:

The political assumption is that an actual distinction from within this category can be made between labour migrants and refugees, and the premise of this assumption is a realist perspective. In contrast, a nominalist perspective holds that the institutionalisation of the category asylum seeker simply serves the political purpose of excluding immigrants generally. (Koser, 1997, p 592)

If this tension is considered in terms of dispersal of asylum seekers and their social exclusion, the realist approach would more closely follow a discourse where asylum seekers are considered to be distinct, not on the basis of their 'culture' per se but on the basis of their trauma, circumstances and experiences and subsequent, assumed or real, behaviour. Asylum seekers in this way are distinct because their situational identity often requires presentation of a particular set of circumstances to access advice, support and other services.

From the 'realist' perspective, the 'refugee experience'[5] (Ager, 1999, p 2) is a term that has been widely used in the field of refugee studies to denote the human consequences – personal, social, economic, cultural and political – of forced migration. As outlined earlier, understanding the social exclusion of refugees entails examination of not only UK-based policy, but also spatial expansion to incorporate factors from the countries of origin. It also requires viewing the variety of socioeconomic backgrounds and differences in terms of nationality, age, gender and other variables. In order to understand a refugee's experience of settlement in a country of asylum, it is also necessary to understand the causes of initial flight. Without this, any potential sense of the ability (enabling factors) or willingness (constraining factors) of the individual to 'belong' in a new country is speculative. As Joly (1996, p 150) argues, it is not possible to fully understand the refugee situation without viewing conditions in the country of origin, flight and reception in countries of asylum.

Prior to the 1970s, forced migration was often conceived of as fitting into a simple 'push–pull' model. Kunz (1973, p 128) attempted to provide a more generally applicable theory of forced migration in a model that differentiated between 'anticipatory' and 'acute' refugee movements. He distinguished between 'anticipatory' migration – those who anticipate persecution and plan their flight – and 'acute' forced migration – those who are coerced, often at gunpoint, and forced to flee, arguing that identifying recurrent patterns would allow for advice and assistance to refugees to be provided more effectively (1973, p 131). He also drew attention to 'vintages' of refugees, with each 'vintage' having its own set of political circumstances and therefore being different from previous or subsequent outflows of refugees, while arguing for the need to look at refugee situations not as individual occurrences but as recurring phenomena with identical causes (1973, pp 141-6). Thus began a more complex understanding of the dynamics

---

[5] The term 'refugee experience' is used because it emphasises the centrality of refugees themselves in any analysis.

involved in forced migration that has since been extended by theorists such as Richmond (1994b, pp 55-6) by placing theories of voluntary/forced migration along a continuum of 'proactive' to 'reactive' migration and incorporating a recognition of agency.

When Zolberg (1983, p 24) wrote about the 'formation of new states as a refugee-generating process', he focused on an analysis of persecution directed against groups – racial, religious, national or social – to which individuals belong by birth. These root causes of forced migration arising from historical processes of the secular transformation of empires into nation states result in refugee flows in the contemporary third world. He argued that political trends could explain the existence of refugees and that refugee situations were 'a general phenomenon that is as much a concomitant of world politics as ordinary migration is of world economics' (1983, p 25). This historic look at what causes refugee flows highlights how even during the period of threat and while the decision is being made to leave the persecuting country of origin, the process of becoming a 'refugee' has already begun.

Once a person decides to flee and survive, their 'primary ontological security' – their self-confidence, which is derived from a sense of permanency – is vastly threatened, if not taken away (Richmond, 1994b, p 19). This generates extreme 'ontological insecurity' (1994b, p 19). Their everyday life, which is dependent on routine and assumes a 'degree of predictability and trust in others' (1994b, p 19), has changed potentially forever. If a social contract exists between the individual and the government, an event may occur at an individual or societal[6] level that splits this. Once this split has occurred, flight is often imminent as the refugee no longer trusts their own government with their own life. Trust at the primary and secondary ontological levels is lost.[7] With both the primary and secondary ontological security of refugees lost during displacement, control over everyday lives, normal routines and ordinary living patterns need to be regained and trust restored.

At what point a person decides to flee can mean the difference between life and death as well as whether international protection will be available. The journey, or 'flight', can range from walking across a physical border into a neighbouring country to flying to another country to seek asylum. During flight, the refugee is forced to trust various agents, be they travel facilitators, passport brokers or other brokers. They do this as a survival strategy and to ensure that 'as few people know you are leaving is important, so you trust no one' (Robinson, 2002, p 64), often

---

[6] For example, the events of August 1988 in Burma where students watched as fellow students were gunned down by the military.

[7] Secondary ontological insecurity 'arises when particular spheres of social life are threatened' (Richmond, 1994b, p 19), for example bereavement, divorce, loss of employment, etc, which 'generate extreme anxiety.... The duration of the feelings of insecurity will depend upon the individual's ability to restore normal routines, re-establish trust, and achieve confidence in himself and others' (1994b, p 19).

not knowing which country they will arrive in and what will occur upon arrival. Once an asylum seeker arrives in the UK, and applies for asylum and support, these past experiences, different socioeconomic backgrounds and individual histories will be confronted by the asylum and dispersal processes, which may negate, dehistoricise and take no account of an individual's background. Compulsory dispersal and potential further relocation to another city is often repeated more than once, continuing the cycle of displacement.

Or are all forced migrants just 'ordinary people'?

Turton (2003) argues that forced migrants have distinctive experiences and distinctive needs and that emphasising the common experiences and needs of forced migrants means that there is a risk of homogenising refugees and perceiving them as a 'mass of needy and passive victims'. He also argues that there is no such thing as 'the refugee experience' or 'a refugee voice' and that there are only the experiences and the voices of individual refugees (Turton, 2003, p 6). For Turton, the way in which refugees are portrayed and perceived is important: if perceived as a group of 'victims' they may be able to access services, advice, assistance or gain status otherwise reserved for other 'vulnerable' populations; if considered a threat, expulsion and exclusion from national territories may be the ultimate outcome. Turton (2003) proposes that refugees and asylum seekers are 'ordinary people' who have been through extraordinary circumstances and it is argued herein that currently in the UK this view can be expanded to:

> ordinary people who have been through extraordinary circumstances in their country of origin and continue to experience extraordinary circumstances in their country of asylum.

Globally, the prevailing image of refugees is of large numbers of helpless, vulnerable, burdens who are dependent. Zetter (1999, p 74) has argued that this perception maintains the international refugee regime and its interests are 'best served by containing and controlling refugees'. Focusing on the traits and characteristics of individuals avoids recognising that redistribution of resources is a factor in the logic behind the containment of refugees. The result is that largest numbers of refugees remain in their regions of origin or first country of asylum and the 'burden' of refugee protection is therefore not borne by industrialised countries. Those who do manage to arrive in industrialised countries are met with rapidly declining entitlements. Given this geopolitical constraint, Zetter (1999, p 75) outlines the challenge of 'recasting refugees in a non-dependent image' and 'perceiving refugees proactively, as a resource', pointing out that 'refugees are demonstrably a positive economic asset, even where social and economic exclusion are the prevailing attitudes of the host community'.

Considerable diversity of descriptions of refugees exists, and these descriptions are often polemic. Perceptions of refugees and asylum seekers largely oscillate between positive, sometimes celebratory, images and victimising, threatening, negative images, something often referred to as the victim–hero dichotomy. Both globally and within the UK, various labels have emerged (Zetter, 1988, 1999; Kushner and Knox, 1999). Positive labels include refugees being perceived as assets, a resource (Zetter, 1999), being agents of development, agents of democracy or agents of change in their countries of origin. Negative labels focus on refugees as a problem[8], burdens, dependent, threats, bogus or vulnerable or powerless victims.

Framing refugees as 'asylum seekers' who are outside society in some way forces them to have what de Voe (1981) describes as a 'situational career' in that their particular circumstances are forgotten once such a label has been assigned. As Waldron (1987, p 1) suggests in his influential essay 'Blaming the refugees', refugees in camps are provided with aid to treat nutritional and health problems but are separated from political expression and become converted to 'clients of the relief effort'. Reducing individuals to 'clients' or 'cases' during dispersal is akin to this type of labelling, with history and heterogeneity forgotten.

For asylum seekers who are now dispersed, Robinson (2003a, p 175) argues that the 'public mindset' of seeing asylum seekers as 'burdens' needs to be challenged so that local communities realise the benefits from having refugees in their communities. He cites the example of Ugandan Asians revitalising the local economies of cities such as Leicester. However, stereotyping in either direction can be dangerous as the portrayal of 'success' stories fails to highlight racism or the lack of welfare provision for particular groups (Robinson, 1993a, p 245). On the other hand, the perception that refugees are 'scroungers', 'bogus' or 'vulnerable' does not address their individual agency or resilience. Refugees are not a homogenous group – they are divided not only by race, religion, nationality, membership of a particular social group or political opinion but also by class, educational or professional background, social status, being single or married, ad infinitum. Box 2.1 illustrates some of the positive and negative labels commonly assigned to refugees and asylum seekers who have been dispersed within the UK over the past few decades.

---

[8] One example of refugees framed as a problem within academia was a conference entitled 'The Refugee Problem and the Problem of Refugees', co-sponsored by The British Academy, Birkbeck, University of London, University of Cambridge and the Wiener Library, The British Academy, London, 23 March 2004.

Box 2.1: Positive and negative labels of refugees and asylum seekers

Survivors	Victims
Angels	Devils
Anti-communists	Communists
Assets	Burdens
Capable	Vulnerable
'Movers and shakers'	Threats
Autonomous agents	Problems
Agents of development	Dependent
Agents of democracy	Undeserving
Agents of change	Terrorists
Deserving refugees	Bogus
Champions	Powerless
A resource	Mobile

As well as this oscillation between positive and negative images there is also an arbitrary distinction between being 'undeserving' and 'deserving' (Sales, 2005, pp 445-62). The prevailing image, promoted by the media, is currently one of refugees being a 'burden' or a 'problem' (Robinson, 2003a), 'bogus' (Sales, 2002), 'scroungers' or a group dependent on handouts. This polarised debate is reflected by the emergence of myth-busting literature that seeks to provide contradictory evidence to the problem of the misuse of statistics by right-wing think tanks opposed to immigration.

The Refugee Council speaks of refugee 'champions'[9] as representatives of local strategic partnerships. RCO newsletters speak of the achievements and positive contributions that refugees make. This includes the way in which refugees fight against the tightening of restrictions and loss of rights – not a positive in itself but demonstrating the resilience of refugees (Hynes, 2003d). Individual achievements are also highlighted, stressing the diversity of the refugee population, the differing needs and the subsequent diversity of achievements (Refugee Women's Association, 2003). RCOs and, in some cases, refugee service providers (RSPs) provide a counter perception of refugees as being 'resourceful' or 'capable'. However, lack of financial resources, among other reasons, means that the impact of these newsletters and campaigns have limited impact on the prevailing image. Refugees and asylum seekers can also find themselves being simultaneously 'victims', 'threats' and causes for celebration of 'diversity'. Spanning these poles, there are also descriptions of the ability of refugees to 'cope in adversity' (Colson, 1991) and the resilience of refugees.

---

[9] Term used by a representative of the Refugee Council, workshop on Social Inclusion, Impact of Change conference, Refugee Council, London, 28 January 2003.

The UK context of deterrence as an overarching factor in asylum policy creates this situation. Debate framed in the language of deterrence can only culminate in polemical images and inadequate policies based on inaccurate perceptions of asylum seekers. The social exclusion of asylum seekers is dependent on the maintenance of negative perceptions of refugees. Among the general public in the UK the perception of the rights of asylum seekers, as found in a recent report by the Institute for Public Policy Research (IPPR), is that inequality is considered legitimate: 'Even those who supported the principle of asylum did not necessarily believe that asylum seekers should receive equal treatment' (Lewis, 2005, p 27). The report also found that 'Although other forms of racism are increasingly considered socially unacceptable, there is no social sanction against expressing extremely prejudiced and racist views about asylum seekers....' (Lewis, 2005, pp 44-5). Asylum seekers are thus far removed from the perception of being ordinary people. Instead, they continue to experience extraordinary circumstances in the UK, with the common experience of being socially excluded and with little opportunity for these experiences to be understood.

Conclusions

The socially constructed perception of asylum seekers as 'burdens', as a group to be mistrusted, allowed for the 'sharing' of the 'burden' to areas outside London and the South East of England. Social exclusion, liminality, mistrust and social networks emerged from grounded data analysis as paramount facets of the dispersal system (Glaser and Strauss, 1968). Asylum seekers are now seen as 'outside' society and therefore not able to receive equal treatment to others. Perceived and portrayed as simultaneously positive or negative, victims or causes for celebration of diversity, 'deserving' or 'undeserving', they are rarely regarded as ordinary human beings who have or are going through extraordinary circumstances. Instead, they are regarded as being in transit, being between statuses and occupying liminal spaces in the imagined communities they inhabit.

In the next three chapters it will be highlighted how dimensions of social exclusion for this population relate to the *structure*, *geography* and *processes* of dispersal. It is argued that each of these different dimensions is key to the social exclusion of asylum seekers as a result of dispersal.

THREE

Dispersal

Introduction

In the previous chapters we saw how the legislative and policy framework has contributed to the social exclusion of asylum seekers. The history of dispersing refugees across the UK was also examined and it was suggested that the contemporary dispersal of asylum seekers is taking place within a qualitatively new environment that has emerged since the mid-1990s and been manifest through several Acts of Parliament. The exclusionary processes resulting specifically from the introduction, structure and implementation of dispersal are the main topics of this chapter. It is suggested that there was an in-built element of deterrence in the design of dispersal, which meant that tensions were inherent in its implementation from the outset.

Separating asylum seekers from mainstream welfare provision created a more visible group and entrenched the distinction between asylum seekers and recognised refugees. It is suggested that this separation and the provision of parallel services specifically for asylum seekers is itself a form of social exclusion. Whereas the role of supporting asylum seekers had previously been undertaken by local authorities, with the introduction of dispersal this became centralised by the Home Office and ultimately administered by the now-disbanded NASS. This centralisation and the speed of its implementation did not allow time for adequate consultation or planning in the early stages. The high number and conflicting roles of agencies also involved power imbalances and tensions between organisations with a hierarchical structure for implementation denying adequate representation from asylum seekers themselves.

Compulsory dispersal is now taken for granted as being entrenched as a policy and the founding rationale for its introduction rarely questioned. Robinson (2003a, p 165) has argued that 'apologists for dispersal are curiously silent about the rights of the asylum seeker'. The right of freedom of movement is the most obvious breach. That dispersal is based on a 'series of contestable assumptions' (Robinson, 2003a, p 167) is the basis of this chapter.

Pre-1999 'informal dispersals'

As in Chapter One, the Asylum and Immigration Act 1996 introduced new social security regulations and imposed severe restrictions on welfare entitlements. Using an 'in-country' and 'at-port' distinction, benefits were withdrawn from 'in-country' applicants. This resulted in local authorities, mostly in London and the Southeast, having to provide support for destitute asylum seekers (Audit Commission, 2000a, p 9). With this came a perceived shortfall of suitable accommodation in these areas and the practice of informal, ad-hoc dispersal (hereafter referred to as 'informal dispersal') emerged.

> Once New Labour was elected in 1997, the perceived political exigencies of formulating policy on asylum seekers in a context of deterrence ultimately led to the Immigration and Asylum Act 1999, which incorporated these informal dispersals. Thus, prior to the formulation of formal dispersal arrangements, policy debates within the Home Office were around the spreading of 'burdens' and addressing this as a national issue: "A lot of the political rhetoric at the time was that asylum was a national issue and we needed a national solution. So dispersal, if you like, is the embodiment of that".[1]

The inherited backlog of cases and the need to "be seen to be doing something"[2] about asylum generally led to the idea that responsibility for both support and RSD should come under the umbrella of the Home Office, providing an internal "incentive"[3] to turn cases around faster. The evidence that a policy of dispersing asylum seekers nationally could work came from several existing informal arrangements with the Local Government Association (LGA) lobbying for a national dispersal system that would redistribute asylum seekers away from London and the Southeast: "using their existing experiences of sending asylum seekers to places like Birmingham, Newcastle and the seaside towns as evidence that such a system would work".[4] By 1998, areas close to ports and airports in the UK such as Dover were considered by the LGA to need pressure on their local population eased and transferring responsibility for asylum seekers to the Home Office rather than local authorities would enable this. The concentration of asylum seekers in Dover[5] was highly significant in prompting the introduction of a national dispersal policy (Fekete, 2001; Robinson, 2003a, p 7).

The Refugee Council had been involved in policy making with central government and local authorities from the mid-1990s when a policy team was formed within the organisation. Before NASS came into operation formally, the deputy chief executive of the Refugee Council was seconded to the Home Office, to work on the development of the NASS system. At a staff conference in July 1999 to discuss Refugee Council policy towards NASS, the general view was that if the Council did not become involved, it would "consign itself to oblivion"

---

[1]   Interview with a representative of the Home Office, London, August 2003.
[2]   Interview with a former employee of the Refugee Council, London, February 2005.
[3]   Interview with a representative of the Home Office, London, August 2003.
[4]   Interview with a former employee of Refugee Council, London, February 2005.
[5]   Interview with a representative of the Home Office, London, August 2003.

and that if they did not bid for contracts, services would be provided by "Group 4 or the British Red Cross instead".[6]

When initially outlined, dispersal was controversial and criticisms of the segregated nature of social support, the cost of implementation and the advisability of dispersing people to unsuitable locations were numerous. The Refugee Council publicly called the arrangements 'a massive experiment in social engineering' (Refugee Council, 2000b, p 6; Robinson, 2003a, pp 126-7). While publicly denouncing the scheme, the decision to bid for contracts rather than have more involvement by private companies was made. Thus, no sustained campaign against the idea of dispersal was made from the voluntary sector agencies,[7] many of whom ultimately undertook a contractual and frontline role in local-level implementation.

Dispersal under the Immigration and Asylum Act 1999

In July 1998, the-then Home Secretary, Jack Straw, set out his ideas for a comprehensive approach to immigration control and new arrangements for supporting asylum seekers in the White Paper *Fairer, Faster and Firmer: A Modern Approach to Immigration and Asylum* (Home Office, 1998a). A key point was the introduction of new support arrangements separating asylum seekers from the mainstream benefit system (1998a, para 8.18). In this document, reference was made to minimising 'the attractions of the UK' of those asylum seekers not considered to be 'genuine' (1998a).

The key objectives of this White Paper were elaborated in an 'information document' setting out proposals for the new support scheme for asylum seekers in genuine need and inviting expressions of interest from potential support providers in March 1999 (Home Office, 1999). It spelled out how the new system would meet international obligations for those with a 'genuine need' while 'deterring' those without 'a well-founded fear of persecution' (Preface, p 3):

> [T]hose who are genuinely fleeing persecution are looking for a safe and secure environment which offers a basic level of support while their applications are being considered. Such people will not be overly concerned about whether that support is provided in cash or in kind, nor about the location in which they are supported. (Home Office, 1999, para 1.6, p 5)

This distinction between 'genuine' and other cases was explicit in both the White Paper and the information document. The assumption that 'genuine' asylum seekers would not be concerned about how they received support or where

---

[6] Interview with a former employee of the Refugee Council, London, February 2005.
[7] One exception was the Medical Foundation for the Care of Victims of Torture, which managed to gain an exception for victims of torture using their services in London.

they lived was also explicit. The reference to minimising the attractions of the UK acknowledges that a period of hardship may deter and reduce the number of asylum seekers. This built-in element of deterrence at the policy design stage was then expanded upon and a system of support was created with an inherently exclusionary logic at its inception. The benefits system was also considered to be a 'pull factor' with a chapter on support packages outlining the proposed provision at 70% of the equivalent in Income Support levels (Home Office, 1999, para 4.19).

The information document also spelled out that it was not an aim of dispersal to evenly distribute the 'burden' of asylum seekers to all council areas in the country – rather it was intended to disperse asylum seekers on a no-choice basis to relieve the 'current burden' on London and councils in the Southeast of England (Home Office, 1999).

Another aim of dispersal was to avoid adding to problems of social exclusion and racial tensions as was the avoidance of secondary migration and adoption of 'rough sleeping as a preferred method of survival' (Home Office, 1999, para 1.18). The selection criteria for locations included areas with minority ethnic populations, some supporting infrastructure and availability of accommodation.

Expressions of interest from the voluntary, public and private sectors were sought on the basis of these arrangements. RSPs and RCOs were considered to have much to 'contribute to the new arrangements' (Home Office, 1999, para 7.4) and it was recognised that this represented a significantly greater role than their current roles (1999, para 7.5).

The White Paper and information document formed the backdrop to the Immigration and Asylum Act 1999, which received Royal Assent on 11 November 1999.

From April 2000, asylum seekers arriving in the UK and claiming support were 'dispersed' outside London and the Southeast of England to locations in England, Scotland, Wales and Northern Ireland. This was carried out on a compulsory basis if financial support and accommodation were needed and the individual had been classed as 'destitute or likely to become destitute' under section 95.2 of the 1999 Act. Sections of this Act detailed how asylum seekers could share accommodation and dispersal was therefore to temporary and, potentially, shared accommodation on a 'no-choice' basis to cities and larger towns. This 'no-choice' basis encompassed both the location and type of accommodation.

This compulsory dispersal for 'destitute' asylum seekers existed in parallel to a system whereby those able and willing to arrange their own accommodation with family or friends and who wished to remain in London and the Southeast could opt for 'subsistence-only' (SO) support wherein financial support was provided without support for accommodation costs.

Initially, dispersal away from London and the Southeast raised a number of service issues, including access to employment, education, training, medical care, specialist care, housing, legal representation and language support (Audit Commission, 2000a). It was also suggested that impacts were felt disproportionately by women who were cut off from support networks (Sales, 2002, p 467).

On 12 August 2001, shortly after his appointment as Home Secretary, David Blunkett announced an internal review of the NASS dispersal arrangements. This announcement followed discussions between the voluntary sector and the Home Office and the stabbing of a 22-year-old Kurdish asylum seeker in Glasgow's Sighthill housing estate. It was clear by this time that dispersal was not running smoothly and there were concerns about the quality of housing. In a statement to the House of Commons on 29 October 2001, David Blunkett suggested that the dispersal system was perceived as unfair by both asylum seekers and local communities, was too slow, vulnerable to fraud, created social tensions and put pressure on local services in dispersal locations (Blunkett, 2001). He also stated that while the government believed that the principle of dispersal remained correct, it was its aim 'to phase out the current system of support and dispersal' (Blunkett, 2001). A proposed structure of a new asylum system was to include a three-tier structure of Induction Centres, Reporting Centres and Accommodation and Removal Centres,[8] the last of these being for fast-track removal with this system initially running in parallel to the existing system of dispersal. These expensive plans for accommodation centres were ultimately scrapped on 14 June 2005 when Tony McNulty was appointed Minister for Immigration.[9]

Published studies of contemporary dispersal are critical (Robinson et al, 2003a; Griffiths et al, 2005). Robinson et al (2003a) provide a comparative analysis of dispersal in the UK, Sweden and the Netherlands. Arguing that asylum seekers and refugees have become defined as a 'problem' due to their spatial concentration, they explore contemporary dispersal and aspects of its implementation, reaching the conclusion that the 'problem' leading to dispersal was socially constructed during a time of 'moral panic' and 'the ability to maintain the purity of our national and local space' (2003a, p 177). They argued that 'Dispersal is nothing more than the necessary response to appease a fearful white electorate and satisfy the local charge payers in those localities that naturally attract asylum seekers in the absence of planned dispersal' (2003a, p 177).

Griffiths et al (2005) focus on RCOs and dispersal, in the geographical areas of London, and the regional consortia areas of the West Midlands and the Northwest.

---

[8] Details during this announcement included: Induction Centres to accommodate new applicants for two to 10 days, enabling initial screening and health checks. Reporting Centres would mean that refugees could stay with relatives but would need to report on a regular basis. Failure to report would result in loss of eligibility for support. Accommodation Centres would initially accommodate 750 people in four centres throughout the country, i.e. 3,000 spaces. If successful, 10 further centres would be opened. They would be open access with full-board accommodation. Education and health facilities would be provided on site. If a space was refused, the refugee would not be eligible for further support. There are currently 2,800 spaces within Removal Centres (Detention Centres were renamed Removal Centres in the 2002 Act). Expansion of these is being proposed to provide 4,000 spaces (Houses of Parliament, written Ministerial Statements).

[9] See www.parliament.the-stationery-office.co.uk/pa/cm200506/cmhansrd/cm050614/wmstext/50614m01.htm#50614m01.html_sbhd3

They examine the role of RCOs in integration, how asylum sits within the 'race relations' framework of 'racialised immigration control' as well as networks and social capital (2005, pp 7, 11–36).

Practitioner reports written about dispersal tend to focus on specific geographical areas (Wilson, 2001; Carter and El-Hassan, 2003). For example, Carter and El-Hassan (2003) focused on refugee housing and community development for various nationalities of asylum seekers in the Yorkshire & Humberside region.[10] Funded by the Joseph Rowntree Charitable Trust, Wilson (2001) focused on services for various nationalities of asylum seekers in West Yorkshire[11] with the aim of identifying achievement and areas of provision where development was needed. The research found gaps and shortcomings in service provision, such as poorer legal representation and the varied quality of accommodation.

Other geographically specific accounts of dispersal have been provided (see, for example, Stansfield, 2001, for an account of dispersal in Nottingham; Temple and Moran et al, 2005, for an account of dispersal in Salford and Manchester; ICAR 'mapping the UK' project for accounts of individual cities across the UK). A gender-sensitive report from Refugee Action – *Is it Safe Here?* (Dumper, 2002) – addressed refugee women's experiences of living in the UK based on the views of 149 refugee women living in either NASS or emergency accommodation (EA).

Exploding and busting myths

There has also been an emergence of 'myth busting' or 'exploding myths' literature surrounding dispersal highlighting the very polarised debate on asylum in the UK and the misinformation and negative perceptions of asylum seekers dominating this debate. Lewis (2005, p 47) noted this plethora of factsheets and myth-busting leaflets, commenting that their impact on the general debate was negligible, partly because they did not reach the right audience and because they were not 'necessarily trusted'. It also suggested that the publication of these factsheets was frequently considered to be the whole solution.

Across the country, local authorities and service providers have published material explaining 'the facts' about asylum, including defining who is an asylum seeker;[12] how many asylum seekers arrive in the UK in proportion to other countries; how the UK is not a 'soft touch';[13] how asylum seekers receive only 70% of the rate of benefits provided to the general population; and how asylum

---

[10] Some 10,500 asylum seekers at any one point in time. The study focused on three cities – Hull, Sheffield and Wakefield.

[11] Some 2,100 asylum seekers at any one point in time in Bradford, Calderdale, Kirklees, Leeds and Wakefield.

[12] See, for example, *Asylum Seekers … The Facts*, Wigan Council, www.wiganmbc.gov. uk/pub/council/asylum/asylumseekers.htm

[13] See, for example, Emms, P. (2003) *Asylum Seeking in Stoke-on-Trent: The Facts*, a report of the Elected Mayor's enquiry into Asylum Seekers in the City of Stoke-on-Trent.

seekers do not drain resources from the National Health Service (NHS) and other services.[14] Gender-specific myths and facts have been addressed by the Refugee Women's Resource Project at Asylum Aid.[15]

NASS also published a factsheet in May 2004[16] focusing on how 'asylum seekers do not "jump the queue" for social housing that would otherwise be available to UK nationals'. Responding to negative media portrayal, this factsheet illustrates how asylum seekers are housed under separate arrangements, funded and administered centrally by the Home Office, that accommodation is not better than that provided to UK nationals and that it did not provide telephones, televisions, hi-fi equipment, new electrical goods, new furniture, cars, cleaning, gym or leisure club membership or computers.

Structure of dispersal: past and present

Until the mid-1990s, refugee resettlement policy for recognised refugees was 'based on two key approaches in social policy; equal access to general state provision and the support of community self-help' (Duke, 1996, p 7). Statutory services met the needs of asylum seekers and refugees in the same way as the needs of the general population and there was 'no permanent, central programme for the resettlement of refugees' (1996, p 7). Access to financial support, accommodation, employment advice, health and education services were each through mainstream statutory services, with 'refugee specific initiatives' (1996, p 13) from specialist voluntary organisations, RCOs and adapted statutory services for those needs that could not be met through mainstream provision alone (Carey-Wood et al, 1995). Figure 3.1 represents this past structure of provision diagrammatically

The introduction of dispersal represents a departure from this structure, with asylum seekers negotiating a more complex system prior to becoming recognised refugees. For asylum seekers, equal access to state provision ended with the creation of NASS. The support of community self-help was limited due, initially at least, to the lack of RCOs in the new dispersal locations across the UK. Lack of funding for RCOs was also a factor.

The current structure of service provision is more complex (see Figure 3.2) due to the high number of agencies involved, whereas in the past the availability of mainstream services to refugees kept the number of agencies involved in resettlement relatively low.

As can be seen, the present structure involves a number of statutory and voluntary organisations. Service provision to asylum seekers is carried out by

---

[14] See, for example *Myths about Asylum Seekers*, a leaflet produced by the Campaign to Stop Arbitrary Detention at Yarl's Wood.
[15] *Myths and Facts Leaflet*, Refugee Women's Resource Project, Asylum Aid, www.asylumaid.org.uk/New%20RWRP/RWRP_Campaigningandlobbying_Myths/
[16] *Dispelling the Myths, Telling the Facts*, a factsheet from NASS, Home Office, 10 May 2004.

'partners' in the public, private and voluntary sectors under contract to NASS and asylum seekers are 'signposted' to essential services. These services are coordinated by regional consortia, established at the outset of dispersal. Housing contracts are awarded by the Home Office to private and public accommodation

Figure 3.1: Past structure of provision for refugees

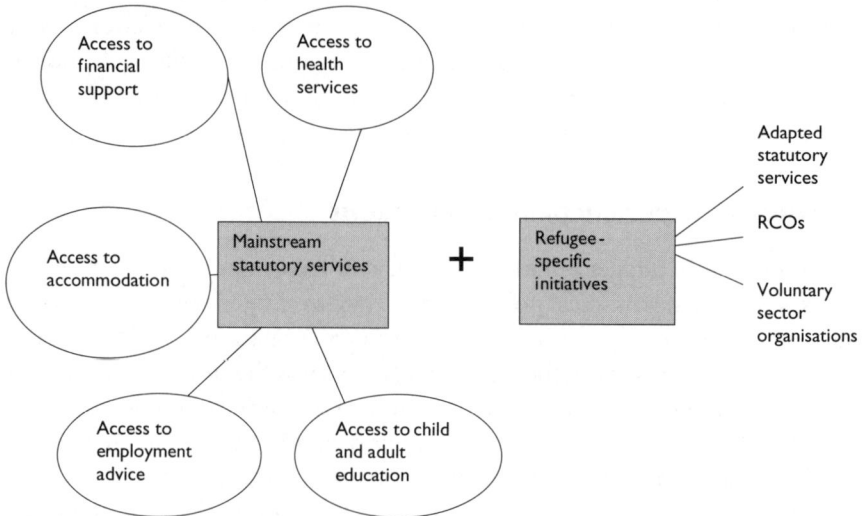

Source: Adapted from Duke (1996)

Figure 3.2: Present structure of provision for asylum seekers

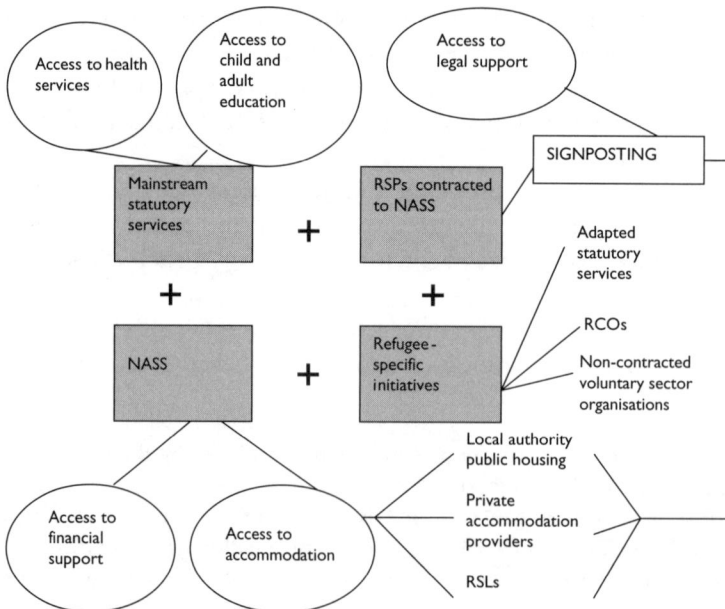

providers as well as some RSLs.[17] A significant characteristic of this dispersal is the privatisation of services to asylum seekers, in particular for accommodation. All accommodation providers are contractually bound to facilitate access to certain services for their tenants. A number of non-refugee-specific organisations have also become involved over time, ranging from mainstream service providers to faith-based organisations.

Access to legal support, which for 'quota refugees' was not a necessity, now occurs through 'signposting' from accommodation providers and RSPs to suitable legal representatives.

Dwyer (2005) discusses what he terms the 'hollowing out' of the welfare rights of forced migrants – asylum seekers; those with Humanitarian Protection (HP), Discretionary Leave (DL) or refugee status; failed asylum seekers; and overstayers – charting the complex situation in Leeds for each of these groups. He argues that 'The state's allocation of a specific sociolegal category is itself an instrument of governance defining an individual forced migrant's welfare rights' (Dwyer, 2005, p 630). These hierarchies of status and the power to define welfare rights based on legal status will be examined later. However, it is important to note here that it is only once an asylum seeker is granted some form of legal status that they are able to access provision similar to that presented in Figure 3.1, in common with the rest of the population of the UK, leaving behind the complex structure of service provision within contemporary dispersal.

The period of being an asylum seeker is therefore one of needing to engage with a complex array of agencies and parallel services. Being in receipt of only 70% state financial support and not having access to community self-help if RCOs have not been established in dispersal areas are far removed from the previous key approaches prior to the mid-1990s outlined by Duke (1996).

Agencies in the dispersal system

Building on the groupings provided by Sales (2002), the range of agencies involved in dispersal is complicated and divergent. There are considerable power imbalances between these groups and outlining their respective roles allows for emerging tensions to be explored.

The range of agencies

Central government agencies

Central government agencies include the Home Office and NASS. NASS is part of the IND and before the establishment of NASS there was no separate

---

[17] Registered social landlord is the technical name for a social landlord registered with The Housing Corporation.

programme for asylum seekers, with ad-hoc, temporary programmes developed for groups of 'quota refugees'.

Public sector organisations

Regional consortia,[18] or 'migration partnerships', and local authorities are the main public sector organisations involved in dispersal. Regional consortia were established at the commencement of dispersal to facilitate inter-agency coordination and bring together agencies in each region to share expertise, information and resources. Although there are regional variations in the membership, size and character of the consortia, they are generally composed of representatives of local authorities as well as representatives from health authorities, housing providers and the voluntary sector agencies dealing with dispersal. The organisations involved have different priorities and experience of working with refugees. Local authority representatives, who lead the consortia, prioritise the interests of their individual cities.

For example, in the East Midlands, the East Midlands Consortium for Asylum Seeker Support (EMCASS) was formally constituted in March 2000 to respond to dispersal. It is a partnership between local authorities, the Refugee Housing Association, Refugee Action, refugee organisations and voluntary organisations, with Leicester City Council as the lead authority. In the Southwest of England, the initial regional consortia disbanded but an informal organisation, the South West Asylum and Refugee Forum (SWARF) emerged from members of the disbanded consortia.

Public sector mainstream service providers

Public sector mainstream service providers include the NHS, schools and further education colleges. Access to these services is through 'signposting' by RSPs and accommodation providers. Access to financial support, initially through vouchers issued by a private company, Sodexho, was through post offices. This system later transferred into a system whereby cash vouchers were provided, which were then redeemed at post offices.

Private sector organisations

Prior to dispersal, the private sector was involved in the detention of asylum seekers. The role of private sector organisations expanded considerably at the commencement of compulsory dispersal as private sector provision of services, through contracts with the Home Office, created a role for this sector in transporting and accommodating asylum seekers. There are several private accommodation providers (PAPs), and subcontractors, who have contracts with the

---

[18] Regional consortia are now referred to as 'migration partnerships'.

Home Office to provide accommodation to asylum seekers in dispersal locations. The contracts with PAPs often involve shared housing with shared bedrooms, although 'warring factions'[19] are not meant to be accommodated together. The contracts also incorporate an obligation to 'signpost' asylum seekers towards health, dental, educational and legal services and specify that the properties need to be "in certain areas close to post offices, local facilities and close to support groups, so they are all within five miles of the city centre".[20]

Voluntary sector, non–user-led refugee service providers (RSPs)

The Refugee Council and Refugee Action are the main formally constituted organisations with charitable status working on behalf of refugees. This sector expanded at the commencement of dispersal with a number of offices and teams within RSPs set up specifically for dispersal.[21] NASS funded RSPs to undertake 'reception assistant' and 'one-stop services' roles. The 'reception assistant' role is to give advice and information on the NASS system to asylum seekers and help clients examine all the options available. The 'one-stop services' role differs in that it is about providing advice, information and 'signposting' to asylum seekers already dispersed and provision of 'a focal point for local voluntary and community effort within cluster areas' (Refugee Council, 2004b).

At the commencement of dispersal the Refugee Council formed the IAP of agencies contracted to NASS to coordinate the work of the voluntary agencies funded by NASS.[22] The Refugee Council was the dominant agency involved with the planning and subsequent implementation of dispersal and is based in London, with regional offices. The other major agency involved in dispersal is Refugee Action, which is a member-based organisation and registered charity founded in 1981 to work with refugees. Refugee Action has a more regional history than the Refugee Council, having played a major role in the Vietnamese, Bosnian, Montserration and Kosovar programmes. It also runs the 'Choices' project, providing information to asylum seekers and refugees on the Voluntary Returns Programme.

Voluntary sector, user-led, refugee-specific organisations (RCOs)

RCOs tend to be based on existing communities and, therefore, exist mainly in London and larger metropolitan areas where the majority of asylum seekers are living (Carey-Wood et al, 1995; Audit Commission, 2000a). The term RCO

---

[19] The term 'warring factions' was used in a Home Office Dispersal Strategy supplied to the author by the Home Office on request.

[20] Interview with a subcontractor of a PAP, dispersal location, June 2003.

[21] Interview with a representative of the Refugee Council, London, August 2003.

[22] Members of IAP are the Refugee Council, Refugee Action, Migrant Helpline, Refugee Arrivals Project, the Scottish Refugee Council and the Welsh Refugee Council.

provides a shorthand term for the 'complex, diverse and fragmentary social forms' (Griffiths et al, 2005, p 11) of organisations set up by and for refugees. They vary considerably in size, scope and range of activities and expertise on which they can draw, but are largely informal and depend mainly on voluntary work by members of their community. They focus on providing advice and information to new arrivals as well as providing a safe meeting place where people can speak their own language and celebrate their own cultures. Some provide formal or informal support to members seeking employment in local ethnic business and in gaining access to housing.

Kelly (2003, p 41) describes RCOs as 'contingent communities' in that they are 'a group of people who will, to some extent, conform to the expectations of the host society in order to gain the advantages of a formal community association, but the private face of the group remains unconstituted as a community'. This was based on research into refugees from Bosnia-Herzegovina but the term does assist in the explanation of the ambiguous and contested notions of 'community' plus factionalism within refugee populations versus the existence of formally constituted RCOs.

RCOs are increasingly involved in service provision in partnership with other agencies (Zetter and Pearl, 2000, p 676). Funding for RCOs is obtained primarily through charitable funds and 'special' statutory funds, which tend to be short term, insecure and often subject to annual review. Some of this funding is channelled through the Refugee Council and Refugee Action.

Voluntary sector, not-for-profit accommodation providers

The Refugee Housing Association and other RSLs or housing associations also provide accommodation to asylum seekers in dispersal locations and in some areas also manage properties for local authorities. As well as providing "single sex"[23] accommodation for single asylum seekers and "family"[24] accommodation, some RSLs are contracted by NASS to signpost asylum seekers to essential services. Allocation of accommodation for asylum seekers is carried out by placement officers who are dependent on the institutional knowledge of the particular RSL in order to avoid 'warring factions' being housed together. These organisations house asylum seekers on a temporary basis and thereafter may offer tenancy support services or 'floating support' teams for recognised refugees.

---

[23] Interview with a representative of an RSL, dispersal location, October 2003.
[24] Interview with a representative of an RSL, dispersal location, October 2003.

Voluntary sector, non-refugee-specific service providers that may have refugee-specific projects

The Citizens Advice Bureau or legal advice centres that were established before dispersal as well as projects such as the Red Cross Orientation Project that was set up for dispersal are examples of these agencies.

Voluntary sector, campaigning organisations that involve users and non-users

Organisations focusing on a specific theme (for example, anti-deportation, detention, the media or gender) are examples of these. They may be locally based or national campaigns, with their thematic characteristic drawing a broad spectrum of individuals and organisations.

Faith-based organisations

There are some organisations associated with religious organisations that have been set up to provide advice, support and assistance in emergency situations to individuals as well as some campaigning work. Issues around insurance policies and the legality of providing support to asylum seekers have imposed some limitations on the work of churches.[25]

The imbalances of power between these organisations and agencies are highlighted in the next five subsections, which look at the tensions of implementing dispersal, early negotiations between NASS and other agencies, the specific roles of the voluntary and private sectors and the 'buffering' role that RCOs undertook throughout the process.

The tensions of implementation

Tensions between these agencies during implementation of dispersal were common. The conflicting agendas of agencies involved were summed up by an individual who was closely involved in the early stages of planning dispersal:

> 'You have got refugee advocacy values among Refugee Council staff but everything that the Home Office was doing was bad. It was nasty, repressive organisation, which had no commitment to the welfare of vulnerable people. Then you had essentially administrators in NASS

---

[25] The issue of asylum seekers sleeping on the floors of church halls was a prominent part of the discussion during a workshop entitled 'Support and benefits for asylum seekers: section 55 and human rights' at the conference 'Refugees, asylum seekers and human rights – the balance sheet so far', British Institute of Human Rights and JCWI, London, 11 November 2003.

making operational decisions with targets from their own organisation and then you had private landlords who basically wanted to make money with the least possible hassle.'[26]

The power imbalances and different interests of agencies were clear. It was unsurprising that a representative of an RSP does not believe the Home Office to have the best interests of asylum seekers at heart as is the criticism of private accommodations providers.

A "hierarchical"[27] relationship between agencies within regional consortia emerged, as did a hierarchy of agencies nationally, particularly those involved in influencing policies. At the pinnacle of the national hierarchy was the Home Office and NASS, the centralised power for creating and maintaining policies. The regional consortia emerged next with the highest level of influence, although often tense, with the Home Office and NASS. Local authorities and accommodation providers vied for position below this. RSPs were low down and RCOs were included on an ad-hoc basis, if at all. Voluntary sector organisations that campaigned directly on behalf of asylum seekers and refugees were at the bottom of the hierarchy. Those with the most experience and knowledge about refugees who worked closest to asylum seekers had less influence on NASS policies than those higher up the hierarchy. This is not to say that attempts were not consistently being made by the voluntary sector, with ongoing attempts by RSPs through the IAP evident.

Asylum seekers were effectively outside of this 'hierarchy' and had no participation in the structures of support and were not able to represent their own concerns (Indra, 1989, p 223).

The suggestion was that RSPs were perceived as "a bit liberal and woolly" due to their "hands–on approach" with asylum seekers. It was also suggested that the regional consortia approach to RCOs was unrealistic: "At the beginning they wanted one person from the community they could lift the phone and speak to … in practice, RCOs are represented by the voluntary sector".[28]

Some RCOs were involved in monthly meetings but the size and scope of this involvement varied dependent on the specific region, meaning that RCOs struggled to develop an independent voice within the system and tended to be marginalised (Zetter et al, 2005).

The role of local authorities in implementation of dispersal was critically examined by Cohen (2002, p 518) when he suggested that 'the integration of the local state into internal immigration controls' transformed 'local government into an arm of the Home Office'. Private sector organisations were largely outside the hierarchical structure with their own direct links to NASS (Zetter et al, 2002).

---

[26] Interview with a former employee of the Refugee Council, London, February 2005.

[27] Focus group with representatives of an RSP, dispersal location, July 2003.

[28] Focus group with representatives of an RSP, dispersal location, July 2003.

Early negotiations between NASS, the regional consortia and the private sector

The wide-scale involvement of the private sector distinguishes contemporary dispersal from past cases of dispersal of recognised refugees. In 1998, the Home Office invited local authorities to form themselves into regional consortia in order that contracts for accommodation and support could be negotiated. A number of tensions during the negotiation of these contracts were evident, often relating to the different speeds with which contracts were negotiated between the Home Office and public and private sector agencies. In some cases, negotiations between the Home Office and regional consortia took some months and, in the meantime, contracts between the Home Office and private accommodation providers were signed. This meant that, in many cases, contracts with the private sector were negotiated faster than those with regional consortia, with the private sector already fully operational, creating tensions between central and local government (Harrison, 2006).

EMCASS signed its contract for accommodation in March 2001 following negotiations and renegotiations over implementation arrangements, price levels and legal arrangements (Harrison, 2006). The Refugee Housing Association (RHA) was contracted by EMCASS to manage accommodation rather than individual local authorities allocating time and resources to this task. However, by the time the contract was due to start on 30 April 2001, private accommodation providers were already providing accommodation to asylum seekers. In Leicester, the International Hotel, run by Accommodata, had already been the scene of a suicide of an Iranian man in January 2001 whose asylum claim had been rejected (Hingorani, 2001, p 129). Other PAPs in Leicester included Roselodge, Angel, Clearsprings and Leena Corporation.

In the Southwest of England, the regional consortium disbanded early on in the process due to lengthy negotiations with the Home Office breaking down. All the main local authorities who accommodated asylum seekers were involved in these negotiations from the early stages for around eight months. As a representative of the reformed SWARF commented while relaying the history of this:

> 'I don't think it is unfair to say that a lot of the time they [NASS] didn't have a clue how to negotiate with local authorities. Eventually a deputation of elected members and senior officers from the Southwest went up to meet with the Home Office minister, to try and sort these things out. They got halfway through the meeting and she said, well, I am not actually sure we need your accommodation anyway.... So, that in effect, at that point in time, was the end of the consortium.[29]

---

[29] Interview with a representative of a regional consortium, September 2003.

The tensions between central and local government revolved around a lack of understanding of how local authorities operated, with the Home Office approaching this from a centralised perspective. Local governments were often willing to negotiate with central government to accommodate asylum seekers but a lack of communication often denied this occurring. Explaining how one county council's negotiations were proceeding, a representative of a regional consortium commented on this perplexing arrangement:

> 'Ironically, the same day that I got a letter from NASS inviting [...] county council to reopen negotiations because they very much wanted NASS to work in partnership with local authorities, totally out of the blue I had a phone call from the police to ask if I had ever heard of Clearsprings. I said yes why? They said that apparently they are going to start bring asylum seekers here. Exactly the same day! Clearsprings had been given the go-ahead by one arm of NASS. No consultation with us whatsoever.'[30]

That the private sector was able to negotiate its contracts with NASS more quickly than local authorities was not surprising. There were regional variations but the private sector filled the "vacuum"[31] when NASS was either slow or unable to negotiate contracts with regional consortia. A considerable proportion of contracts negotiated by NASS in the early stages was directly with PAPs.

The lack of understanding by the Home Office and NASS of the regional variations in the UK was replicated with other regional consortia also unable to complete negotiations. A consortium made up of 21 councils in Wales that had agreed the terms of a contract, advertised and appointed staff, and were awaiting the signing of the contract, ultimately withdrew due to not receiving confirmation from NASS by April 2002.[32] By this time, Adelphi Hotels had a contract for around 70 'bedspaces' in Wrexham and Clearsprings was beginning to locate suitable accommodation in the area.[33] Cardiff, Newport and Swansea also accommodated asylum seekers dispersed by NASS.

While the regional consortia were seen as being "powerful", having considerable "clout" and giving "credibility" and a "higher profile"[34] to agencies within their structures, their ultimate role was, however, strictly determined by central government policy. One representative of a regional consortium broadly agreed with Harrison's (2006) characterisation that they had 'responsibility without ownership' of the policy:

---

[30] Interview with a representative of a regional consortium, September 2003.
[31] Interview with a representative of an RSP, dispersal location, July 2003.
[32] Press release issued by Wrexham Council, April 2002.
[33] Email correspondence with the Housing Department, Wrexham Council, October 2002.
[34] Interview with a representative of an RSL, dispersal location, October 2003.

'We are consulted by NASS and we attempt to influence policy but we do not set the policy. It is government, Home Office, policy. There are a lot of difficult issues that NASS is still tackling and we constantly try to influence NASS to resolve these.'[35]

Frustration about the way in which NASS operated was evident across the board, bordering on total disillusionment. One representative of a regional consortium went so far as to comment: 'I think some time, somebody will make a film of NASS and, I mean, it can't be true, because nobody would believe it!'.[36] A representative of an RSP commented that "the general level of incompetence is high" and its inefficiencies were "enough to make your jaw drop".[37] A representative of a voluntary sector organisation not contracted to NASS, laughing loudly, exclaimed: "do you want to turn the tape off because you don't want swearing on it!".[38]

During 2002, NASS established a working party to look at the viability of regionalising its services, acknowledging that the dispersal system meant that its services should also be available nationwide. It has been considered that the remoteness of NASS from the impact of its service has limited the organisation's effectiveness and the expectation is that an increased NASS presence closer to the point of delivery would improve efficiency.[39] Regional offices are to be located in several cities[40] and some 440 NASS staff are to be located in these regional offices.

The NASS system was problematic from the outset and the focus on improving the NASS system by the voluntary sector in their campaigning work and attempts to influence policy were clearly necessary due to the inefficiencies and inadequacies of the process. Considerable energy and time was dedicated to this, with several commentators arguing that this has meant that refugee-centred services have now been marginalised.

The voluntary sector: their role and the perception of independence

Representation by the voluntary sector was another tension emerging from the study given its dual advocacy and implementation roles. Cohen refers to this engagement of parts of the voluntary sector in a punitive system as 'dining with the devil' (2003, pp 157-74; see also Cohen et al, 2002). He also suggests that a central role for local authorities means that they act as 'internal immigration

---

[35] Interview with a representative of a regional consortium, January 2004.
[36] Interview with a representative of a regional consortium, September 2003.
[37] Interview with a representative of the Refugee Council, London, May 2003.
[38] Interview with a representative of a voluntary sector organisation, dispersal location, November 2003.
[39] IAP News, April 2003.
[40] Birmingham, Bristol, Cardiff, Croydon, Dover, Glasgow, Leeds, Manchester, Neastle and Peterborough.

controls', which transforms them 'into an arm of the Home Office' (2002, p 518). Others have suggested that a considerable range of agencies has been co-opted into a system of support that is also a form of policing asylum seekers (Zetter et al, 2005; Squire, 2009). Squire (2009) has suggested that these processes of co-option effectively depoliticise the exclusionary politics surrounding asylum seekers.

From a pre-dispersal position of being 'advocacy' (Refugee Action, 2003) and 'care-giving' (Refugee Council, 2004b) organisations with considerable empathy for refugees, involvement with dispersal meant that RSPs took on the role of providing EA and were placed in the front line of implementing the dispersal policy. Their role in making sure that asylum seekers could access services, be given advice as well as 'signposting' them to services was hampered due to other aspects of the system failing: "We are spending most of our time managing emergency accommodation and processing far more applications for NASS support than we ever expected to".[41]

Upon implementation of section 55, the 'landlord' role placed RSPs in the difficult position of not being able to provide EA to those clients approaching them who did not hold the correct documentation.[42] This meant that RSPs were forced to turn away a proportion of asylum seekers in need of support. Also, the numbers of asylum seekers were refused support, and were therefore not 'presenting' to the offices of RSPs for advice, remained unknown to the agencies (Refugee Action, 2003). The processing of applications for support involved completion of a form that posed sensitive questions, which could be seen to replicate the role of the state as these same questions would have been posed by immigration and Home Office officials:

> 'We help them to fill in NASS application form, which is a big form in English – 13 pages. And there are some immigration questions as well that we have to ask – where did you come from? Did you pass any country before you came to Britain? What time did you arrive here? Have you claimed asylum in port? If yes, which port, if not, how did you claim asylum? And all these kind of questions that immigration ask are included on that form as well.'[43]

This led to difficulties in distinguishing their role from the Home Office and the difficulties in sustaining their independence in the eyes of the client group were also acknowledged: "When people come here they can mix us up with

---

[41] Interview with a representative of the Refugee Council, London, August 2003.
[42] Applications 'at port' needed to be in possession of an IS96, which is a document stamped by an immigration officer at port, a Standard Acknowledgement Letter (SAL) or an Application Registration Card (ARC) and/or 'in-country' applicants in possession of a letter from NASS.
[43] Interview with a representative of Refugee Action, dispersal location, July 2003.

---

immigration".[44] This view that RSPs were seen as a function of the Home Office was recounted by asylum seekers and refugees. The issue was also commented on by a member of an RCO, explaining why her organisation did not get involved in contracting for NASS, while also raising other concerns about the possible constraints on independence:

> 'Had we signed up for the NASS contract, then we would have become like a little branch of the Home Office. And no doubt they would want to have all sorts of information about the community. And we knew that if we had done that then the people would mistrust us and therefore we let it pass – although it would have meant getting one full-time worker and running costs.'[45]

Thus, while RSP staff stressed their independence from the Home Office and challenged this perception at every opportunity,[46] they were often perceived by refugees to be part of the system rather than as advocates. The term "NASS in Brixton" was used by asylum seekers to refer to the Refugee Council's advice office. This mistrust was evident among refugees who had been in contact with RSP staff: "I appreciate their caseworkers, they are nice and caring people, but no, all they are is just a part of the Home Office".[47] This perception undermines the trust of refugees in RSPs, an issue that is crucial in work with refugees. As a solicitor working in a dispersal area commented, this was also an issue surrounding the perception of the organisations: "It is not only whether they are independent but whether they are perceived to be independent. It is something that they are very aware of and they know that it is precious to keep this independence".[48]

The tension between these roles was clear and, while RSPs had no role in decision making on applications for support, their role as a bridge to that service and their involvement in NASS contracts made it difficult to sustain the perception of independence from the Home Office. Over a decade earlier, a similar argument was made by Hitchcox (1987, p 5) about the voluntary sector role with regard to the Vietnamese dispersal when the sector's function as a pressure group was constrained because of conflicting roles. Contracts with NASS created questions about its real or perceived independence. Voluntary sector staff were often aware of this and many argued that there was no evidence that the government attached strings to contracts:

> 'I would say that no, there isn't. They recognise something, they have this voluntary sector compact, this government has been interested

---

[44] Interview with a representative of Refugee Action, dispersal location, July 2003.

[45] Interview with a female representative of an RCO, London, November 2002.

[46] Interview with a representative of Refugee Action, dispersal location, July 2003.

[47] Iranian participant in a focus group, dispersal location, July 2003.

[48] Interview with a solicitor, dispersal location, July 2003.

in promoting, which is about providing a framework for a better partnership between the voluntary sector and explicitly recognises that the voluntary sector is independent and needs to be independent.'[49]

This same representative later acknowledged, however, that working to contracts involves different forms of working: "If we are delivering a service on behalf of the government, then we have to deliver that to the specifications that are required by the contract".[50] The 1998 'compact' referred to (Home Office, 1998b), meant to ensure that the impact on voluntary organisations is taken into account during policy formation, did not mean that their involvement and contact with the Home Office and NASS meant they were consulted on the introduction of section 55 – the Refugee Council calling it a 'clear breach of the Compact' that 'undermines any intention it might have had to strengthen links with the voluntary sector' (Refugee Council, 2004c, p 32).

Refugee agencies can – often successfully – carry out advocacy work while involved in these contracts. The Refugee Council was, for example, the lead player in the successful campaign against the use of vouchers and lobbied against forced returns to Zimbabwe. It also campaigned against section 55[51] while simultaneously involved in negotiating new contracts. Balancing these two roles, however, creates tensions, which can undermine the trust between voluntary organisations and refugees and thus limit advocacy work:

> 'It is very limiting. And you do give the impression that you are not on the refugee service but rather the establishment's service. I think the [a refugee agency] has a very bad reputation within the refugee community and they do see them as agents of the government. They see them as a "strainer" … for the Home Office.' [52]

This tension for the voluntary sector between simultaneously campaigning against and implementing the raft of restrictive policies that have emerged over the past decade has led to heated public controversy.[53] There have also been visible examples of resistance made regarding this. For example, a group of some 35 asylum seekers who had been refused assistance set up camp in a car park behind the Refugee Council offices to demand support.[54]

---

[49] Interview with a representative of the Refugee Council, London, August 2003.
[50] Interview with a representative of the Refugee Council, London, August 2003.
[51] Successfully overturned on appeal in August 2004.
[52] Interview with a representative of an RCO, London, November 2002.
[53] For example, at a conference at the London School of Economics in 2003, an allegation was made that the Refugee Council had asked *The Guardian* to omit a paragraph in an article that discussed the refusal of the Refugee Council to house asylum seekers refused support under Section 55 (Fesshaye, 2003). Viewed on 1 December 2010 at www.allwomencount.net/EWC%20immigrant/semrearticle.htm
[54] For more details, see www.inhumananddegrading.info

Arguing that the benefit of contact and involvement with NASS provided 'added value' to asylum seekers who otherwise might be provided services by the private sector, representatives of RSPs considered that even under the terms and conditions of the contracts the voluntary sector was likely to provider a better service. The practical benefits of this involvement were presented:

> 'Certainly we can demonstrate this – a lot of people would have lost their NASS support, were it not for appeals that caseworkers do. We do have an extremely good record on appeals, NASS do listen. So that is a lot of clients, still accommodated, still supported because we helped them.'[55]

If an asylum seeker is refused asylum, RSPs cannot provide support to them. In EA, they are obliged to evict those who become ineligible, for example when an appeal is turned down. This activity requires them to be in agreement with, or at least to accommodate to, the criteria that dictate whether people get support or not. They are constrained to take on the norms of the system in which they operate, while often trying to make it better for individuals. While RSPs are not involved directly in deportations, their involvement with the Home Office undermines their independence in the eyes of many refugees, so that they are in danger of appearing to be part of the system that forcibly returns people.

Involvement in contracts creates an organisational interest in the continuance of the system, since jobs, and the future of the organisation, become dependent on them. It also places more general constraints on how organisations operate and has implications for the priorities of the organisation. This includes an accommodation to the culture and expectations within the partnership, for example that staff should not criticise NASS.[56]

Private sector involvement in dispersal

The privatisation of services for asylum seekers in dispersal has been largely unchallenged, sometimes due to the secrecy of commercial terms and agreements. Compared to the extent of challenge that private partnerships in the health and education sectors have seen, this is itself a comment on the social exclusion of asylum seekers, whose needs are perceived as secondary to, or below, those of the wider population.

In terms of private accommodation, the maintenance of properties was identified as the primary consideration. In the view of a representative of a voluntary organisation, in these terms their involvement was beneficial:

---

[55] Focus group with female representatives of the voluntary sector, dispersal location, July 2003.
[56] Information conversation with a former IND policy advisor, June 2003.

'The sub-contractor is very good. In other areas it is the local authorities that provide housing whereas here it is the private sector. In this instance, the houses are brilliant. I mean, they are first class. They have spent a lot of money on them. They have their own maintenance team who turn up the next day mostly if something needs fixing. They are a property company so it is in their interest to have well-maintained properties. When dispersal ends they will have good property to sell. That is a big motivation. It is not the right motivation but it does mean that asylum seekers get better accommodation here.'[57]

However, this was an isolated incident of praise for a PAP, with the general consensus being that private accommodation was inadequate and inappropriate. Dispersal ended in this dispersal location very soon after this interview with the property company mentioned above reallocating the housing to students who were the other body of tenants in their property portfolio. The asylum seekers who were moved out of these properties were rapidly relocated to alternative accommodation in other dispersal locations. The provision of accommodation to asylum seekers based on the fluctuations in the housing market was in this way capricious.

In Leicester, the use of the International Hotel to accommodate asylum seekers was widely criticised. This hotel had been previously used to accommodate Kosovan refugees and had since been condemned. In July 2003, there were some 400 asylum seekers accommodated and it emerged that there had been no hot water in the hotel for over a week. This was one of many complaints, others including the food, the rooms and the painted-over windows in the hotel. The private accommodation provider – Accommodata – has since had its contract terminated by NASS.

Further implications of private sector involvement were recognised by a regional consortia representative: "They go to the properties to check maintenance. They would not necessarily be able to tell, or be interested, if an asylum seeker needed counselling or therapy".[58] Thus, while maintenance may be catered for in private accommodation, it is clear that the end of accommodation contracts and subsequent relocation was problematic. PAPs were not caregivers or advocates for refugees and their role in that sense was relatively straightforward. Significant variations in standards of private accommodation were a feature of dispersal (Zetter et al, 2002). The deterrence element of dispersal was also recognised by a subcontractor to a PAP: "In a way it gives them a chance to find out about the country they are currently living in and asking to stay in. It may influence

---

[57] Interview with a representative of a voluntary organisation, dispersal location, November 2003.
[58] Interview with a male representative of a regional consortia, September 2003.

—

their decision as to whether to stay, because there is a programme, a voluntary programme to encourage them to go back".[59]

The awareness of the voluntary programme and use of the words 'encourage them to go back' was indicative of the lack of understanding about the reasons for asylum seekers arriving in the UK. The suggestion that the system 'may influence their decision' to return illustrated the implicit in-country deterrence element of dispersal. That a clear signal, through accommodation and other aspects of the NASS system, 'may influence their decision as to whether to stay' demonstrates this. That asylum seekers are 'asking to stay' and are only 'currently living' in the UK indicated a liminal state. Organisations new to the provision of services to asylum seekers commenced their involvement at this point when asylum seekers were provided with so-called incentives to return to their countries of origin and it is unsurprising that these organisations considered asylum seekers as being temporarily in the UK.

RCOs: the buffer?

Marx (1990, p 201) argued that 'refugees organise as "refugees" in order to better negotiate with the state'. Such 'community self-help' (Duke, 1996, p 7) had been a key approach in social policy-based notions of 'diversity' and 'multiculturalism'.[60] With refugees this self-help was through RCOs.

When dispersal first began there were scarce pre-existing RCOs or community support structures available. Pre-existing RCOs in London and the regions were also not considered as implementers of dispersal even though they were well placed in knowing the distinctions between members of refugee 'communities' that NASS, local authorities, RSPs and other agencies had to go through 'a steep learning curve'[61] to discover. They also already knew about issues surrounding translation and interpreting. One RCO representative argued that they already had "a pool of interpreters talking three different dialects" and knew about "differences" between what were perceived to be 'communities' from the outside, with one community worker commenting:

> 'You might have a situation where Somali groups are unable to come together. Social services and refugee organisations funded by the Home Office, local government or institutions are unable to understand that. Similarly, there was difficulty understanding Kurdish people from

[59] Interview with a representative of a PAP, dispersal location, June 2003.
[60] The term 'diversity' is used in a general sense and does not relate to the current debate surrounding 'super-diversity' (Vertovec, 2006). 'Multiculturalism' is used in its historical anti-racist sense rather than the current emphasis on identity politics and 'faith communities'.
[61] A phrase repeatedly used to describe how agencies had learnt about their 'clients' during the initial phase of dispersal.

Turkey, Syria, Iraq and Iran. They didn't understand that. We were not objecting to dispersal but we were objecting to the way they did not think it through. The host community was not prepared. They had never seen a Kurd before. They don't know the differences between Kurds.'[62]

At the outset of dispersal, London-based RCOs – without additional funding – supported asylum seekers outside London. One large London-based RCO, for example, received 3,302 enquiries between April 2002 and March 2003 from locations outside London. This 'buffer' was not considered during the subsequent implementation of dispersal and funding for dispersal concentrated on advice and service provision to RSPs and to the detriment of community development activities across the UK. Several representatives of RCOs commented on receiving telephone calls from the newly set-up dispersal areas. Having to resolve issues and telephone social services departments hundreds of miles away from dispersal areas was highly problematic. This unacknowledged and unfunded 'buffer' role for RCOs was a feature of the early stages of dispersal. Authors such as Wren (2007) continue to contend that responsibility falls on voluntary and community organisations in cities such as Glasgow to fill in gaps in statutory service provision.

In one dispersal location the RSP had considerable links with RCOs in the city and directed newly arrived asylum seekers to their 'community'. While this would appear to be a positive action, handing over the responsibility to the RCOs meant that unpaid individuals worked lengthy and inhospitable hours to assist new arrivals in accessing services. Calling on this sense of "duty" of co-nationals, the "voluntary work"[63] carried out by the organisation included locating solicitors, locating opportunities for further education, form filling and delivery of informal advice services. As a Sudanese asylum seeker commented on the way in which this operated:

'It was very difficult the first time because we don't know how to use the phone either. So when we have been given the numbers to call we still didn't know how to use the phones. We found a Kurdish person who helped us to make the call to the Sudanese organisation. Once we were in contact they have sorted out a lot of problems through them. If we have any problem we go to them.'[64]

The experience of this asylum seeker of being directed to their own 'community' for assistance and support was repeatedly recounted. This approach certainly benefited this asylum seeker, giving them "access to friends – we have a social

[62] Interview with a male representative of a Turkish/Kurdish RCO, London, August 2004.
[63] Conversation with a representative of a Sudanese RCO, dispersal location, November 2003.
[64] Interview with a male Sudanese asylum seeker, dispersal location, November 2003.

life and everything".[65] He continued to explain that now he had contact with a Sudanese organisation he would no longer need to contact the RSP and could be supported by the RCO. As the representative of the RCO commented, "if it is your community you can't just stand and watch so you have to do it".[66] Thus, while both the RSP and the asylum seeker benefited greatly from this arrangement, the representative of the RCO was left with the task of providing not only advice and support but also access to social networks and, upon the detention or eviction of another asylum seeker from NASS accommodation upon termination of his support, alternative accommodation:

> 'I am sure that we can find him somewhere to stay. We have of course seen the same problem before. Sometimes we pay about £3,000 for someone for bail from detention. The community has to find it. We can manage to find him a place. This is going to be a short-term solution, not a long-term one. He is not going to be all his life living with people without permission to work. Sometimes it is very difficult. There needs to be a long-term solution really. But I am certain that in the short term we will find something for him.'[67]

Thus, the system of handing over responsibility for co-nationals to RCOs is dependent on goodwill, a sense of 'duty' and not being able to 'stand and watch' what is perceived to be their 'community'. This direction towards and subsequent reliance on 'community' support was largely unquestioned. While there are certainly benefits to this approach, the assumption that the particular 'community' will respond effectively to all asylum seekers is questionable, something that has also been queried in work on destitution in Leeds (Lewis, 2007a). Placing the longer-term responsibility onto co-nationals also has the effect of steering newly arrived asylum seekers into a limited 'bonding' form of social capital. The potential mistrust a newly arrived asylum seeker may have in approaching an organisation that may or may not represent their political opinions or 'vintage' (Kunz, 1973) of migration requires further consideration. It is of interest in the case cited above that both the RCO and the asylum seekers followed the same religion, spoke the same dialect and came from the same region of the country of origin. For others of different faiths, dialects and origins, the outcome may have been different.

Asylum seekers are outside the hierarchy of organisations involved with dispersal and RCOs offer the best possibility for what is sometimes referred to as a 'voice'. The 'voice' of asylum seekers in the punitive NASS system was not apparent. Griffiths et al (2006) outlined how dispersal arrangements meant RCOs

---

[65] Interview with a male Sudanese asylum seeker, dispersal location, November 2003

[66] Conversation with a representative of a Sudanese RCO, dispersal location, November 2003.

[67] Conversation with a representative of a Sudanese RCO, dispersal location, November 2003.

were marginalised as a result of political experiences of the broader race relations framework.

Although some RCOs have contracts with RSPs to provide culturally specific services, they have remained largely unfunded for the volume of work they perform. Given the sheer numbers of different nationalities of asylum seekers dispersed to different locations, it is not possible that each nationality could set up an organisation in each dispersal location. Access to a RCO is therefore dependent on several factors, including proximity. Several refugee-specific issues that have arisen have been dealt with through RCOs rather than contracted agencies. The voluntary sector representing asylum seekers would not therefore necessarily be aware of all the issues that RCOs have been approached to deal with.

In a deterrence environment where there is little room to negotiate with the state to improve conditions for asylum seekers, it is unsurprising that 'users' of the system do not place emphasis on this type of organisation. Even if requirements of day-to-day survival would allow, formally organising as 'asylum seekers' would not necessarily bring benefit. The notion that community self-help is available to all is questionable.

Conclusions

Evidence from past dispersals was not considered during the policy formulation of dispersal – rather, pressures in the policy arena provided the evidence that contemporary compulsory dispersal could work. The history of the dispersal policy was framed by deterrence and therefore involved an inherent exclusionary logic. The lack of consultation, and speed at which the policy was designed, planned and implemented, meant that dispersal was flawed from the outset. These deficiencies at a national level had great effect on implementation at a local level. Past dispersals placed refugees into mainstream service provision but contemporary dispersal separates asylum seekers and other migrants from mainstream services. The power to define access to services based on a complex hierarchy of centrally devised statuses is a form of social exclusion that cannot be overcome at a regional or local level.

Widespread disillusionment with NASS and the Home Office was strongly felt by many working within the system. The seeds of this disillusionment were sown even before contemporary compulsory dispersal began and continued to remain a feature of subsequent negotiations. The proliferation of agencies, including the decision by the voluntary sector to take part in a punitive system for asylum seekers and a new role for the private sector characterise this dispersal. The high number and conflicting roles of agencies means that tensions have been inherent in the relationships between NASS and other agencies. Power imbalances between agencies have played out through a hierarchical structure with those agencies at the top of the hierarchy least likely to be involved with asylum seekers and agencies working locally on a face-to-face basis with asylum seekers having the least influence on policy. The emergent hierarchies have been led by central government and framed by the environment of deterrence. The legislative base for dispersal means that agencies cannot break the law by refusing to provide information to the Home Secretary or implement dispersal once contracts with NASS have been signed. While contracts between public, private and voluntary organisations specify clear responsibilities towards asylum seekers, power imbalances, as well as lack of communication between agencies holding conflicting values, have meant that tensions built into the structure of dispersal are difficult to address at a local level.

Redirection towards the asylum seeker's own 'community' for support has been an unquestioned assumption, with the role of RCOs in 'buffering' dispersal largely unrecognised, unfunded and with little emphasis on using this channel to support subsequent integration strategies.

The position of asylum seekers is outside the hierarchy of the dispersal system. They are represented by the voluntary sector, which undertakes dual roles of 'advocacy' and 'implementers' of dispersal. The voluntary sector is effectively at the interface between asylum seekers and in-country deterrence and therefore inhabits the most visible and contested space within the system. The tensions and replication of the role of the state by various agencies mean that an asylum seeker's experience of institutions – from NASS downwards – has seldom been positive and has not provided space for the restoration of institutional trust.

A moral underclass discourse of social exclusion was evident from non-user-led agencies when descriptions of the actions of asylum seekers were focused on. The imposed constraints of the system were in this way often disregarded in favour of focusing on the behaviour of individuals.

FOUR

The evolution and geography of dispersal

Introduction

Key design principles of dispersal that may have made the policy more user-friendly were abandoned or unfulfilled early in its implementation. One of these principles was the idea of 'clustering' asylum seekers according to their language groups or nationality. There was also a shift from dispersing asylum seekers individually – or in official terms 'self-write'[1] – to dispersal by group. Maybe most importantly, suggestions made during the design stage to ensure that asylum seekers were not placed in areas of multiple deprivation were also disregarded. This, and other design elements that may have made the lives of asylum seekers less harsh, are detailed below.

To do this, this chapter views the design and evolution of the dispersal policy, illustrating the geographical spread of cities involved. The ultimate *geography* of dispersal reflected the availability of unpopular or low-demand accommodation encompassing also the exclusionary policy context towards asylum seekers in which the policy was designed. Compared to the available alternative of claiming SO support, compulsory dispersal created a different pattern of settlement. SO support can be regarded as an indicator of existing social networks and it is revealing that the geographical spread of asylum seekers was radically different under this option than dispersal with its mechanisms of 'institutionalised redistribution' (Thielemann, 2003b, p 228).

Locations chosen for dispersal feature heavily in the list of the 88 most multiply deprived districts in England. This link between dispersal and multiple deprivation is explored through the voices of asylum seekers, refugees and voluntary sector practitioners working at grassroots level. It is suggested that the dispersal policy was bedspace-led and that this accommodation, being mainly in multiply deprived areas, was, and remains, key to the reinforcement of formal and informal social exclusion of asylum seekers in the UK.

---

[1] The terms 'self-write' (individuals) and 'group' dispersal originate from NASS and are used by RSP staff.

Evolution and implementation of dispersal

Original design elements of the dispersal policy disappeared during the early stages of implementation of the policy and the criteria unfulfilled or abandoned are addressed below.

Cluster area idea abandoned

The idea of 'clusters' of asylum seekers based around available accommodation, multicultural environments plus supporting infrastructure and services was originally a major element of the design of dispersal (Refugee Council, 2004b). Documented[2] suggestions were made by the Refugee Council of which cities would be suitable and the idea of 'clusters within clusters', that is, specific cities within regions, was considered more practical than even distribution across regions.

A focus on language-based clusters was a logistically useful idea for local authorities and RSPs given the requirements of translation and interpretation. However, this became an ongoing tension between regional consortia and the Home Office. Lists of agreed languages for dispersal to particular cities grew as extra languages were added onto local authority lists. As the policy evolved, arrivals of asylum seekers speaking other languages than those listed were prevalent and the clustering of language groups did not occur in any real sense. For example, by mid-2003 in Leicester, of a total of 1,217 asylum seekers in NASS accommodation, there were 63 different nationalities of asylum seekers, many of whom did not speak the 28 different agreed language groups.[3] It was widely considered that reducing the number of interpreters and translators would have benefited implementing agencies within designated cities.

Wider issues around notions of 'community' and 'integration' were not considered. The assumption that speaking the same language would make compulsory dispersal more sustainable in the longer term was fraught with difficulties, implying an imagined community based on language alone (Anderson, 1991). Such an idea would not account for historical antagonisms with bordering countries or factions within one nationality. The basis of an individual's asylum claim is often along religious or political lines that divide groups who speak the same language. One Iranian male mentioned that he was sharing his room in Leicester with an Iraqi Kurd and while they spoke the same language, "history" denied them the possibilities of conversing.[4] The complexities of this combined and often simultaneous contact and conflict warrant further research and it is

---

[2] *Some Thoughts on Clusters*, Refugee Council, October 1999.
[3] Leicester initially had 12 languages – Gujerati, Polish, Latvian, Ukrainian, Kiswahli, Serbo Croat, Swahili, Hindi, Mandarin, Turkish, Somali and French – as agreed languages. Another five languages were suggested by NASS in late 2002 – Farsi, Dari, Arabic, Pushto and Czech.
[4] Focus group with male and female asylum seekers, Leicester, November 2003.

possible that an entire spectrum of outcomes would be highlighted. Sharing a room and having day-to-day close proximity with someone would not necessarily depoliticise or dehistoricise individuals. This idea that 'warring factions' would be kept apart during dispersal had been outlined in a NASS Dispersal Strategy to avoid 'any tension spilling over from their countries of origin' but was largely left out of decisions over where to accommodate asylum seekers.

Zetter et al (2003) suggest that the idea of language-based clusters had only limited practical success due to 'twin pressures of speed and economy with the socially and logistically complex task' involved in such an idea. The logistical task was certainly complex and dependent on accurate information being available within the system. The social task was as complex and overridden by the requirement to find accommodation.

A Home Office report published in December 2005 identified 'linguistic clustering' as potentially contributing to emerging 'ghettos' of asylum seekers and refugees in deprived areas, in turn hindering refugees' future 'integration' into communities (Home Office, 2005, p 7). The politics of language and ability to integrate into the UK based on an ability to speak English is part of a much broader race relations framework (Bhavnani et al, 2005; Finney and Simpson, 2009). References to 'ghettos' are unsubstantiated by evidence available (Peach, 1996; Finney and Simpson, 2009) and, given the high number of different nationalities dispersed to each city, the feasibility of such 'ghettos' emerging was unrealistic.

One in 200

In line with this thinking about the dangers of concentrating minority ethnic groups, a ratio of asylum seekers was outlined in the early stages of consultation between the Home Office and local authorities. A ratio of one asylum seeker per 200 head of population was outlined. Quite how this crude method of quantifying and allocating asylum seekers arose remained unknown but this ratio of 1:200 became another source of contention between agencies within dispersal and the Home Office. It was considered that the Home Office may have "regretted" outlining the ratio but it was often referred to:

> 'So much depends on the local resources, the back-up support, the make-up of the host community, all those sorts of things. That figure one to 200 has sort of haunted the Home Office ever since and people throw it back to them at time to time. Then it becomes cast in stone.'[5]

This tension between national and local government and the number of 'bedspaces' in each city according to this ratio became an issue that on occasions resulted in suspension of dispersal to particular cities due to their exceeding the 'quota': "It has only recently emerged, when NASS has started looking at the actually number

---

[5]   Interview with a representative of a regional consortium, September 2003.

of bedspaces they have got contracted in each place, that they have contracted for far more bedspaces than their own guidelines".[6]

The 1:200 ratio was also essentially ignored to some extent because private accommodation providers largely operated outside the regional coordination structures and it was a common suggestion from representations of regional consortia and other agencies that they did not always take the ratio into consideration: "The private providers all piled in and bought up cheap rented property where they could, and offered it to the Home Office, those guidelines have been largely exceeded".[7] In this way, the provision of accommodation by the private sector had considerable impact on the way in which dispersal evolved over time.

'Group' and 'self-write' dispersal

There were two ways in which dispersal was implemented – 'self-write' of individuals and 'group' dispersal where groups were picked up, usually by coach, from their initial accommodation. At the outset, 'self-write' dispersal of individuals was the main method utilised. The idea being that each individual would be provided with a set of instructions from NASS along with a dispersal pack containing information about dispersal, their address, vouchers and tickets if they were travelling on public transport with reception arrangements and a named individual to meet in their dispersal city. This method, however, proved difficult to implement because NASS found the allocation of individuals to specific accommodation difficult to arrange in practice. Also, the database from which these arrangements were made did not contain information regarding family members who may already be in the country in different dispersal locations. NASS staff did not meet asylum seekers face to face and decisions based on this partial access to information led to numerous mistakes and inefficiencies.

This system gave way to 'group dispersal' with asylum seekers picked up mainly in London and the Southeast. Explaining this system, a representative of an RSP commented:

> 'Group dispersal contained coaches arriving outside the emergency accommodation and, if accommodation had been allocated for 20 Iraqi single men, then 20 Iraqi single men would be assigned to this coach and they would drive to wherever. The accommodation provider would meet them and they would allocate individual accommodation when they actually got there as to who would share with whom, who did not want to share with anyone, etc. ... because NASS did not have that information available to them whether these two are brothers,

---

[6] Interview with a representative of a regional consortium, January 2004.
[7] Interview with a representative of a regional consortium, January 2004..

or these two are best friends or whatever. They weren't making that type of decision.'[8]

The potential for problems with this system were often summed up in one phrase – 'failure to travel'. This term was used to described how asylum seekers would 'fail' to turn up to be dispersed, something that occurred for a multitude of reasons, including people not wanting to share rooms: "Because people couldn't travel with their friends or because they were being put into a shared room and they didn't want to share, they were not travelling. Which is why the system started to break down".[9] Individuals' not wanting to share rooms with strangers and being unable to maintain social networks due to dispersal was repeatedly raised in discussions about why dispersal was not working. The more structural failings and imposed constraints of the system itself were often disregarded in favour of focusing on the behaviour of individuals.

The switch to group dispersals did facilitate, for example, two Iraqi friends in EA choosing to get on the same coach knowing its destination. Another representative of an RSP in a dispersal location also commented on the reasons and method involved in this switch from 'self-write' to 'group' dispersals, suggesting that it was effectively the inefficiency of NASS that pre-empted this shift:

'So the number of people in emergency accommodation waiting to be dispersed started to rise and went up so NASS asked us. They said we have to do something about it. We have to lower the number of people in emergency accommodation, so you have got the people in emergency accommodation, you have got the names, can you just make the list. For example, 20 people, and we'll send a coach and we'll disperse all these people together somewhere. And we did that, and after that then they started to develop this group dispersal system. They sent us a timetable of group dispersals in that whole week.'[10]

This switch was due to NASS being "unable to cope"[11] and greater involvement from the voluntary sector was required to make the system work. This new method allowed RSPs some "room to manoeuvre" in that the "choice" of the "place" to send "singles" or "families" was given to refugee service providers. However, the choice of people was more complicated as RSPs were unable to refuse dispersal and "had to fill in the people to go".[12] The perceived benefits of this were that RSPs knew the clients because they worked closely with them and therefore knew who was likely (or fail) to travel: "We know if someone really doesn't want

---

[8] Interview a representative of the Refugee Council, London, May 2003.
[9] Interview a representative of the Refugee Council, London, May 2003.
[10] Focus group with representatives of the voluntary sector, dispersal location, June 2003.
[11] Focus group with representatives of the voluntary sector, dispersal location, June 2003.
[12] Focus group with representatives of the voluntary sector, dispersal location, June 2003.

to travel because they have got friends or family and then we don't put them on the list at all. We wait until we have got in-region dispersals. Then we disperse those people".[13]

For asylum seekers, forming relationships with the new decision makers, RSPs, became necessary if preferences were to be taken into consideration. These agencies, operating "not exactly a gentlemen's agreement, but trying to accommodate preferences",[14] were able, therefore, to try to put people together. Some "good relationships around the country" between RSPs, local authorities and city councils could be utilised to move asylum seekers who were "desperate" to move. The inadequacies of the NASS system put RSPs in a position whereby they did more of the negotiations among themselves. As a result, an even more complex dynamic – of providing the best service to their clients while at the same time making decisions on their ultimate dispersal location and type of accommodation – emerged.

Regional variations in approaches, based on local conditions and relationships between NASS and local implementers of the policy, made it difficult to generalise about the overall impact of this shift from individual to group dispersals. What was clear, however, was that the initial system designed to facilitate dispersal was inadequate. As a result, local agencies took on the dual role of advocacy for individual asylum seekers as well as taking a frontline role in the implementation of a policy that was unpopular with many asylum seekers.

Unpopular housing: a bedspace-led policy

The geographic concentration of social exclusion has a long history in the UK as has the degree of concentration of minority groups (Mohan, 1999, p 128; Lupton and Power, 2002, p 118). The inferior quality of housing available to minority groups through 'residential clustering' has been a distinctive feature of accommodation patterns (Lee, 1977, p 1; Mohan, 1999, p 129; Sim, 2000, p 93). Dispersal of minority groups has also been a part of 'the racialized social policy interventions that occurred in response to the black post-war settlement in Britain' (Bloch and Schuster, 2005, p 203).

As well as concentrating on particular groups, social exclusion has been conceptualised in a geographical sense to implement social policy interventions by identifying geographical areas that require regeneration or renewal. In 1999, the availability of low-demand accommodation or unpopular housing in England was investigated by the Policy Action Team of the Social Exclusion Unit (SEU) of the recently appointed Labour government. The published report, *Report by the Unpopular Housing Action Team* (DETR, 1999) (hereafter 'the PAT report')[15] identified low-demand housing stock of local authorities, RSLs and the private

---

[13] Focus group with representatives of the voluntary sector, dispersal location, June 2003.

[14] Interview with a representative of the Refugee Council, London, May 2003.

[15] Underpinned by a research project from Heriott-Watt University.

sector. The report showed that local authority dwellings in unpopular areas were concentrated in the North West, North East, Yorkshire & Humberside and West Midlands.[16] Unpopular private sector housing was concentrated in the North West, West Midlands and Yorkshire & Humberside.[17] The distribution of RSL properties was concentrated in the North West, South East, West Midlands, North East and Yorkshire & Humberside.[18]

Team members of the PAT report included the head of the pre-NASS team who subsequently became the first director of NASS and information about accommodation being collected by DETR was also mentioned in the 'information document' (Home Office, 1999). Lists of these vacant properties were available in meetings between the Home Office and the Refugee Council before dispersal began.[19] Although a much smaller number than the 838,500 low-demand public and private sector properties, the distribution of 12,320 asylum seekers in England by December 2000 reflected patterns of unpopular accommodation. Table 4.1 illustrates this initial distribution of asylum seekers in Yorkshire & Humberside, the North West, the North East and the West Midlands.

Carter and el-Hassan (2003, p 24) suggest that RSLs were expected to take a substantial role in providing temporary accommodation to asylum seekers but were ultimately a 'relatively small player in the UK overall'. It was also initially anticipated that approximately 60% of accommodation would be provided through private contractors and 40% by public providers (Harrison, 2006).

Dispersal was considered to be a source of income for local authorities with unpopular housing stock. The ability of the Home Secretary to use powers under section 100 of the Immigration and Asylum Act 1999 to force local authorities to release empty council accommodation was also a factor cited in the decision to participate in dispersal. One regional consortia representative commented how "people thought, well, we had better go along with this, for fear of having it forced upon us".[20]

Glasgow also accommodated larger numbers of asylum seekers. It was suggested that the availability of unpopular housing also influenced the speed at which contracts were signed, with Glasgow City Council signing the first contract

---

[16] 377,000 local authority dwellings in areas of low demand: the North West (31%), North East (17%), Yorkshire & Humberside (16%), West Midlands (11%), East Midlands (8%) and South West (2%) accounting for just 10% of the unpopular local authority housing stock (DETR, 1999, p 3).

[17] 461,500 private sector properties were in the North West (38%), the West Midlands (15%) and Yorkshire & Humberside (15%), with the East Midlands (8%) and South West (4%) accounting for 12% of low-demand properties (DETR, 1999).

[18] 89,500 RSL properties in low demand were in the North West (28%), South East (14%), West Midlands (14%), North East (11%) and Yorkshire & Humberside (10%), with low-demand RSL properties in the East Midlands (6%) and the South West (5%) accounting for 11%.

[19] Interview with a former employee of the Refugee Council, London, February 2005.

[20] Interview with a representative of a regional consortium, January 2004.

Table 4.1: Regional distribution of asylum seekers accommodated in England by NASS, end of December 2000

Region	Number supported in NASS accommodation (as of end December 2000)
Yorkshire & Humberside	3,550
North West	3,420
North East	2,420
West Midlands	1,350
East Midlands	760
Greater London	250
South West	380
South Central	200
East of England	0
England total	12,320

Note: South Central encompasses East of England.
Source: Home Office, www.homeoffice.gov.uk/rds/immigration1.html

"because they had large amounts of housing. Tower blocks that they might otherwise consider demolishing if they hadn't had the contract with the Home Office. It brought in rent, Council Tax and revenue to the local authorities".[21]

When originally devised, there was public housing in Leicester that was 'hard to let' – this situation changing later alongside changes in the housing market. In the South West of England the availability of public sector housing was low and the allocation of this was considered likely to create a "political backlash" if it were perceived that asylum seekers were being allocated housing that was "already in great demand".[22] The position of asylum seekers in any hierarchy of needs was thus widely regarded as low, unlike much of the historical support provided for 'quota' refugees.

Considerable regional variations in the anticipated 60:40 private/public split were apparent: in Bristol, for example, provision of accommodation was 100% private. In these areas, provision of accommodation to asylum seekers was a political issue at both regional and local level as well as the predominant national issue it was initially devised to address (see Chapter One).

As with the dispersal of Vietnamese refugees, contemporary dispersal was led by the availability of accommodation. However, contemporary dispersal was led by the need to find 'bedspaces' for 'singles' or 'families' and these were largely in shared accommodation. It was also led by the availability of unpopular housing,

---

[21] Interview with a representative of a regional consortium, January 2004.
[22] Interview with a representative of a regional consortium, September 2003.

procured through contracts with the public and private sectors and a small number of RSL properties. The basis of these contracts was provision of 'bedspaces'.

Deprivation and dispersal

Suggestions by the Refugee Council and other voluntary sector agencies that dispersal should be to areas with unemployment levels at, or below, the national average (Refugee Council, 2004) were disregarded. The right to work had not, at this stage, been withdrawn[23]:

> 'The original idea was to pick areas that were relatively appropriate, in terms of being multicultural initially. Also we suggested using some basic criteria like employment rates that were lower than or at least at the average. But, as far as I know, the indices we suggested were never actually used.'[24]

The indices discussed here are the Indices of Deprivation 2000, which provide data on rates of deprivation and unemployment at district and ward levels. Phillimore and Goodson (2006) addressed how the dispersal policy focused on sending asylum seekers to these excluded urban areas with high unemployment. They argued that the high levels of unemployment and underemployment experienced by asylum seekers and refugees exclude them from society in dispersal areas and, crucially, in doing so exacerbate the general levels of social exclusion in those areas.

The 88 most deprived local authority districts in England are often referred to in the literature on neighbourhood renewal and regeneration. These 88 districts were identified in a SEU report in 2001 entitled, *A New Commitment to Neighbourhood Renewal: National Strategy and Action Plan* (SEU, 2001, p 13). Figure 4.1 shows these 88 most deprived districts in 2000.

A Home Office study, *An Exploration of Factors Affecting the Successful Dispersal of Asylum Seekers*, published in December 2005, identified a 'significant association' between levels of deprivation and dispersal (Anie et al, 2005, p 10). It is also the case that some 70% of all black and minority ethnic communities live in the 88 most deprived districts, compared to 40% of the general population (ODPM, 2004, p 5).

In addition to the requirement for accommodation that would otherwise be hard to let or unpopular, the requirement of the dispersal policy to place asylum seekers in multicultural areas resulted in a high proportion of the areas being in these same multiply deprived districts. Nearly 80% of the initial dispersal locations in England were in the 88 most multiply deprived districts identified by the Indices of Deprivation 2000. This reduced to just over 70% by June 2004, due in part to the inclusion of Greater London in the statistics.

---

[23] Permission to work was denied from 23 July 2003.
[24] Interview with a representative of the Refugee Council, London, August 2003.

Figure 4.1: 88 most deprived districts in England, 2000

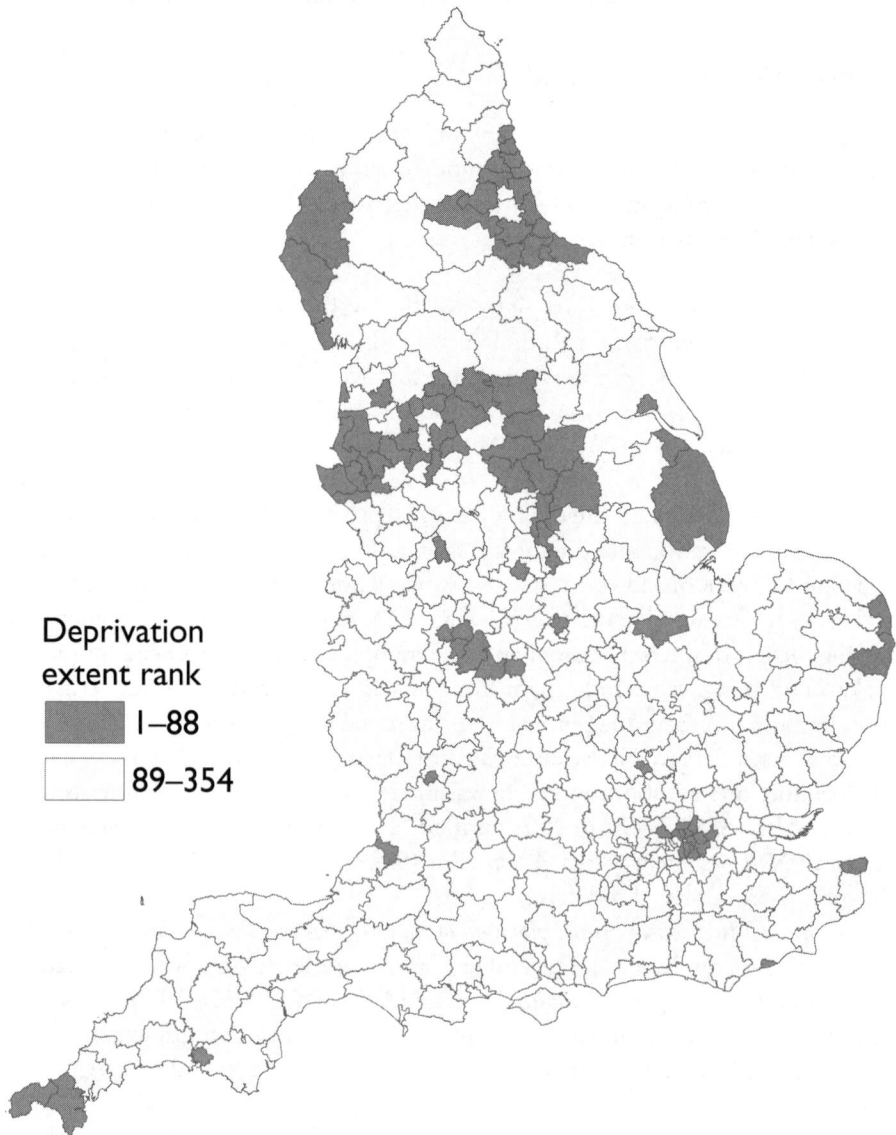

Deprivation
extent rank

1–88

89–354

Source: DETR, Indices of Deprivation 2000

Figure 4.2: English map of dispersal, June 2001

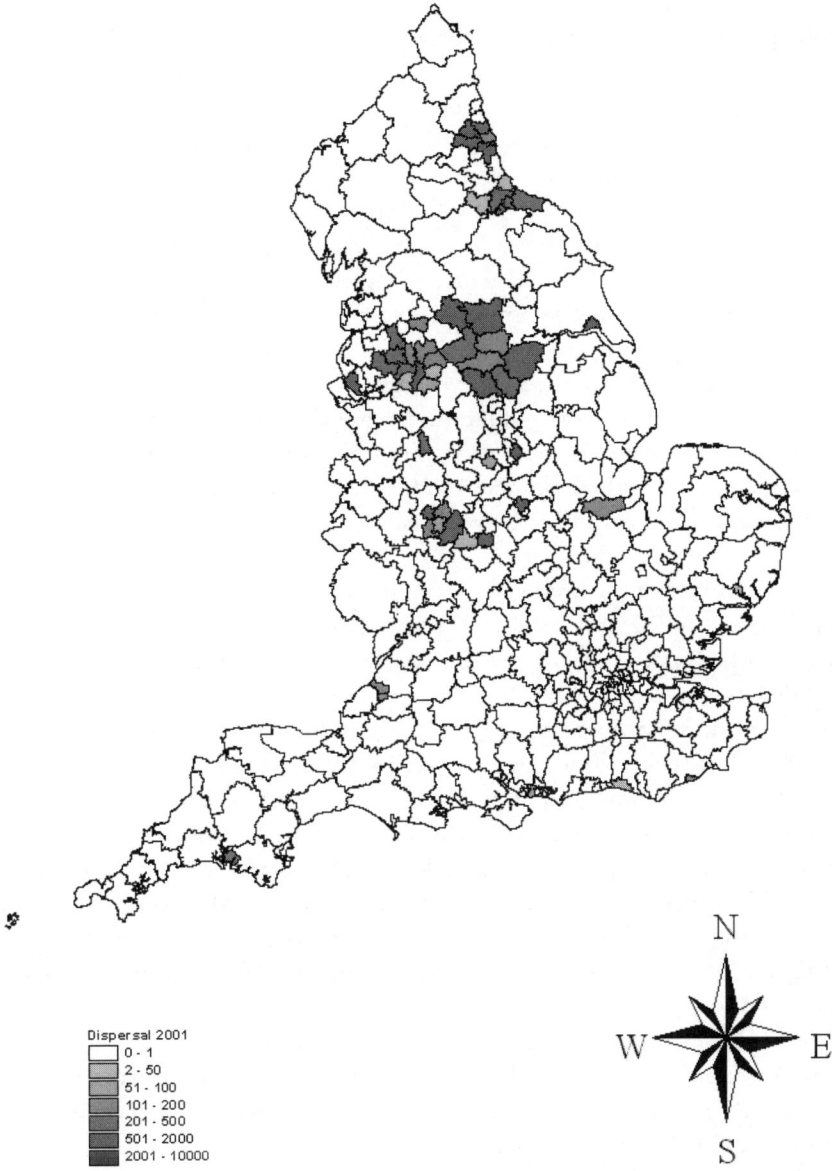

Source: Figures for June 2001 provided by the Home Office

Dispersal

Avoiding adding to the problems of social exclusion and creating racial tensions was a stated aim of dispersal but asylum seekers were placed in areas already designated as areas of multiple deprivation and social exclusion. In practice, dispersal brought concentrations of asylum seekers to particular locations, shifting the concentrations from London and the South East of England to these areas. Separating them further from mainstream support without adequate representation meant that asylum seekers in these areas became visible targets for exclusion. This was a commonly held view by representatives of agencies implementing dispersal at a local level, outlined in the words of one representative from a regional consortium:

> 'It was one of the unfortunate things that it was the more deprived areas that had available public sector housing. Councils saw that as an ideal opportunity of actually utilising that vacant housing, getting some income and whole streets suddenly became asylum seeker areas. You are half way to disaster, you really are.'[25]

This perception that the presence of whole streets of asylum seekers equated to being halfway to disaster is explored further below.

Viewing the pattern of dispersal in England shows how, by June 2001, it had expanded in each region with 22,620 asylum seekers in NASS accommodation, with the North West and Yorkshire & Humberside regions each supporting close to 6,000 asylum seekers. Both regions were involved in the Kosovan Humanitarian Evacuation programme and thus had recent experience to draw on (Audit Commission, 2000a, p 17) as well as available accommodation. It was never the intention to evenly disperse asylum seekers to all districts across the country and by the early stages dispersal was uneven and had a marked urban bias. Scotland, Northern Ireland and Wales also received asylum seekers as a part of this policy. In England, as illustrated in Figure 4.2, by June 2001 dispersal was to 54 local authority districts.

These concentrations of dispersal locations remained relatively fixed over time due to the contracts awarded, which were generally for periods between three to five years. By June 2003, 81 locations[26] were a part of the dispersal policy. At the end of June 2004 there were 37,070 asylum seekers in NASS accommodation in 78 locations[27] in England. Figure 4.3 shows these concentrations as of the end of June 2001 to the end of June 2004, showing how Yorkshire & Humberside, the West Midlands, the North West and the North East accommodated most of the asylum seekers dispersed during this period in England. Table 4.2 illustrates

---

[25] Interview with a representative of a regional consortium, September 2003.
[26] Including 12 Greater London dispersal locations.
[27] Including 10 Greater London dispersal locations.

Figure 4.3: Regional distribution of asylum seekers in NASS accommodation in England and Wales, end of June 2001–end of June 2004

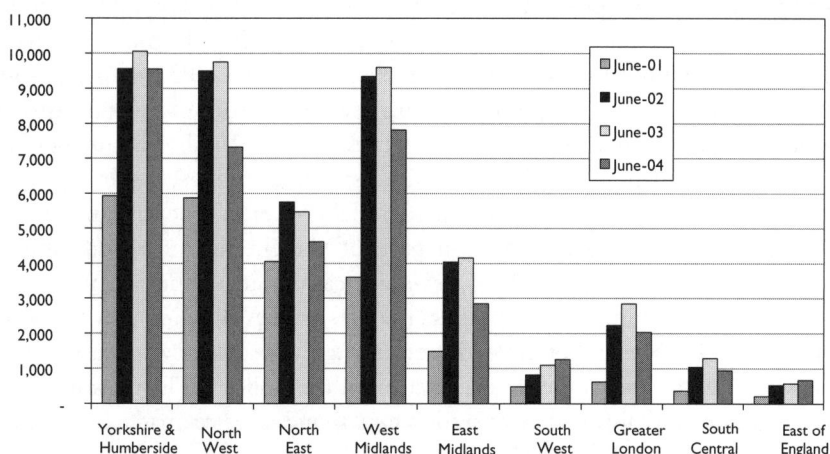

Source: Home Office website (quarterly statistics). Figures for June 2001 provided by email from the Home Office

Table 4.2: Regional distribution of asylum seekers in NASS/BIA accommodation, June 2001–June 2007

Region	June 2001	June 2002	June 2003	June 2004	June 2005	June 2006	June 2007
Yorkshire & Humberside	5,930	9,560	10,055	9,555	8,000	6,610	7,745
North West	5,870	9,500	9,755	7,325	6,155	4,655	6,810
North East	4,060	5,750	5,475	4,620	3,620	2,925	3,310
West Midlands	3,610	9,340	9,600	7,820	5,530	4,020	5,685
East Midlands	1,490	4,054	4,165	2,850	2,210	2,055	2,220
Greater London	620	2,230	2,845	2,035	1,225	1,190	1,545
South West	480	815	1,095	1,255	920	995	1,135
South Central/ South East	360	1,040	1,290	940	610	545	460
East of England	210	520	570	670	540	490	465
England total	22,620*	42,805*	44,850*	37,070*	28,810*	23,490*	29,385*
Northern Ireland		90	165	110	120	155	190
Scotland		5,040	5,885	5,580	5,640	4,730	5,230
Wales		1,150	2,130	2,375	2,285	2,335	2,475
UK total		49,085*	53,050*	45,135*	36,855*	30,710*	37,280*

Notes: * total includes 'disbenefited' cases. Disbenefited cases refer to those cases that were previously supported by local authorities or the Department for Work and Pensions (DWP) but became supported by NASS when it began operating in April 2000.
Source: Home Office website (quarterly statistics). Figures for June 2001 provided by email from the Home Office

how asylum seekers were dispersed over the period between June 2001 and June 2007 across the four nations of the UK.

Between June 2001 and June 2002, cases of dispersal grew in areas around the original concentrations as of December 2000, with only minor decreases in Burnley and Plymouth. Between June 2002 and June 2003, there was some reduction in numbers of dispersed asylum seekers in some areas and growth in others, with the main reductions in cities such as Bradford, Burnley and Manchester. In December 2002, several dispersal locations were suspended at the request of the police, local authority or regional consortia. The suspended cities listed were Blackburn, Burnley, Nelson, parts of Manchester and Huddersfield.[28] Between June 2003 and June 2004, several locations receiving asylum seekers experienced some reduction in numbers in cities such as Birmingham, Coventry and Liverpool. By November 2004, dispersal of asylum seekers was ceased, either partially or fully, to eight cities at the request of the police.[29] Fluctuations in the fixed geography of dispersal occurred when requests were made by agencies involved when social tensions were perceived.

Mohan (1999, p 128) suggests that there has been a welcome move from the mapping of minority groups to 'charting the geographies of racism' by geographers since the 1960s. However, charting any relationship between racism and dispersal of asylum seekers is not straightforward. A report by the IPPR found that concern about asylum seekers was often in areas where there were 'few or no asylum seekers' (Lewis, 2005, p 1) and that '[a]ttitudes were most positive in areas with larger numbers of asylum seekers, refugees and BME [black and minority ethnic] communities than in places with small numbers of asylum seekers and migrants' (2005, p 17).

The report also suggested that the British National Party (BNP) and other right-wing parties were 'more active in areas of the country where there are few minority ethnic communities and few asylum seekers' (2005, p 22). The 'moral panic' (Robinson, 2003a) surrounding the issue of asylum in the UK is thus played out nationally and locally regardless of the actual presence of asylum seekers. The imagined threat posed by asylum seekers is thus simultaneously constructed within dispersal areas and areas where asylum seekers are not dispersed to.

SO support

Asylum seekers opting for SO support were heavily concentrated in Greater London and the South East of England. This reflected the availability of family

---

[28] Asylum support information, 18 December 2002. Although Bolton was also listed as a suspended city, confirmation sought with Bolton local authorities asylum team confirmed that dispersals were not suspended, with the confusion arising due to dispersals in a few postcode areas in Bolton being stopped.

[29] These cities were Bootle, Burnley, Derby, Doncaster, Manchester, Nelson, Nottingham and Swansea.

---

or wider social networks. Greater London hosted the highest proportion of SO cases – 84% as of June 2003.[30] SO support can be regarded as a proxy indicator of social networks in that the receipt of only financial assistance requires some connection with family, friends or acquaintances able and willing to provide accommodation.

This maintenance and utilisation of social networks was in areas that dispersal aimed to move asylum seekers away from. Dispersal may well contain a high proportion of individuals and families who have had their social networks destroyed or severely disrupted during their forced migration and are unable to opt for SO support in the first instance. Accommodation allocated in dispersal areas did not allow for relatives claiming SO support to be accommodated within it, with 'bedspaces' being strictly allocated and monitored by landlords for the Home Office.

The element of 'choice' – a word used cautiously here given the limitations of the system – in opting for SO support shows a different pattern of settlement to dispersal.

The concentration of minority ethnic groups in housing patterns has been explained in terms of 'choices' and 'constraints'. Studies emphasising 'choice' focus on cultural preferences, arguing that minority groups prefer to live within concentrations of their own groups for social and linguistic support. Studies focusing on 'constraints' surround the economic position of the individual and notions of institutionalised racism, arguing that minority groups have been prevented from moving outside these areas because of, for example, discriminatory practices in the wider processes of allocation of accommodation (Lakey, 1997). This distinction resonates with the MUD and RED frameworks of social exclusion (Levitas, 2000).

Dispersal was premised on a 'no-choice' basis and any focus on cultural preferences was largely tokenistic. That cultural preferences could be prevalent if the alternative SO support option was chosen sat uncomfortably with the realities of the day-to-day lives of asylum seekers in receipt of this. In the words of one RSP representative, asylum seekers opting for SO support usually ended up "sofa surfing" (moving between friends to find accommodation) and the potential for exploitative relationships to occur as a result of this practice remains unresearched.

Having said this, SO support usually occurred in larger cities. For example, in Leicester virtually a third of the asylum seekers supported by NASS were SO cases.[31] There were also a number of larger cities in England that were not dispersal points but had cases of SO support such as Luton, Milton Keynes and Oxford. SO support also appears to provide a proxy indicator for where asylum seekers "feel comfortable"[32] in the UK. The lack of a SO presence of asylum seekers was largely

---

[30] Of a total of 27,350 in receipt of SO support.
[31] 600 cases of SO compared to 1,185 dispersed at end of June 2003.
[32] Participant in focus group, Leicester, July 2003.

in areas without a history of hosting black and minority ethnic communities.[33] The issue of visibility, therefore, affects the choices of locations asylum seekers made if left to disperse themselves.

Figure 4.4 shows that SO support was still a main source of support for asylum seekers and remained concentrated in London some years after dispersal began. The total number of dispersed asylum seekers was 37,070 and those in receipt of SO totalled 25,085, demonstrating a high proportion of cases of social networks being utilised in London rather than entering the dispersal system.

Figure 4.4: Regional distribution of asylum seekers in NASS accommodation and in receipt of SO support in England, end of June 2004

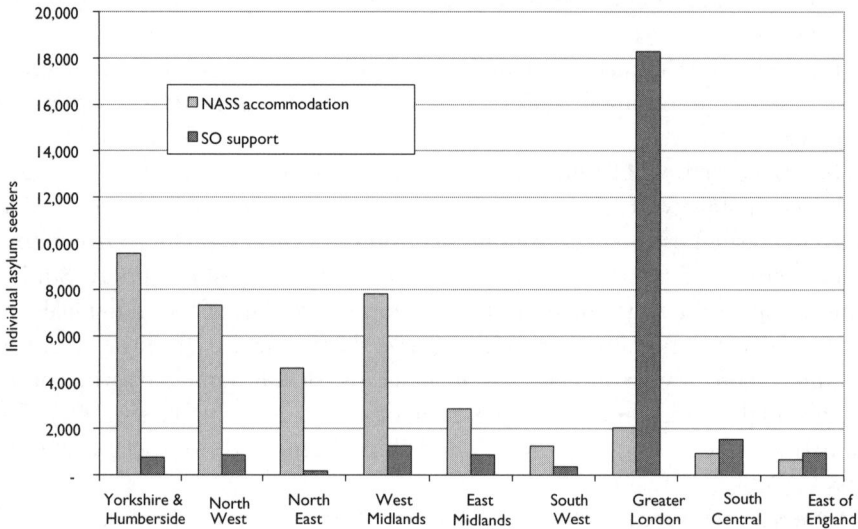

Source: Home Office (quarterly statistics)

Several London boroughs with no dispersal had high numbers of SO cases and these were concentrated in areas of London such as Brent, Ealing, Enfield, Haringey and Newham.

Deprivation, dispersal and SO support

Table 4.3 reveals that the geography of deprivation was closer to the pattern of dispersal than that of SO support.

There were also more cities receiving asylum seekers under the SO support arrangement than the number of dispersal locations, suggesting that asylum seekers disperse themselves more effectively than social policy interventions or efforts at institutional redistribution. While a number of these locations were also

---

[33] For example, Cleveland, Hartlepool, Lincoln and Redcar.

in deprived districts, the proportion was lower – 50 to 60% rather than 70 to 80%. This challenges notions that asylum seekers choose to live in the same areas considered by the designers of dispersal to provide room for cultural preferences. Proportionately, half of the areas chosen were not in the top 88 deprived areas.

Table 4.3: Dispersal, district-level deprivation and SO support

	Dispersal (June 2001)	Dispersal (June 2002)	Dispersal (June 2003)	Dispersal (June 2004)	SO (June 2003)	SO (June 2004)
Total number of dispersal and SO support locations in England	54a	57	81b	78c	111d	98
Total number of dispersal and SO support locations in 88 most deprived local authority districts in England	43	45	58	55	57	57
Percentage of dispersal and SO support locations in 88 most deprived districts in England	79.63%	78.95%	71.6%	70.5%	51.35%	58.16%

Notes: a Excludes Greater London.
b Includes 12 Greater London dispersal locations.
c Includes 10 Greater London dispersal locations.
d Does not include 'disbenefited' cases.
Source: Home Office website (quarterly statistics). Figures for June 2001 provided by email from the Home Office

Dispersal and local-level deprivation

At a local level in Bristol, for example, a higher number of asylum seekers were accommodated in the wards of Easton and Horfield – two areas with historical associations with immigration. In the words of one PAP, Easton was being used to fulfil the criteria of accommodating asylum seekers in multicultural areas: "It is standard accommodation in houses in residential parts of Bristol. Ideally, in areas where there is support networks for refugees. So, typically, areas like Easton and the surrounding area, which is the Muslim area".[34]

As Harrison and Phillips (2010, p 20) argue, discrimination in the private sector housing market has historically witnessed the 'steering' of minority households away from areas favoured by white people. They argue that forms of direct or

---

[34] Interview with a PAP, dispersal location, June 2003.

indirect discrimination were fairly easy up to the end of the 1980s given the lack of monitoring or equality codes (2010, p 20). The above quote from a PAP, with its association between asylum seekers and Muslims, bore little resemblance to the religious identities of individuals actually dispersed to Bristol. At the end of March 2003, there were 48 different nationalities in NASS accommodation (Refugee Council, 2003b) in the city, with a high proportion necessarily Muslim given their countries of origin.[35] There were not necessarily shared religious, linguistic or cultural traditions for all asylum seekers in these areas. The assumption that support networks for asylum seekers were automatically available in areas such as Easton was therefore dubious.

In another example, in Leicester, asylum seekers were accommodated in North Braunstone, an area ranking highly in the ward-level Indices of Deprivation 2000 (rank 57). Other wards mentioned were Mowmacre, Eyres Monsell, Spinney Hill, West Humberston, Rushey Mead, Belgrave and Beaumont Leys wards. With the exception of Rushey Mead, each of these wards was in the top 10% of deprived wards in England. These areas in Leicester that have historically housed immigrant communities are now being used to house asylum seekers, with areas '[o]ften chosen because of their unpopularity, [which] has led to vacancies in the housing stock' (ICAR, 2003). Concerns were expressed about asylum seekers being accommodated in areas of economic and historical disadvantage (ICAR, 2003). These areas were also mentioned in a study on settlement patterns of Ugandan Asians who arrived in the 1970s (Martin and Singh, 2002).

The principle that asylum seekers would automatically be best accommodated in multicultural areas was a central tenet of the initial design of dispersal. In practice, areas perceived to be appropriate areas for asylum seekers were deprived areas.

Social exclusion and neighbourhoods

The perception from a representative of a regional consortium that whole streets of asylum seekers equated to being halfway to disaster requires exploration as it contains an assumption that the damaging characteristic of streets was the arrival and concentrated presence of asylum seekers. Lupton and Power (2002, p 138) call this a 'trigger point' – an identifiable moment when neighbourhoods begin to spiral into decline. They argue that the 'nature of neighbourhoods actually contributes to the social exclusion of their residents' in three ways: the intrinsic characteristics of neighbourhoods; residential sorting that concentrates the most disadvantaged in the least advantaged areas; and once this concentration of disadvantage is established, areas acquire more damaging characteristics, which

---

[35] Also, given that religion is a basis of persecution, the number of non-Muslim asylum seekers originating from majority Muslim countries would need to be taken into consideration.

---

include the reputation of the neighbourhood. In their study,[36] the decline of Thanet's popularity over time is outlined as a decline in tourism, which meant that hotels were converted to bedsits and hostels, seeing an influx of the unemployed, homeless and, most recently, asylum seekers. They identify how high levels of crime impact on people's sense of control over their own environments, their trust in neighbours and their confidence in the authorities to resolve problems and the loss of a sense of power, control and inclusion results in mistrust of public service providers generally (2002, p 134).

Asylum seekers often focused on high crime levels in dispersal areas as well as mistrust of the ability of the police to assist in these areas and mistrust towards their neighbours. For example, for one female asylum seeker, the link between dispersal and deprivation was outlined when she described the area they had initially been accommodated in before being relocated to Leicester:

> 'It was a very bad area. You see people drunk in the street. Very bad. That is why we have come here. If they throw stuff in our windows, we had to wait until they broke your head or something. The area was known to the police. The police came to our neighbours. When we rang them [the police], they said they would come but they did not come until the next morning and say, are you OK? They didn't like to come to this area because too many things happen. We had problems where we were. We were not sleeping at night. We didn't say where we want to move to, they moved us here. They moved us to a better area now − it is a very quiet area.'[37]

This illustrates the characteristics of Lupton and Power's negative acquired characteristics of deprived areas (2002, p 134). They also associate a process of diminishing social capital with smaller social networks and mistrust (2002, p 136). Mistrust of neighbours, service providers and authority figures is a broader feature of social exclusion with resonance beyond dispersal of asylum seekers. That an asylum seeker with no history of living in these deprived areas reached the same conclusions in a matter of weeks or months was revealing about the experience of living in deprived areas. The loss of control over lives due to dispersal, if seen in this sense, entrenches mistrust of the police, neighbours as well as service providers. The asylum seeker described how teenagers in the area were causing trouble and how she did not want her own children to become like them. For this family, taking their children out of the environment of deprivation and social exclusion was paramount. All was resolved once the family were moved to a better, very quiet area, demonstrating how social exclusion does not need to be perceived as static. The potential for restoration of social and institutional trust

---

[36] The dynamic processes of social exclusion in neighbourhoods in Birmingham, Blackburn, Caerphilly, Leeds, Redcar and Cleveland, and Thanet are explored.

[37] Lebanese female participant of a focus group with asylum seekers, Leicester, July 2003.

began for this family once they reached an area in which they felt comfortable. Mistrust is therefore a key concept in social exclusion as it is in forced migration. However, in this context it is less about the behaviour of individuals than about their economic position and circumstances.

Several asylum seekers had specific problems with the condition and type of accommodation allocated. Problems with the type of accommodation were a recurring feature of the interviews and for single asylum seekers accommodation in hostels was a persistent issue: "They sent me to Newcastle before I came here. They forced me, they put me with other people. All of them were smoking and drinking. I have a problem with that. You have no choice, you have to go. It was dirty."[38]

The wider link between deprivation and dispersal was also clearly perceived in a majority of cases. The impact of this link for another family who had received refugee status was ongoing. During the dispersal process they had been relocated a number of times and found that having several addresses in areas with "bad" postcodes meant that they had problems obtaining credit, bank accounts, loans, credit cards and mobile phones. The sheer number of postcodes they had to remember was also related to excluding them from job applications:

> 'If you are a refugee, you have to have a good memory because you have to know your old postcodes. When you fill in the form they just assume that you only need three spaces because they can't believe that someone could move more than three times in three years. Every time when you apply for a credit card you fail. That is how this system is putting you down.... They think you are hiding something.[39]

The impact of the postcodes of hostel and temporary accommodation recurred in other interviews with refugees who had obtained legal status. Given the historical associations of areas where asylum seekers were accommodated that emerged, this had a broad resonance. Asylum seekers also recounted a link between dispersal and deprivation in the areas where RSPs were located:

> 'This area is a very bad area. I had a really bad experience there. One time I phoned my friend from a broken phone box and someone put his hand in my pocket and took my wallet out of my pocket. When I opened the door, he punched me here, I didn't expect it, so I fought with them until he threw a bottle against me. I was very angry. I didn't know at that time that the number was 999. I was bleeding and I tried to follow them. Another person told me not to follow them.

---

[38] Libyan male participant of a focus group with asylum seekers, dispersal location, July 2003.

[39] Afghan male participant of a focus group with asylum seekers, dispersal location, July 2003.

The police came. It is not a good idea to go to a bad area like this that is provided.'[40]

This brought to the forefront the structural aspects of the dispersal policy by recognising that deprived areas were an inherent part of the implementation.

Conclusions

None of the initial criteria for implementation of dispersal, other than the majority of locations being in multicultural areas, was ultimately accomplished. The abandonment of language clusters, wanting to have asylum seekers individually dispersed, a 1:200 ratio of asylum seekers per head of population, 'warring factions' being kept apart and employment levels not below average were each unfulfilled aspects of the initial design.

The structure and implementation of dispersal did not allow for adequate representation of asylum seekers and 'failure to travel' was one way in which asylum seekers could make their 'voice' heard in the absence of any meaningful participation or inclusion in the structures of support they were receiving.

In this chapter the link and implications of the link between dispersal and deprivation has been explored from the perspectives of agencies involved in the system and asylum seekers. It has been shown how compulsory dispersal, particularly at the outset, was to areas of deprivation at a national level with between 70 and 80% of dispersal locations also included in the 88 most deprived local authority districts in England. This was because the geography of dispersal was based around the availability of unpopular or hard-to-let accommodation. This accommodation was largely in multicultural areas that already experienced a high degree of deprivation.

Because of this, dispersal will have a legacy on asylum seekers. The legacy of the dispersal system will ultimately affect the future social exclusion of asylum seekers because 'bad' postcodes affect credit ratings, employment opportunities and other potential routes to 'integration'.

Asylum seekers and refugees interviewed were conscious that the places allocated for implementation of dispersal were largely in deprived areas and the impact of this was already being felt by refugees who had received status. Mistrust of neighbours, the police, service providers and other officials are recognised as an indicator of social exclusion beyond dispersed asylum seekers. In the UK, social inclusion is often about 'partnership' and 'participation' – both of these require mutual trust to be built.

Asylum seekers are heterogeneous and yet dispersal was designed on a one-size-fits-all basis. It was clear that larger cities and areas in London and the South East are more popular with asylum seekers, particularly illustrated by those in receipt of SO support. The suggestion that people feel 'comfortable' in these areas

---

[40] Libyan male participant of a focus group, Leicester, July 2003.

by being able to use 'strategies of invisibility' (Malkki, 1995b) will be explored further in subsequent chapters.

FIVE

The process and experience of dispersal

Introduction

> 'We have our roots in our hands. We carry them from place to place. Then we put them down and have to pull them out again. You are waiting for life for years. You have no rights to define what you do.'[1]

It has already been argued that social exclusion of asylum seekers occurs due to the structure for implementation and geography of dispersal. This chapter begins an exploration of the lived experiences of asylum seekers and *processes* of social exclusion resulting from their dispersal and claims for asylum. Each phase of the dispersal system is outlined using qualitative data from asylum seekers and refugees and then the overall impact of the dispersal and asylum systems is discussed. While NASS has been officially disbanded since 2006, many agency staff and asylum seekers still refer to it to describe the dispersal system and reference to it is therefore retained.

The earlier stages of the 'refugee experience' within countries of origin are considered to show how the focus on an administrative process did not allow for an understanding of the prior experiences and subsequent needs of asylum seekers. While this has now been partially addressed with the introduction of a single 'case owner'[2] under the NAM introduced in 2006, there is considerable scope for improvement in understanding contexts of origin and how prior experiences of asylum seekers require consideration. The NAM involves 'segmenting' asylum claims into different categories according to their perceived 'credibility' with different procedures for assessing their claims. This involved greater control over asylum seekers during the process of status determination to enable them to be arrested if their asylum application failed. During dispersal this control was exercised by having asylum seekers attend reporting centres on a regular basis and by a 'policing' role written into the contract of accommodation providers (see Chapter Six). Detention on arrival became more common and those detained had their applications heard through fast-track procedures.

---

[1] Participant in a focus group, dispersal location, July 2003.
[2] The 'case owner' is responsible for every aspect of contact between the Home Office and asylum seeker, with both the asylum claim and support brought together in one file.

It is argued that the dispersal system is a study in liminality – or more precisely, 'policy-imposed liminality' – because the top-down, 'one-size-fits-all' character of dispersal has added an extra layer of liminality to the already difficult asylum process that asylum seekers negotiate. It is suggested that this has implications for the restoration of social, institutional and political trust and that asylum seekers resist this policy-imposed liminality using techniques that avoid direct confrontation with authority.

The dispersal process: aka 'the NASS system'

Table 5.1 shows the distinct phases of early accounts of dispersal from their arrival into the UK to the ultimate decision on their asylum claim and, in a small proportion of cases, their ability at this stage to officially 'integrate' into the UK.

Table 5.1: The early process of dispersal

Arrival in the UK	Period in emergency accommodation	First dispersal location	Relocation	Decision on asylum claim	Resettlement
'Spontaneous' arrival of 'asylum seeker' either 'at port' or 'in-country' Applies to Home Office for refugee status Applies to NASS for support and/or accommodation	'Asylum seeker' Possible 'failure to travel' to dispersal location	'Group' or 'self-write' dispersal of 'asylum seeker' Remains in first dispersal location until decision on asylum claim or leaves prior to decision	'Asylum seeker' Relocation 'in-region' or other dispersal location	Becomes a 'refugee' and obtains 'ILR' Given temporary right to stay and obtains, 'ELR', 'HP' or 'DL' Not given right to stay and is termed a 'failed asylum seeker' Appeals process	'Integration' of 'refugee' in dispersal location 'Secondary migration' or 'driftback' of 'refugee' to location other than dispersal location 'Failed asylum seeker' either deported or may 'go underground'/become 'undocumented'

From 2003, Induction Centres were introduced to speed up the transition from arrival to first dispersal location. It is also the case that in a small number of cases, not every phase was experienced – for example, an asylum seeker may not have experienced relocation from their first dispersal location.

The views of asylum seekers and refugees are highlighted throughout this chapter, underlined by views of caseworkers from the voluntary sector and representatives of RCOs.

Arrival in the UK: "This is where the suffering begins"

Upon arrival, if not detained, asylum seekers were, until 2006, required to apply to the Home Office for RSD and to NASS for either SO support or financial support and accommodation, which meant compulsory dispersal. Finding information about these offices could prove difficult, with asylum seekers not always informed of the right to apply for financial support and even if they knew about this right, they did not always know immediately how to claim this support.[3] The process of claiming asylum was and is confusing and the expectation that asylum seekers would know, or be able to distinguish, which agencies were connected to or funded by the Home Office was unrealistic. One asylum seeker at the beginning of his process commented how difficult it was to know who was assisting him: "It is very difficult. You don't know what the process is. You know people come to you and say, this is from [rapid tone adopted] and you just know you need to follow. You can't do anything, because you don't understand the system".[4] When this asylum seeker adopted a rapid tone to denote the name of the agency, he was demonstrating how agencies in the system were largely indistinguishable from each other. The same interviewee compared himself to a newborn baby who did not know anything about the world around them or, given the language barrier, how to ask for assistance. He added that he did not know what the problems with the process were and that "If you are a baby, even if someone throws you in the river, you can't understand why they did that".[5] The inability to predict what would happen next or where the process would lead, left him feeling as though he had no control over the process. This loss of 'social competence' is what Marx (1990, p 197) refers to when discussing 'severe disruption' of social networks.

For another individual, who arrived in the UK on his own, his first days in the country were, like many others, recounted as being extremely difficult: "The first day I didn't know where to go, where to sleep, where to live so it was very difficult for me. No place to live, no place to sleep".[6] This confusion about the process can be dangerous. Describing how their newborn baby was burned on their first day in the UK, another asylum seeker explained how she did not know the area they had been placed in or what to do in the case of an emergency. Exhausted from their journey to the UK, they ran into the street with the baby: "English neighbours, they don't want to help us. They say sorry, sorry I can't help.

---

[3] Joint interview with male representatives of voluntary sector, dispersal location, June 2003.
[4] Joint interview with male asylum seekers, dispersal location, November 2003.
[5] Joint interview with male asylum seekers, dispersal location, November 2003.
[6] Joint interview with male asylum seekers, dispersal location, November 2003.

We didn't understand why. The baby was shouting and he was crying, he was burned, it was an emergency". This comment about the mistrust encountered from their neighbours when they asked for help placed them in a position of extreme vulnerability. When they managed to find another neighbour to assist and get them to a hospital they were disappointed with the response from agencies involved:

> 'It was very hard those first days. We don't know where we are or which area we are in. Also, nobody has a telephone. Nobody came to come to get us from NASS, nobody came to get us out from the hospital. We didn't know where we were. We had no money. We didn't know our address because we arrived during the night. So the same neighbours they wait for us, they come and pick us up. We go from the hospital to the caseworker who was taking care of us. They said we can't come now; you can wait about three or four hours. We have the baby there. We cannot do anything, not eating anything, the baby was crying.'[7]

Their inability to distinguish whether the caseworker mentioned was from a RSP or from NASS, referring to them all as from NASS, highlights initial confusion about the agencies involved in the process and their roles. This was common with asylum seekers with comments such as:

> 'We don't know really who is giving us money.'[8]

> 'Maybe NASS, maybe the refugee agency, both are NASS anyway.'[9]

The NASS caseworker referred to would have been the caseworker from the RSP and their lack of response in the case of an emergency involving a baby was problematic. The family's need to subsequently rely on a neighbour whom they had not previously met did not give any confidence in the NASS system from the beginning. They did not know what to do in an emergency – this was a dangerous oversight on the part of whoever had allocated the accommodation and not knowing to call 999 was not an isolated incident. Not knowing their address or the area they were in was again indicative of loss of control over their lives.

Upon arrival, asylum seekers will not know who they are able to trust. As one participant in a workshop on accessing legal advice commented: "When you get here, you don't know who you can trust".[10] This was met with general agreement in the workshop and the survival strategy of mistrust (Hynes, 2003a)

---

[7] Female focus group participant, dispersal location, July 2003.
[8] Joint interview with male asylum seekers, dispersal location, November 2003.
[9] Comment from a translator during an interview with asylum seekers, November 2003.
[10] Refugee participant in an 'Access to Legal Advice' workshop, International Women's Day, Action for Refugee Women, London, 6 March 2003.

was a common theme. At a social event in one dispersal area, a refugee who had been in the country for nearly three years suggested not to speak to a Ukrainian women who had recently "arrived in a box" (a container): "She would not trust anyone who started asking her questions … [and would] just clam up if anybody attempted to speak to her".[11]

Further explanation of the reasons for this mistrust referred to interviews with the Home Office, which were conducted in an atmosphere of suspicion and were considered a defining feature of the experience more generally:

> 'People are mistrustful of everything. If you think that refugees are people running, running for their lives. They have had to do this to survive. They mistrust everyone, including their own community groups. Only once the basics are sorted, the basics for survival – roof and work – then they can begin looking around and seek additional support.'[12]

The perceived power of the Home Office and NASS was ever present, with one interviewee describing the Home Office as an unapproachable "monster".[13] NASS was described as being as "another head of the same creature".[14] The NASS system commenced at a point when the individual felt as though the Home Office disbelieved them and this was also pervasive in dealings with NASS. One refugee who had encountered problems with NASS explained how this mistrust manifested itself in the availability of original birth, marriage and death certificates:

> 'When I first came I went to NASS. My father was killed sometime last year when the rebels took him away. And they said my claim was false because I could not get papers, let alone a death certificate. Where am I supposed to get references to prove my father's death?'[15]

That NASS, the system for supporting asylum seekers, attempted to deny support to an asylum seeker based on an assumption made about the credibility of his asylum claim was inappropriate. Disbelieving the death of a parent also illustrated the lack of basic understanding of the conditions and contexts from which asylum seekers are arriving from. This Liberian asylum seeker had given up attempting to access support from NASS and had taken employment before permission to work was denied. His perception was: "The system is the barrier to integration".[16] He went on to elaborate that the difficulties he had encountered had stopped

---

[11] Informal conversation with a refugee, Lincoln, May 2004.

[12] Interview with a female representative of an RCO, London, November 2002.

[13] Interview with a female representative of an RCO, London, June 2003.

[14] Talk by a representative of a London-based user group, London, March 2004.

[15] Interview with a male asylum seeker, Leicester, July 2003.

[16] Interview with a male asylum seeker, Leicester, July 2003.

him from wanting to belong in the UK. Another asylum seeker, despairing of the requirement to provide original certificates to NASS, commented:

> 'They said if he is your husband you must provide a marriage certificate. I was searching for my certificates – when you are in Africa you only get one copy of certificates, you have no copies, only the original. I didn't bring all my certificates with me.'[17]

Again, this lack of understanding of the circumstances under which asylum seekers arrive in the UK and disbelief of the marriage of a man and woman with three children was inapt.

Overall, confusion about the agencies involved in dispersal and their roles, difficulties experienced during the first few days of arrival, the loss of control over their lives and not knowing who could be trusted characterised this first stage. The perception that arrival was the point at which "the suffering begins",[18] while on the face of it dramatic, was in many cases an accurate reflection of this early stage.

Emergency accommodation: playing the waiting game

'Liminality' or 'limbo' was most clearly evident during an initial period in EA. The provision of "a bad roof or no roof"[19] was, until November 2003, used to describe EA in London. The new role of 'landlord' from a 'care-giving organisation' (Refugee Council, 2004b) was, after this date, affected by the decision of the Refugee Council to stop providing EA in London for new arrivals in order to improve the quality of its services. This decision was due to the anticipated time spent in EA escalating from an initial seven to 10 days to 'months, if not years'.[20] Short-term accommodation therefore became long term and the number of beds rose from an initial 500 to over 4,500. These hostels, run by a private accommodation provider, contracted by the Refugee Council, were previously hotels and were not identifiable as hostels from their appearance alone.[21]

A single asylum seeker had difficult experiences of the NASS system as they were more likely to be accommodated in hostels than families. David,[22] who was within the mainstream benefits system upon implementation of dispersal in 2000, commented that in order to enter into the NASS system he was required "to attend the Refugee Council and declare myself destitute ... [which was]

---

[17] Female participant in a focus group, Bristol, July 2003.
[18] Joint interview with male representatives of the voluntary sector, dispersal location, June 2003.
[19] Interview with an RSP, October 2003.
[20] Email update from the Refugee Council, 2 October 2003, via frank.corrigan@asylumrights.net
[21] Sites visited October 2003.
[22] David is a pseudonym.

dehumanising". He was told to go to Heathrow to join newly arrived asylum seekers from Dover and waited for four hours before "being delivered to a hotel, allocated a room with two others in the same room on the third floor".

Families, however, were also placed in EA. A female asylum seeker with a small baby commented that this was inadequate in many respects:

> 'They put us together with singles, about four singles. And no one knows how to clean or to take care of themselves. There was only one shower for all of us. The singles would sit in the sitting room, drink and watch television. They would watch football and not let the baby watch anything. Putting their legs up on the table, putting things everywhere. Holding the baby, playing with him, we did not like it. We cannot keep him in the small room we had. It was a dirty place with no outside space for the baby.'[23]

In the above quote, the first 'they' referred to the RSP. The description of no one knowing how to keep the accommodation clean and it being a dirty place was indicative of liminality and loss of control, with a few interviewees commenting how this temporary accommodation was not cleaned by anyone, especially those accommodated within it. Not being able to control their own environment or have a place where children could play was again not appropriate. Sharing a sitting room with four singles while waiting to be dispersed to more suitable accommodation proved to be frustrating and inadequate for this family.

During time in EA, asylum seekers received £10 in cash per week. With this lack of financial independence, uncertainty and boredom characterised time spent in EA, with awaiting dispersal considered by many participants to be a waste of their time. Few attempts were made by adults at this stage to access education or other services unless essential. As David commented:

> 'While I was in there, I never went to a GP [general practitioner]. There were no signs to tell you how you were supposed to spend your time. The question of education did not come into it before dispersal, because the uncertainty of the length of time you were going to stay there. You never knew. Some people came; there was no particular definite length of time, no precision. Some people came one week and they went the next day. Some people came in and were like me. I was one of the longest. You don't know what is going to happen next. You could start by going to school today but then there could have been a delay. If I was to start college or school one day, I might be dispersed the next day.'

---

[23] Female focus group participant, Leicester, July 2003.

Not wanting to begin education or access medical services during this time was a clear indication of the sense of liminality being experienced. This uncertainty and the theme of wasting time created a sense of 'temporariness' that several participants recounted. It also resonated with the temporary character of the Vietnamese holding centres that Bousquet (1987) describes and the expulsion from normal existence encountered. The inhabiting of this liminal space and not crossing from one status to another (Malkki, 1995b) was made worse by the unpredictability of time left prior to dispersal. People arriving and leaving in no particular order suspended normal activities.

There was a pervasive perception by asylum seekers within the NASS system that time in EA was about just being left by the agencies and NASS. The regulated character of days spent in EA was also a feature of this stage, with several asylum seekers using the phrase of not wanting 'to bite the hand that feeds' to describe the relationship between themselves and agencies involved.

The 'lottery' aspect of dispersal and lack of choice of the type of accommodation and dispersal location was problematic. Awaiting news about which dispersal city he would be dispersed to, David commented:

> 'Every morning at 9 o'clock, somebody would come in from the NASS, and pin up names, lists of names on the walls. Your name would be put against your NASS number and the area you would be going to. Good heavens! Whether they disperse you to Newcastle, Lincoln, we had no choice. But every day in the morning at 9 o'clock, you could come and look. You had to come in a check through a whole list. There used to be an average of about 150 dispersals every day. So you are looking at the movement of people coming and going everyday. I spent September, October, November, December, until the 6th of December. During that time, every day I looked. The rest of the day you go back to your room and just wait. Not a very good system.'

Again, he did not distinguish between the staff of the RSP and NASS. Again, 'they' indicated the RSP and the 'we' were other asylum seekers. The lack of choice and element of luck involved was repeatedly raised. Asylum seekers often did not know who was accommodating them, just that they had been placed in accommodation. Even local community workers with considerable knowledge about the system and local areas often did not know the name of the landlords. Confusion over the agencies and their roles in the NASS process operated at many levels.

This system was inappropriate for individuals fleeing persecution who had already lost much control over their lives in their countries of origin. This uncertainty did, however, sometimes provide the basis for a bond between people. These bonds and the social trust built up in this way were subsequently dispersed to different locations. For David, his experience was illustrative:

'You come down; you go through the list of about 100 names. They
were never in alphabetical order for some reason. I don't know what
criteria they used. Sometimes I would not go and search. Sometimes
you build among yourselves friends, if you stay in a place like that
you start getting people you identify with, people that talk to you,
where if somebody saw my name they would come and let me know.
Then, one day somebody came up to me and said your name is there.
I couldn't believe it, I said now I am coming down. So I went there
and I checked on the wall – Lincoln. I had never been to Lincoln.'

Dispersed on a 'self-write' basis, he was not given any information about Lincoln
but was given tickets and a printed timetable with details of train connections.
Another asylum seeker who was in the International Hotel in Leicester
commented on this lack of information provided:

'I was in London when I arrived. I went to Refugee Action [sic] in
London and they told me you must go to the hotel for six weeks and
after that we must find house for you. I said OK. I went to hostel
for six weeks and I was waiting. Waiting, waiting. It is going on two
months. More than two months. I went to them and asked what was
happening because I am waiting for a house. They said to me, "Would
you like to go to Leicester?". I said, "Yes, yes, I go anywhere but not
to a hostel. … I don't like hostel, because I saw trouble there". They
told me, "You have to go to Leicester, you have to take the key, you
have a house there". I said, "Yes, I am very happy, I am very happy
[laughs]". When I come here, they said to me, "This is your house".
International Hotel! I said, "This is hostel. That is not good".'[24]

His mistake about the name of the agency in London illustrated the confusion
over agencies involved in dispersal. He had been led to believe that suitable
accommodation was available in Leicester but upon arrival found himself in a
hostel called the International Hotel. Again, the 'bad roof or no roof' philosophy
that stemmed from the contractual obligations between RSPs and NASS had
resulted in uncertainty.

Overall, lack of control over finances and the ultimate destination of dispersal
characterised this stage of the system. Asylum seekers within this system waited and
subsequently had any social trust built up literally dispersed to different locations.
A lack of institutional or restorative trust was clearly apparent between 'them'
(NASS and the generally indistinguishable agencies involved) and 'we' asylum
seekers within the system. The welcome introduction of Induction Centres post
2003 speeded up this phase but the fulcrum of trust (Daniel and Knudsen, 1995)
on which social policies for refugees was based still did not tip favourably.

---

[24] Participant in a focus group, Leicester, July 2003.

First dispersal location: dispersal, the national lottery

Compulsory dispersal is a lottery and the odds are not good. Asylum seekers awaiting dispersal will not know which city they will be dispersed to or whether they will be arriving in a city where they have family or friends and they will be dispersed regardless of gender or age.[25] The dispersal city may or may not have RCOs of their same nationality and these organisations may not be representative of the individuals' personal politics or may have origins in a different 'vintage' or 'fate-group' (Kunz, 1973, pp 138-41). The city may or may not be largely tolerant towards asylum seekers, have appropriate mainstream service provision or have an RSP presence. One participant had been dispersed to a city she could not even pronounce. Thus, the compulsory nature of dispersal was highly problematic. For asylum seekers who expressed a preference of location, this could be taken into consideration but there was no obligation even for brothers to be dispersed to the same location (Refugee Council, 2004). One asylum seeker commented: "Once I had my interview they sent me. It depends where they send you, sometimes [dispersal location], sometimes London, you don't know. Sometimes it is another town. It is just a matter of luck where you are sent".[26]

The dispersal process for 'singles' and 'families' was similar in that both received one offer of accommodation, one opportunity to travel to dispersal accommodation and both were expected to live in dispersal accommodation until the outcome of their RSD process (Refugee Council, 2004b). However, if single asylum seekers 'failed to travel' without a 'reasonable excuse',[27] this led to termination of support and eviction from their EA. Families who 'failed to travel' were also evicted from EA but the offer of support in the dispersal location would be kept open indefinitely, which meant that the support was never discontinued and the family were therefore not, technically, homeless or able to appeal to the Asylum Support Adjudicators (ASAs).[28]

Lack of control over finances was also an imposition of dispersal – with only 70% of the standard rate of financial support provided for asylum seekers in dispersal accommodation. Utility bills and Council Tax were paid for by the accommodation provider, meaning that the management of the lives of asylum seekers placed asylum seekers in a position of reliance on the accommodation provider to be responsible for all aspects of budgeting at every stage of dispersal. This inability to gain financial control over their lives was compounded by other aspects of the process. Setting off to his dispersal location and having been told

---

[25] Except in cases of extreme or special needs.

[26] Joint interview with male asylum seekers, Bristol, November 2003.

[27] Medical Foundation or urgent medical problems with evidence from a GP.

[28] ASAs are funded by the Home Office to adjudicate appeals regarding NASS support. They are the only people you can appeal to about NASS support. View at www.asylum-support-adjudicators.org.uk

that somebody would be waiting for him at the train station, David found nobody there to meet him:

> 'I got there, nobody was waiting for me. Nobody knew I was coming. I did not have an address. It was the middle of winter, 6th of December. I had run out of money and I actually phoned [the RSP who had accommodated him in EA] to say I am stuck here, and I have been stuck here for about three or four hours and nobody has been waiting for me, I don't know where to go. They said, "You are out of our hands. You have a new accommodation provider now to take care of you".'

That coordination between the RSP who had accommodated him in EA and his new accommodation providers had not occurred illustrated the type of problems occurring. The complexity of the structure for implementing dispersal often led to a lack of coordination. David sought assistance in a police station as he could communicate fluently in English and did not fear the police:

> 'I had run out of money on my mobile phone. I had to find a police station. It was very difficult. A black man stuck in a country environment like this in [dispersal location]. It was very difficult. I was very ill-equipped in terms of dressing for the weather. It was snowing. I was in a very sorry state. I had put on a very nice summer suit to arrive there. I must have looked a sight. I walked to the police station, the police helped me four hours later and I went to the address. They directed me to address I was supposed to go to. I went there. I was waiting outside, they hadn't opened the door. It was raining, my luggage got wet. I got wetter, I was angry. NASS had assigned me that accommodation.'

From this we begin to see how what Malkki (1995b, p 155) calls 'strategies of invisibility' are regarded as a positive coping strategy for asylum seekers within the system. Arriving in a new city dressed in a suit could have meant that the label of asylum seeker was 'supplanted by a series of alternative identities and labels' (Malkki, 1995b, p 156). Attempts to negate the asylum seeker label by taking on new identities in this way were a recurring feature in the narrative accounts provided by asylum seekers. The resourcefulness of David was the only reason NASS accommodation was located that day.

Two asylum seekers in Bristol felt comfortable in the city due to the availability of a mosque, support from the community[29] and the multicultural character of the city: "It is like a smaller London, you don't feel like an outsider here".[30] Asylum seekers in Leicester also discussed how they were "comfortable" in the city, noting

---

[29] Joint interview with male asylum seekers, Bristol, November 2003.
[30] Participant in a focus group, Bristol, July 2003.

the "multicultural"[31] character of the city. Several of these participants had been accommodated, had visited for immigration purposes or had been to court in other cities so were glad of this characteristic.

The heterogeneity of asylum seekers, alongside the range of experiences of dispersal encountered, highlighted how notions of there being a distinct 'refugee experience' were not apparent.

A beneficial aspect of dispersal put forward by a refugee was that they would ultimately be able to afford to buy a house in the city and that their children would benefit from cheaper property prices:

> 'We would be able, let's say in five years' time, to buy a property here because property is cheaper here than in London. Those who are able to get a job in London will struggle because of property prices. But now we can, if I am working, probably we can buy something.... Dispersal is better for the second generation. Those who come the first time face trouble but those who come later will benefit.'[32]

Thus, for a small number of asylum seekers ultimately granted refugee status, dispersal was seen as beneficial in the longer term. However, the person making this comment was engaged rapidly in conversation by another asylum seeker who remarked that it was easier to live outside London but that the above participant "shouldn't forget that they take away your right to choose" where you live.[33]

The same element of luck applied to the nature of accommodation provided. Prior to dispersal, the type – private, public or social – of property would be unknown to the asylum seekers. They were also unaware whether or not they would be required to share the same room in that accommodation. The already difficult process of awaiting a decision on an asylum claim was magnified due to the uncertainty around accommodation:

> 'It is not easy here, especially for the children. You do not know where you will go, where they will put you. We do not know if our decision will be OK or not. If it is OK it will also be very hard because you don't know which house they will give you. Maybe it will be empty and dirty and you have to start from the beginning, painting and buying things.'[34]

The suggestion here was that the end of the liminal period was the point at which dispersal accommodation was no longer used and some ability to "start" began.

---

[31] Participant in a focus group, Leicester, July 2003.
[32] Participant in a focus group, Leicester, July 2003.
[33] Participant in a focus group, Leicester, July 2003.
[34] Participant in a focus group, Leicester, July 2003.

Complaints to NASS about the inadequacies of accommodation were met with disbelief. A Kosovan participant commented: "They don't accept our problem, they don't believe us".[35] He pointed out that complaints would not be listened to and that even in extreme cases such as older people becoming ill because of the inadequacies of their accommodation, NASS would not listen. He cited the example of an elderly couple accommodated in the International Hotel in Leicester, several complaints to NASS and the RSP had not been responded to: "They are very old. They told them that they would be living there for one week. They have been there for five months now. The woman is 65 and the man is 75 years old. The woman is very sick".

As with the period spent in EA, in a number of cases, participants did not know who the landlord was, instead referring to the first name of the individual they had dealings with. Several issues emerged regarding the first and subsequent allocation of dispersal accommodation. These included issues around privacy whereby landlords held keys and entered accommodation unannounced; control over their own finances; and sharing accommodation and bedrooms with other asylum seekers with conflicting views. The requirement to 'sign' for accommodation and the practice of making children 'sign' for accommodation in the absence of their parents was questionable. Each of these issues involved issues of power and control and the imbalances of patron–client relationships.

Asylum seekers in dispersal were required to 'report' to police stations during dispersal, which was something that separated them from other migrants or quota refugees. Letters from the Home Office detailed these reporting requirements and outlined their 'temporary admission', being provided 'emergency accommodation' and later 'temporary accommodation' pending their asylum decision. The centrally devised character of the policy thus continued to impact on the regional and local implementation of dispersal; the ability to assume new identities other than 'asylum seeker' being effectively denied. Attempts at avoiding the stigma of the label at a local level were dependent on an interplay between the character of the city dispersed to and the type of accommodation allocated. There was an ability to restore some social trust at this stage but the continuous use of the terms 'them' and 'us' highlighted a system in which any potential restoration of institutional trust was limited.

Relocation, relocation, relocation

Numerous examples of asylum seekers relocating several times were encountered, which exacerbated the sense of 'limbo' or 'liminality' outlined above. Asylum seekers were 're-dispersed' either 'in-region' (within the regional consortia area) or to other dispersal locations across the UK. Some had been relocated to three

---

[35] Participant in a focus group, Leicester, July 2003.

cities in four months;[36] two cities in 16 months;[37] five cities in three years and six months;[38] three cities in two years;[39] and, for David, two cities in five months.

In a few of these cases, relocation was beneficial as they had moved from areas of high deprivation to areas where they felt more comfortable. However, these self-generated moves followed repeated requests to NASS, letters from solicitors and medical reports from doctors. NASS was generally unresponsive to such requests. Relocation was, however, usually a result of being moved, with accommodation providers shifting their tenants, rather than wanting to move.

One of the main complaints about relocation was that it disrupted education of both children and adults. This lack of control over where to live and how to plan the education of children clearly contributes to the social exclusion of asylum seekers.

Having to postpone education and change courses, 'start again when you move'[40] and again when status was obtained was common. As one asylum seeker at the beginning of the process commented, "I wish, I hope that they don't move me from Bristol. It is very hard to start again and find people to help you". Having established links within Bristol, this individual did not want to be re-dispersed, be it within or outside the region.

The issue of privacy was also recounted by another asylum seeker as a primary motivation for seeking relocation:

> 'Because sometimes he [the private accommodation provider] would come into my house. He didn't tell me before he came in. I knew that he would come in the house every morning to pick up papers. I must sign the paper every day. Like a prisoner, like a martyr. Sometimes my children sign it. [Name of private accommodation provider] said to my children to sign it again. I said, "Why?" He said, "You must sign". I say, "OK, no problem". I didn't like him because he come in my house anytime he wants. I had no privacy! In my house! Every time I go to school he went into the house to check everything. One day I was in the toilet. I knew my children were in school – British schools – so I took a shower. I was alone in my house. I only had a small towel around me and he was there! They used to come and see what you have inside your house. No privacy!'

The contractual arrangement between PAPs and NASS for tenants to sign to testify presence in the property was considered by this mother to be a unwanted regulation that made her feel like a prisoner and making her children sign was,

---

[36] Participant in a focus group, Leicester, July 2003.
[37] Participant in a focus group, Bristol, July 2003.
[38] Participant in a focus group, Bristol, July 2003.
[39] Participant in a focus group, Leicester, July 2003.
[40] Participant in a focus group, Bristol, July 2003.

she continued, one of the main reasons she wished to relocate. Her only recourse following this invasion of privacy was to tell the landlord that she was going to go to the RSP office to tell them about this. The power imbalance between landlord and tenant in this instance illustrates clearly how unmonitored use of PAPs opens up channels of potential exploitation. On this occasion, upon hearing that the tenant was willing to complain to the RSP, the landlord said: "'I will send you to Bristol'. He said, 'I will find you a big house if you would prefer' and I said yes. The house in [dispersal location in the West Midlands] was too small. But NASS didn't know that we moved so we missed our money for two weeks'".

These quotes illustrate not only the issues of privacy and control imposed by the contractual obligations between accommodation providers and NASS, but also the lack of communication between PAPs and NASS. The fact that NASS did not know that this family had been relocated highlighted this lack of communication. This was not an isolated incident and the high numbers of different nationalities in each location is partly as a result of this unregulated system of 're-dispersal' or relocation by, in particular, PAPs.[41]

In other dispersal areas, the contractual arrangements for accommodating asylum seekers were highly problematic. Properties let by subcontractors to the NASS contracted PAP often involved relocation to other locations with very little notice. PAPs and their subcontractors operated outside the hierarchy of agencies and communication problems were evident between these agencies.

The relocation of asylum seekers was built into the NASS system. By 2005, questions posed in contract negotiations by the Home Office to regional consortia showed how the management of these relocations had been transferred onto local authorities. Questions included how local authorities would reduce the need for relocation within regions, how families with dependent children would be relocated locally to provide continuity of education, how disruption due to the process of relocation would be minimised for service users, the impact of relocations on local communities and how the relocation would be managed.

The experience of liminality was inherent in the NASS system. Unexpected outcomes of these relocations included the inability to obtain a credit rating, which contributed to social exclusion for many years. Again, any social trust restored through day-to-day or meaningful encounters prior to relocation was lost with each relocation.

Decision on asylum claim: an existence vindicated?

The decision to claim asylum is one of the biggest decisions a person may make in their life and is therefore an intensely personal decision. For an asylum seeker, the transition to becoming a 'refugee' and obtaining ILR or the more temporary status of Exceptional Leave to Remain (ELR), HP or DL can be a cause for celebration and simultaneously involve a recognition of the 'victimhood' of their particular

---

[41] Conversation with a representative of a local authority, dispersal location, June 2004.

circumstances.[42] Morris (2002a, 2006, 2010) has outlined how the structure of legal statuses – which themselves govern eligibility for particular rights – results in an emergent civil stratification of rights that sorts, includes and excludes migrants into different positions. Particular restrictions inherent in the lesser forms of status such as lack of family reunification until after a certain number of years continue to mean stratified access to this universal right.

At a legal level, the granting of one of these statuses may mean that an individual's existence in the UK may be vindicated but each individual may take many years to develop their own sense of vindication. For example, one Chilean refugee described how it was only after Augusto Pinochet was arrested that she personally felt as though she had her existence vindicated in the UK as a "political refugee".[43] The legal process, however, may be extended by an appeals process if status is not granted straight away. This is a very stressful process for the individual, particularly if the proceedings are adjourned for any reason.[44] Issues surrounding the credibility of the asylum claim are addressed by a Home Office respondent during appeals and the overarching character of these proceedings is disbelief and mistrust of the individual by the Home Office, questioning and doubting the accounts provided of lives, family backgrounds, links with the country of origin,[45] time taken to apply for asylum and even the 'Christian name'[46] of individuals. For those who have been opposing human rights violations in their country of origin, this process and judgement as to whether their convictions are real or not is extremely disempowering.

Unsurprisingly, it was evident that decisions on claims for asylum were a vital turning point in terms of liminality. With the exception of problems with the dispersal system, asylum seekers in dispersal areas identified their difficulties as being largely connected to politics in the country of origin. It was clear that those interviewed who felt a sense of temporariness built bridges with the past in the sense that the content of their narratives was largely based on the country of origin. This building bridges to the past sometimes indicated the forced nature of migration as time had not been spent planning new futures in the UK, with the focus being firmly on resolving what had happened in the past. This added to the sense of temporariness and liminality being experienced due to the dispersal system. One interviewee focused on his rapid departure from Iran;[47]

---

[42] Assertion based on discussions with refugees, various dates.

[43] Interview with a female representative of an RCO, London, November 2002.

[44] Discussions with individuals at Immigration Appellate Authority, Feltham and London, November 2004; interview with Liberian refugee, dispersal location, July 2003.

[45] Home Office country reports are available for the top 25 nationalities of asylum seekers.

[46] Home Office respondent's question on the credibility of the Buddhist Burmese individual's name, London, November 2003. In Burma the concept of a surname does not exist and questioning the credibility of a 'Christian name' from a majority Buddhist country highlighted a lack of basic country information.

[47] Interview with a male asylum seeker, Leicester, November, 2003.

another focused on the war in Somalia;[48] two Sudanese asylum seekers discussed political organisations in Sudan as the main reason for their migration[49] and a Congolese asylum seeker considered that French colonialism and globalisation were the reason for her persecution as well as dictating her choice of the UK as an asylum destination:

> 'My country was colonised by French people and when they come into power they take everything out of Congo. They start contracts with French people, American people and English people. French people come and put the war in Congo and there was a *coup d'état* and the new government took over democracy but they were not democratically elected. There is a big oil company because the country has quite a lot of resources. The government signed a new contract with the French oil company and the French government are quite close to [name of oil company]. When the *coup d'état* happened, we had to flee immediately. Not to France because of political grounds.'[50]

These 'new geographies' (Koser and Pinkerton, 2002) of claiming asylum, in this case the active avoidance of claiming asylum in France so as to avoid a future in a country closely associated with the country of origin, warrant further research in order to investigate the forces that impinge on the day-to-day lives and decision-making processes involved. The feeling of being socially excluded largely revolved around issues of immigration status, both before and after RSD. Questions from a user group regarding the difficulties of having a 'voice' for refugees led to an animated discussion and a whole series of examples of ways in which asylum seekers feel socially excluded. The difficulty of forming a group with any remaining members of friends and family who had been dispersed across the UK was prominent in the discussion. There was also a feeling that asylum seekers may not feel as though they have the right to voice an opinion due to the lack of legal status and fear of deportation. As one refugee participant suggested, even after RSD this can be difficult:

> 'Most of them are very scared and they prefer to keep quiet than speak out. Because they know, I don't have the right to speak out. I can be deported, or … I may not be accepted. So maybe that is why. We think that we don't have rights. We need to come together and to form, and start. We need our rights…. You know, one time, I felt as though we should speak out, but then I thought, oh, I could be in trouble, maybe with the immigration.'[51]

---

[48] Participant of a focus group, dispersal location, July 2003.
[49] Joint interview with two male asylum seekers, dispersal location, November 2003.
[50] Participant in a focus group, dispersal location, July 2003.
[51] Participant of a focus group, dispersal location, July 2003.

Stressing the structural position of a refugee and phrased in the language of rights, this quote suggests how asylum seekers within the dispersal process, as well as refugees who had been through the process, adopt as a strategy the avoidance of confrontation, particularly with 'officialdom' (Robinson, 2002; Hynes, 2003a). Notably in the above quote, asylum seekers are referred to as 'them' and 'they', with this recognised refugee distinguishing herself from them but then referring to the 'we' of not having rights and needing to come together to 'speak out'. The reluctance to 'speak out' then becomes a personal issue as she refers to 'I' in relation to her status of 'refugee' being also a position of weakness. Thus, even after RSD, the impact of social exclusion for this individual meant that her ability to participate unhindered in the political process and have rights that other residents of the UK expect were curtailed. This barrier to political participation was corroborated by another refugee when real fears about personal security and the consequences of speaking out to defend others were voiced, with specific examples of encounters with officials and institutions recounted. The ambiguity surrounding legal status and being able to defend themselves once status was granted was mixed with fear of repercussions. For David, receiving refugee status was welcomed with the wish to help others: "Now that I have refugee status, I want to give something back, not just work and forget about everything that happened to me in the past three years". However, daily survival needs meant that he was unable to do this and he moved to a city where he was able to utilise past employment experience and move away from the negative experiences encountered during his time in his dispersal city. This focus on daily survival needs was a continuous theme: "To be realistic. You can't be a strong community because we struggle for our daily life".[52]

It was apparent that the shift from temporary to permanent status often involved individuals focusing on different sources for their present difficulties. Those with refugee status interviewed generally provided accounts that situated their problems in terms of the UK and wider discussions of global politics, history, the world capitalist system as well as the male structures of societies.[53] When describing her situation, one refugee went one step further by perceiving the problem to be due to the international relations and history between the UK and her country of origin:

> 'I had to flee the regime that you [the British] have put into power. You enforce the Islamic regime in Tehran. Being here and what I have been through, made me regret why I didn't prefer prison, going back to prison [in Iran] rather than coming to Europe, England…. Because of the wrong system, unfair system is ruling the world.'[54]

---

[52] Participant of a focus group, dispersal location, July 2003.
[53] Interview with a female refugee, London, June 2003.
[54] Participant in a focus group, dispersal location, July 2003.

This shift was particularly marked with David. Upon gaining refugee status, he asserted how his views had changed about the source of his problems:

> 'I used to look at it – from the inside – as it was NASS being the main body. But NASS is not the main body, it is not deciding. It is the Home Office. Somebody is deciding what to do. NASS comes in between. They are taking directions from the Home Office and ODPM [Office of the Deputy Prime Minister]. NASS does not move in diversity or cohesion or equality circles. When I was in the system I thought NASS was the mother body but now I know NASS is just one organisation, that is not where the blame is. There is a more powerful source somewhere and nobody wants to talk about it. I am now looking from without, seeing that NASS is not to blame.'

The shift from temporary to permanent status had led, in this case, to a demonstrable engagement with UK racism discourses. David's view about the importance of NASS had changed: his view now was that there was a more powerful source directing the agenda on equality and cohesion. Theoretically, this changing viewpoint illustrates how any epistemological privilege assigned to 'insiders' means that the whole picture or process may be left out of any analysis. For this individual, his changing viewpoint illustrates how a 'user' of the NASS system, once out of the system, perceived NASS differently. That users can be considered the experts of their own experience is without doubt but an understandable initial inability to see aspects of the broader processes as they are learning the written and unwritten language of a different country means that their views change over time.

Another refugee asked me candidly: "Why don't you ask me if the Home Office is racist?".[55] This was another indication of engagement with the UK discourse of racism. The argument about NASS having nothing to do with inclusion, diversity, equality and cohesion are particularly relevant given the original aims of the policy to not add to existing social exclusion and tensions. The issues around gaining a sense of 'belonging' or 'inclusion' are discussed in the final chapter.

Unsurprisingly, asylum seekers receiving a negative decision focused on their immediate survival needs and the lack of quality or fairness in the RSD process. The impact of not getting refugee status and thus having to move out of NASS accommodation had an immeasurable impact. As an asylum seeker served with an eviction notice from his PAP commented:

> 'You start getting on well in your life, you make friends, you talk about different topics ... you start having hope that you can be part of the society in a way. We talk about other issues, not related to the police

---

[55] Conversation with a female refugee, dispersal location, June 2003.

or the immigration or whatever, we start living life. Suddenly you get a letter killing all the hope, it changes your life completely and you have to start thinking about the problem of immigration and police.'[56]

This killing of hope obviously did not lead to trust in the political systems of the UK. The word 'lottery' was used by solicitors, asylum seekers, refugees, service providers and others to describe the RSD system and the perceived lack of fairness or justice was often spoken about. Confidence and trust in the asylum system was lacking both among asylum seekers and those who worked with them.

The end of the liminal period for some, and the beginning of the process of moving towards belonging, were inextricably linked to the RSD process. The process of moving away from liminality thus involved the asylum and NASS systems, which were initially dealt with by separate Home Office directorates. With the introduction of NAM in 2006 these functions were adjoined but the speed of the new process then became an issue, as did the bureaucratic 'fractioning' of the 'refugee' label to facilitate the management of 'new' migration (Zetter, 2007).

Resettlement or refusal: the end of NASS support

Regardless of whether a positive or negative decision on an asylum claim was made, at the point of a decision, asylum seekers were required to move out of NASS accommodation. If the decision was positive, 28 days were given to leave the accommodation and at this point 'integration' and the many policy initiatives surrounding inclusion could commence. However, this process, referred to as 'move-on', was problematic for asylum seekers at many levels: "NASS services are really awful. Once you have got your refugee status, they cut everything and you are almost paralysed".[57] In March 2005, pilot projects to administer this move between asylum seeker and refugee status were set up. These projects – the Strategic Upgrade of National Refugee Integration Services (SUNRISE) – were a part of the UK government's refugee integration strategy and were rolled out nationally in 2008.

This sudden necessity to negotiate and access agencies used by the UK's wider population was difficult for many after many months, sometimes years, spent within a different system. NASS support ended and mainstream services needed to be accessed. There was a distinct lack of information provided to asylum seekers about which services needed to be approached at this stage. Both financial support and accommodation needed to be sought as well as paperwork for employment: "When you finish with NASS, you go to the social security office and this is another problem. It is like a Home Office interrogation to have a National Insurance number".[58] Because of the lack of linkage between the NASS system

---

[56] Interview with a male asylum seeker, dispersal location, November 2003.
[57] Participant in a focus group, dispersal location, July 2003.
[58] Participant in a focus group, dispersal location, July 2003.

and national integration programmes, for this refugee moving through the now allowed process was similar to that experienced when claiming asylum. A new set of agencies needed to be negotiated and the impact of the disbelief experienced by the Home Office during her asylum claim clearly impacted on the way in which the social security office was approached and perceived. The loss of trust in institutions generally was clear.

Accessing accommodation following 'move-on' from NASS included putting names on waiting lists for public accommodation. Some 'move-on' teams slowly emerged in local authorities across the country to assist asylum seekers in accessing accommodation once a positive decision was granted.[59] However, the other option – to move to an area close to existing friends or family – did not attract such support and was actively discouraged in later legislation enacting a 'local connection' for asylum seekers to be accommodated within regions of dispersal.

Coordination between the Home Office and NASS was again an issue at this stage. Two interviewees received a letter saying that NASS support had been terminated without receiving their status determination letter. Support was terminated upon receipt of a negative decision but often the Home Office had not notified NASS that an appeal had been lodged and eviction notices were served, creating unnecessary worry and distress. If the decision was negative, an eviction notice from NASS accommodation was served on the individual by the accommodation provider. This drawing in of accommodation providers into enforcing destitution was a highly questionable aspect of the NASS system. As one asylum seeker commented upon receiving a letter to leave his accommodation six days later[60]:

> 'I believe that you are not going to die until your day comes. I have been through lots of things so I am not scared about dying because there is a day I am going to die anyway. But I am thinking about whether I am going to suffer from torture or whether I am going to suffer now that they have asked me to leave this room. If I am going to live in that cold weather. This is what I am thinking about. I don't care if I die. Everybody is going to die. But I am just thinking about that torture and suffering. The future is finished for me now. I am just thinking, what can happen tomorrow?'[61]

This linking of past to present circumstances was common during interviews with asylum seekers moving through the NASS system. The link for this individual was

---

[59] For example, Newcastle has a 'move-on' team and Sheffield has a 'floating support' team.

[60] Accommodation providers receive 10 days' notice of a negative decision and serve subsequent eviction notices.

[61] Interview with an asylum seeker, dispersal location, November 2003.

from past torture and persecution to his current eviction and the implications this would have for his future. For this individual, the period of liminality was not over.

While relocation of asylum seekers by agencies was fairly accepted as a normal aspect of the policy, any 'secondary migration' (Robinson, 2003a) by asylum seekers following RSD was discouraged through the requirement to retain a 'local connection' to their dispersal areas.

A common assumption among asylum seekers, refugees and RCO representatives was that the link between deprivation and dispersal created the impulse for secondary migration. The study by Zetter et al (2005) also found that the experience of the process itself, conditions in receiving locations and the quality and location of accommodation were the main reasons behind secondary migration.

Asylum seekers would 'secondary migrate' either during the process to opt for SO support and stay with friends or once their asylum application had been accepted or rejected and they were required to leave NASS accommodation. This wide variety of times and reasons for secondary migration were largely a reflection of the heterogeneity of asylum seekers. Those in receipt of a negative decision would either go 'underground' or become 'undocumented' – either way the potential for exploitation of their circumstances was great. Thus, the end of the period of policy-imposed liminality of a positive asylum decision brought with it new problems and issues that asylum-seekers-turned-refugees encountered and the feeling that they were 'beginning again' was present. A negative decision meant that beginning again was not an option, with present and immediate survival needs taking precedence over other aspects of their future.

For those with a positive outcome, funding was provided by the Home Office through the European Refugee Fund (ERF) and the Challenge Fund for projects aimed at integration of refugees. However, in a report for the Home Office, Peckham et al (2004, p 2) found that clients of the ERF and Challenge Fund services in 2002-03 were 'an extremely disadvantaged group – more disadvantaged than residents in even the most deprived areas in Britain'. A finding was that the circumstances of these clients were 'much worse than those of residents in Britain's New Deal for Communities areas and/or among black/ethnic minority residents' (2004, p 6). The link between dispersal and deprivation clearly had implications for refugees beyond the move-on stage and this legacy impacted on their levels of social exclusion.

Impact of the dispersal system: policy-imposed liminality and the absence of trust

The main impact of the NASS system for asylum seekers was a feeling of loss of control over their lives and a sense of liminality, or limbo, imposed by the process. The 'one-size-fits-all' character of the NASS system added an extra layer of liminality to the already difficult asylum process. While the NASS support system was not unique in creating an absence of trust, being made to feel temporary, having no choice about which city and what type of accommodation to live in and then being relocated several times contributed to this policy-imposed liminality.

From the point of arrival, asylum seekers did not know who they could trust and the complexity of the NASS system added to the difficulty of distinguishing implementing agencies from the Home Office. It also resulted in a system that was characterised by waiting, not wanting to 'bite the hand that feeds' and an unwilling patron–disadvantaged client relationship. The compulsion inherent in the system was highly problematic and the perception was that dispersal was a 'lottery'. The system of dispersal and relocations integral to the process meant that asylum seekers were often separated at the point where they were beginning to form relationships through meaningful or day-to-day encounters. Importantly, this did not enable the re-establishment of normal routines necessary to re-establish primary and secondary ontological security[62] (Richmond, 1994b), hindering any re-establishment of trust. The need to report to the police on a regular basis also made it difficult to escape the centrally imposed and stigmatising label of asylum seeker and adopt a new identity once they reached a local setting.

A turning point was the award or refusal of refugee status. Together with the lack of confidence in the integrity and quality of RSD, trust in political processes to ensure equitable outcomes was largely absent.

Overall, the experience of being socially excluded and separated from mainstream services and, most importantly, the rights and entitlements of others left little space for the restoration of any institutional or political trust.

The maintenance and creation of social networks (Marx, 1990) were key ways of restoring social trust and for asylum seekers who had recourse to social networks this was the most important way in which a sense of 'belonging' in the absence of political belonging was created. For those without recourse to social networks, dispersal could lead to extreme social isolation and social exclusion and the ability to create social networks took on greater importance. Asylum seekers gained information about the negative or positive characteristics of different dispersal locations largely through family, friends, acquaintances and brief encounters with other asylum seekers. Generally, agencies involved in the implementation of dispersal were not approached to obtain this type of information. Social networks – be they weak or strong – clearly overrode trust in institutions, particularly those associated with NASS. Forms of belonging generated through such trusted social networks were those that evoked the familiar, in some way reconstructed an imagined past and were linked strongly to regaining dignity. These were key ways in which asylum seekers resisted the imposition of liminality during dispersal.

---

[62] Primary ontological security refers to 'an individual's self-confidence, derived from a sense of the permanency of things.... Becoming a refugee ... generates extreme ontological insecurity'. Secondary ontological insecurity 'arises when particular spheres of social life are threatened' such as bereavement or loss of employment that generate anxiety (Richmond, 1994a, p 19).

Clearly, the environment of mistrust in which the NASS system operated disregarded the dignity of asylum seekers from the outset with the process being characterised by compulsion, control and inefficiency. Along with detention, deportation and more recently destitution, dispersal was used as a policy to deter new arrivals. In the process the imposition of the dispersal system hindered resettlement, 'integration' or any sense of belonging. This NASS system represented an extension of the disbelief already inherent in the process of seeking asylum. There was a constant reinforcement of mistrust at every stage of the NASS process with the in-country deterrence aspect becoming a taken-for-granted characteristic of dispersal by agencies involved in its implementation.

Subsequent to dispersal, a range of further legislative measures and mechanisms were introduced to deter new arrivals. Dispersal was implemented at the same time as asylum seekers were denied permission to work, there was withdrawal of social support for asylum seekers applying 'in-country'[63] as well as pilot projects to take the children of refused asylum seekers into care if they did not 'voluntarily' return to their countries of origin. The trajectory of asylum policy in the UK has increased the chances of mistrust and liminality being experienced by asylum seekers. The government's Five Year Strategy for Asylum and Immigration, published in February 2005 entitled *Controlling our borders: Making migration work for Britain* (Home Office, 2005), included reviewing individuals' granted refugee status after five years. Assessments of continuing protection needs – for example potential changes in conditions in their countries of origin – would then dictate whether their LLR could become ILR. While this threat may not be carried out in practice, any increase in uncertainty generated for refugees will equate to yet another barrier to trust.

Subsequent policy initiatives for asylum seeker or refugees to date have not addressed the trust issue. The immovable policy position of the Home Office that integration should only occur once a positive status decision has been granted denies this possibility and effectively runs counter to other Home Office initiatives to promote social cohesion.

The new policy environment for asylum seekers will also impact on levels of trust. Agencies offering SUNRISE services found housing to be a particular difficulty because there was no provision for development of housing resources. It had little impact on finding accommodation, particularly for single refugees who remained or were moved into temporary arrangements, often provided by family, friends or RCOs (Lukes and Hynes, 2008). Support during SUNRISE was conditional on refugees retaining a 'local connection' in their dispersal locations. As a high proportion of dispersal areas are in areas of multiple deprivation and high unemployment, this conditional support denies movement to other areas of the UK where employment could be found that draws on past skills and professions, allowing the rebuilding of trust across space and time.

---

[63] Section 55 of the Nationality, Immigration and Asylum Act 2002 withdrew social support for 'in-country' applicants from 8 January 2003.

NAM was introduced to deal with applications for asylum made after April 2007. Under this model, asylum seekers are segmented into seven different categories, each with their own assessment criteria, which predetermine the outcome of claims (Zetter, 2007) and speed up the deportation process. While NAM has brought about an integrated casework model that allows more focus on the reasons why asylum seekers arrive in the UK, this segmentation is unlikely to increase the perception of fairness of the RSD process.

Overall, there was little confidence in the asylum process from asylum seekers or from the general population during the period this research took place, suggesting a role for an independent asylum board. With fewer asylum seekers arriving in recent years, policies that allow space for the creation of trust would be timely.

It is clear that the environment of mistrust in which the dispersal system operates disregards the dignity of asylum seekers from the outset, with the process being characterised by compulsion, control and, particularly in its early incarnation, inefficiency.

What is lost in the process

Understanding the beginnings of the 'asylum cycle' (Koser, 1997), from the period of threat to the decision to flee and survive and the subsequent journey, allows for a broader consideration of the needs of asylum seekers. It also highlights what is lost if the focus is only about the administrative process of the system. Viewing only the stages once an asylum seeker reaches the UK creates a view that is bleak and dehumanising as it stresses outcomes around vulnerabilities. The focus is on the '*loss* of a place' throughout, ignoring the 'struggle to *make* a place' (Turton, 2004, p 26; emphasis in original). From this position, which emphasises the negative aspects of the experience, acting on behalf of asylum seekers due to their unique needs is justifiable and setting up parallel services is one possible response. In contrast, asylum seekers' perceptions of their capabilities, resilience and ability to make their own place once the liminal period of the NASS and asylum systems were over was clearly apparent.

Malkki (1995b, p 224) suggests that studies of forced migration must not 'dehumanize and dehistoricise refugees' and that the heterogeneity of individuals be recognised. The refugee quoted earlier who connected her claim for asylum in the UK to the history of British involvement in Iran asserted: "It is my right to flee the hell you made for us"[64]. These words echoed the less forceful sentiments of other asylum seekers and refugees who referred to the histories of their countries of origin as well as to their personal histories and circumstances. Reclaiming histories was a recurrent feature and Malkki's reference to not stripping people of their histories was especially pertinent.

During the period of threat, the basis of the asylum seeker's persecution was formed (Zolberg, 1989; Richmond, 2002; Castles and Loughna, 2004) and the

---

[64] Participant in a focus group, dispersal location, July 2003.

decision to flee and survive, once made, involved complex decisions around which country to seek asylum in and which family, friends or acquaintances would be in a position to assist. There were political considerations surrounding historical colonial connections as well as the 'new geographies' of migration due to new patterns of global trade (Koser and Pinkerton, 2002). The flight or journey undertaken involved a number of issues around survival for which mistrust was used as a survival strategy (Robinson, 2002; Hynes, 2003a).

Until the introduction of NAM, the status determination process by the Home Office was based on the pre-arrival stages and NASS on the latter stages post-arrival in the UK. In doing this, much of the detail around socioeconomic backgrounds and differences in terms of nationality, age and gender of asylum seekers and refugees were disregarded by NASS. Whether an asylum seeker was a former minister or a pre-literate farmer, there was effectively an equal distribution of deprivation imposed on them by dispersal and this meant that individual vulnerabilities, capabilities, histories and socioeconomic status were equalised and neutralised by the policy. This also applied to agencies contracted to NASS as outlined by a caseworker:

> 'On the very first day, they have got no idea who we are, and they start to tell us everything, why they left their house. And we just have to stop and say, "Just tell me, do you need a shelter, do you need clothing, do you need food?". We are there to assist as advisors. We can talk to them while we are signposting and we might discover that they need assistance with immigration or legal issues.'[65]

The implementation of dispersal therefore also involved RSPs in negating personal histories. Having to stop a client from talking about the source of their persecution to shift the focus onto immediate survival needs was a product of the limited funding allocated by the Home Office. It also indicated that asylum seekers were not distinguishing between agencies in the system. The period of policy-imposed liminality commenced and future "hopes and needs"[66] were catered for by signposting to other services outside of the RSP.

The personal history and unique circumstances asylum seekers have been through was described by one Sudanese asylum seeker who had been forcibly conscripted to the army:

> 'The problem here is people when they look at your case they expect you to say exact dates, exact times and exact numbers. We have been living in the bush where there is no difference between days, you

---

[65] Joint interview with representatives of the voluntary sector, dispersal location, June 2003.
[66] Joint interview with representatives of the voluntary sector, dispersal location, June 2003.

don't know what the time is and you don't know what the date is. You just live like an animal lives. Animals don't care about the dates because they don't need them. You don't get a salary, so how are you to know dates. So when people here expect you to give exact dates, what the date happened to you, etc. It is very difficult to state that one very accurately.'[67]

This added factor of not knowing dates and times was clearly a factor for this pre-literate asylum seeker. The feeling that his history could not be understood by agencies because of the difference between his country of origin and the UK did not apply to the RCO he had contact with who knew the circumstances of Sudan in depth. However, RCOs were rarely in a position – in terms of funding, 'voice' or ability to influence policies – to affect the process.

Similarly, factionalism – often the basis of claims of persecution – was largely misunderstood. The NASS Dispersal Strategy[68] discussed avoiding dispersing 'warring factions'. In practice, however, this was often the case and factionalism was not considered by NASS during allocation of accommodation and no guidance was provided to service providers on its implications. Different nationalities, clans and opposing nationalities were dispersed together and while that was not always problematic, some consideration would have been beneficial. The same applied to those with different political opinions, religious views and membership of particular social groups. There was confusion and a lack of understanding as to what the term 'warring factions' meant. Several different interpretations of this term were encountered by service and accommodation providers. At a local level this issue had been approached involving a "steep learning curve" and the specific "institutional knowledge"[69] of placement officers of the agencies involved. As one housing officer commented, "It depends on the staff. It is an ongoing process. We specialise in refugees so we know about factionalism. If there are 'warring factions' we move them.... It can be something from 400 years ago that has been dormant but suddenly pops up".[70]

Another provider discussed the "shifting sands" of global conflicts that meant that tensions could not be foreseen between individuals. An opposing view from a mainstream service provider who had previously been a refugee was provided when it was explained how colleagues could not conceptualise this:

'If you have had a gun pointing to your head and they didn't shoot you, you will never know what it means. I know cases where I have been caught in crossfire, come very close to being killed. All because of my ethnic group. If that person was thought to be from my ethnic

---

[67] Interview with an asylum seeker, Bristol, November 2003.
[68] Supplied to author by Home Office on request
[69] Joint interview with an accommodation provider, dispersal location, October 2003.
[70] Joint interview with an accommodation provider, dispersal location, October 2003.

group, your tribe, they would be killed. Just because of your ethnic group you could be dead. Someone can explain this to you but you will never understand it. We explain it to them [colleagues], they think it is a joke you know, I am making up or something like that.'[71]

Thus, an insider/outsider perception had great bearing on this issue. For this individual, explaining the threat posed by a member of another ethnic group to someone who had not encountered this in their lives was clearly considered not possible in this instance. It was therefore unsurprising that the vague issue of "warring factions" and "complex patterns"[72] that asylum seekers operate within and form had not been given serious consideration during dispersal.

Another reason why the process was confusing upon arrival stemmed from political conditions in countries of origin. Distinguishing between the voluntary sector and government agencies was not necessarily something that individuals had done before in countries with a limited space for civil society. Many of the countries from which people flee persecution could be classed as those without a vibrant civil society as a result of dictatorial regimes. It is well known, in cases like Burma for example, that was is sometimes regarded from outside the country to be a civil society are organisations set up to appear humanitarian while being run by the relatives of the ruling regime. Given this experience, upon arrival in the UK, asylum seekers may not separate the voluntary sector from the government in the first place. This related closely to the issue of trust: a solicitor dealing with asylum seekers commented:

> 'It is difficult for them to trust you. Because usually they don't have voluntary organisations in their own country. Usually there is no such separation between the state power and the oppression power. So it takes time to trust me and then they are moved, and then they have to start the process again.'[73]

As Colson (2003, p 6) suggests, 'Good intentions, even if perceived, do not earn trust'. Good intentions alone, in the absence of a fair and just dispersal process and RSD decision to back them up, did not change the lack or loss of institutional trust.

'Cultural somersaults' and the 'hypocrisy of democracy'

Trust was also gendered and dependent on the separation of roles in the country of origin and the new roles encountered in the country of asylum. In the UK, the process women go through when adapting to new power structures inside

---

[71] Interview with an asylum seeker, Leicester, July 2003.

[72] Focus group with female representatives of the voluntary sector, dispersal location, July 2003.

[73] Interview with solicitor, dispersal location, July 2003.

and outside the home was described by one refugee as "cultural somersaults".[74] The realisation that divorce from violent partners was possible or that financial support for children was not dependent on remaining with fathers were examples of such 'cultural somersaults'.

The loss of political trust related to the assumption of fair treatment due to the democratic ideals of the UK. When this proved incorrect and rejection was experienced, it led to anger:

> 'That is fine having democratic rights provided they mean real democratic rights.... There are some aspects about democratic rights that are at the moment ignored. Nobody would believe five years ago that they could be in operation in Britain. To detain someone without charge for indefinite periods. So what democratic values are we talking about? People are far smarter than what the politicians think. They can see the double standard – democracy and the hypocrisy of it.'[75]

The hypocrisy of democracy referred to by this solicitor and a dichotomy of rights for asylum seekers and others based on legal status were present throughout. Two separate human rights systems in the UK, one for the resident population and the other for asylum seekers, were repeatedly raised by asylum seekers, refugees, voluntary sector agencies, campaigning organisations and also accommodation providers in dispersal areas. This 'them' and 'us' distinction emerged during the dispersal system and in the perceptions of individuals.

The system did not take account of the negative or positive experiences people bring with them, nor did it take account of the skills or qualifications of those arriving into the country. The focus on an administrative system was therefore detrimental to any recognition that asylum seekers may be resilient survivors.

Optimism at the beginning of this process was replaced by narratives devoid of optimism regardless of whether the asylum decision was ultimately positive or negative.[76] As one asylum seeker with a negative decision commented on his hopes of rebuilding his life, or making a new place in the world:

> 'When I came here I was happy because I can start finding people and I felt that I was getting support and I could start thinking about the future. I could have new hope that there is a future. Now this has stopped. They have taken that hope from me now. Because in the past I had no future. Because there was killing everywhere, you don't think about the future. When I came here I start thinking about my life, my

---

[74] Interview with a female representative of an RCO, London, November 2002.
[75] Interview with a solicitor, dispersal location, July 2003.
[76] Interviews with various asylum seekers and refugees, various dates.

future. You know, I have retrained, I could get ahead. But suddenly now they have taken that. What is going to happen to me?'[77]

Mistrust of the Home Office and NASS and dependence on needs-tested, selective benefits did not restore, and arguably destroyed, institutional trust at the outset. A strong desire to move away from the NASS system and avoid the agencies involved in the process involved resisting the policy-imposed liminality of these systems for those who ultimately were to remain in the UK.

Resistance to policy-imposed liminality

In his seminal study of everyday forms of resistance in rural Malaysia – *Weapons of the Weak* – Scott (1985) illustrates how everyday techniques of evasion and resistance[78] were utilised that avoided direct confrontation with authority. The silent struggle to define their own lives and the 'constant, grinding conflict over work, food, ritual – at everyday forms of resistance' (1985, p xvi) resonates with general resistance to the asylum system and dispersal-specific forms of resisting the 'policy-imposed liminality' experienced, although care has been taken not to over-romanticise these. Given the status and social exclusion issues outlined above, formal resistance and direct confrontation were not generally utilised but resistance to the NASS system was apparent.

One dispersal-specific form of resistance to liminality encountered was, in the terms of NASS and RSPs involved, 'failure to travel' to dispersal locations. This was largely at the point of the process where they were in emergency accommodation or in their first dispersal location. The assumption that once allocated accommodation by NASS, asylum seekers would comply, was found to be incorrect and thus "secondary casework" of those who had not travelled "took NASS by surprise" with some 'cases' returning 15 times across the desk of NASS employees.[79] The lack of choice in dispersal location was clearly a factor in asylum seekers not wanting to 'travel' and other reasons included inadequate information provided about the proposed dispersal location, the existence of family or other social networks in London and various other complex motivations. A comprehensive account of the characteristics and profiles of those who 'failed to travel' would require further research but social networks were considered influential by those working closely with asylum seekers.

'Failure to travel' to the allocated dispersal location was a form of non-compliance, a form of resistance that avoided direct confrontation with authority, in this case NASS. As a representative of a PAP commented, "They usually don't

---

[77] Interview with an asylum seeker, dispersal location, November 2003.
[78] Everyday forms of resistance included pilfering, arson, subtle sabotage and desertion (Scott, 1985).
[79] Joint interview with representatives of the Home Office, London, August 2003.

bother to get on the coach if they don't want to go. A lot of them don't arrive when we go to meet them at the coach station".[80]

Some other more direct and well-publicised forms of resistance to the asylum process were apparent in dispersal locations. These included extreme acts such as stitching up eyes and mouths in symbolic acts to register disapproval of the way in which asylum seekers were treated. In January 2001, asylum seekers in the International Hotel in Leicester took their beds out onto the streets to protest about inadequate heating and poor hygiene (Fekete, 2001). Hunger strikes against the general conditions of dispersal locations in several areas were another avenue of resistance, with occurrences including a Kurdish hunger strike in Liverpool[81] and an Iranian asylum seeker hunger striker in London.[82] Demonstrations were held in several cities across the UK in April 2005 involving asylum seekers and refugees.[83] A well-publicised case was of an asylum seeker setting himself on fire in the office of Refugee Action in Manchester when he had been refused refugee status[84] and was unable to get a medical report because he had no permanent accommodation and was therefore unable to access a GP.[85] There were also demonstrations outside the offices of the Refugee Council in London.

Some 'anonymous acts of resistance' (Scott, 1985, p 304) were recounted by the one PAP interviewed who was:

> 'teaching these people to live together and to keep the house clean. Maintenance has been a big problem for us – damage, malicious damage to property. We provide cleaning materials to asylum seekers and show them how to clean. We are trying to get on top of this at the moment, which is quite a tough job.'[86]

The cleanliness of properties was a complaint coming from both asylum seekers and the accommodation providers. That asylum seekers felt they had no stake in maintaining or cleaning properties once within this liminal process was clear. Attempting to show asylum seekers how to keep properties clean was in this way a manifestation of the lack of control asylum seekers felt they had over their lives. These direct and indirect forms of resistance were ways in which asylum seekers resisted policy-imposed liminality.

---

[80] Interview with a PAP, dispersal location, June 2003.
[81] Interview with a male representative of an RCO, London, August 2004.
[82] 'Asylum seeker goes on hunger strike', *This is Hertfordshire*, www.thisishertforsdshire... asylum_seeker_goes_on_hunger_strike.php
[83] 'Asylum seekers on the march', *IRR News*, www.irr.org.uk/2005/april/ha000008.html
[84] 'Refugee's fireball horror', *Manchester Online News*, www.manchesteronline.co.uk/news/s/134/134535_refugees_fireball_horror.html
[85] 'Open verdict on asylum seeker who slept in a wheelie bin', Manchester Committee to Defend Asylum Seekers, www.asylumpolicy.info/notsuicideverdict.htm
[86] Interview with a PAP, dispersal location, June 2003.

Resisting liminality was also evident in the way some individuals had already invested in the UK by learning the language, making new friends from the 'settled' population and participating in volunteering schemes in the absence of being able to take up paid employment.

Being able to 'opt out' of the NASS system was another form of resistance. To do this, social networks were necessary as was a willingness to provide accommodation to individuals receiving SO support. Asylum seekers were generally not arriving from countries that had any welfare state and upon arrival in the UK they did not wish to live on benefits any longer than they had to. One asylum seeker commented on his reasons for "opting out" of the NASS system prior to the rule on permission to work being revoked:

> 'I said this is useless. There was no reason to live off public money. I didn't feel good. So, I left the NASS and stayed with a couple of my friends. And then eventually became independent. It was factory work, developing these mechanical engines, preparing the parts that are used to transport the fluid and things like that. It was a really, really difficult job but I didn't really mind because I was working and supporting myself. I have always preferred working and taking care of myself to living off benefits. I don't care for that at all. I don't know what would have happened if I didn't have permission to work. Right now I am contributing a lot of money to the public coffers – taxes are big and National Insurance is big. When I think that I am going to go back home so the National Insurance that I pay is going to be still here to pay for other people. The money can stay in Britain forever and I will go back.'[87]

Employment, as a method of resisting liminality, was for this individual a route to 'social inclusion' even though he anticipated ultimate return to his country of origin. The recognition that 'dependency' is due to structural impediments is closely linked to this as Sen (1999, p 7) argues: 'the rejection of the freedom to participate in the labour market is one of the ways of keeping people in bondage and captivity'. The denial of permission to work thus created a space wherein asylum seekers were controlled.

Conclusions

In this chapter it has been shown how the primary lens for understanding how asylum seekers experience social exclusion during dispersal is policy-imposed liminality. At each stage of the NASS system, a lack of control over the process, a lack of space for the restoration of different forms of trust and the inability to assume new identities other than that of 'asylum seeker' create this lens. Both

---

[87] Interview with an asylum seeker, Leicester, July 2003.

formal and informal processes of social exclusion clearly begin at the point of arrival in the UK and continue throughout the NASS process due to a lack of choice of dispersal location and type of accommodation. The mistrust of asylum seekers in the RSD process is replicated by NASS and the ensuing process of liminality begins. The NASS system involves an unwilling patron–disadvantaged client relationship.

In theory, dispersal imposed an equal distribution of deprivation on all forced migrants regardless of their socioeconomic backgrounds and individual histories. Every destitute asylum seeker was dispersed without regard for the human resources and experiences they were potentially able to mobilise and this means that individuals were effectively equalised and dehistoricised by dispersal. This dehistoricising of asylum seekers was replicated by agencies funded by the Home Office. Dispersal as a 'one-size-fits-all' policy demonstrates the consequences of Indra's (1999) earlier examination of tensions in the theories of forced migration. The centre of gravity on the macro side has important consequences and what is lost in the focus on an administrative process is the heterogeneity, resilience and capabilities of asylum seekers.

Resistance to this policy-imposed liminality is the way in which asylum seekers begin to acquire a sense of belonging or inclusion in the UK. 'Integration' therefore occurs despite asylum policies and not because of them. Resisting policy-imposed liminality was evident throughout this study with 'failure to travel' being the main dispersal-specific form. The foundations for future social and institutional trust are laid during the NASS process and the space for both forms of trust is extremely limited by the policy. Dispersal has added another layer of 'liminality' to the already difficult asylum process and institutional trust is not formed during the NASS system. Subsequent chapters explore how this policy-imposed liminality occurs due to services being provided on a temporary basis and how asylum seekers resist, subvert and challenge this liminality with coping strategies, which include social networks.

SIX

Access to services

Introduction

Dispersal away from London and the South East brought with it questions around access to legal representation, language support, housing, medical care, education, training and employment (Audit Commission, 2000a). This chapter looks at access to services, demonstrating how temporary access to services added to the liminal experience of asylum seekers. The changing entitlements of asylum seekers since the early 1990s are outlined, highlighting how the power to define who can access welfare and other services is now based on legal status. The obligations of agencies contracted to the Home Office to facilitate access to services are explored using qualitative data relating to specific services in dispersal locations. Once gender and the intangible barriers to access services have been explored, emergent issues in dispersal locations such as services for domestic violence and mental health are identified.

It is argued that the temporary nature of services, along with the monitoring and reporting roles of accommodation providers, maintain asylum seekers in a liminal state. It is also argued that the priority for good-quality legal, accommodation and translation services is indicative of the weaknesses of the dispersal and asylum systems.

Changing entitlements and tangible barriers

The decline in entitlements to rights for asylum seekers since the 1990s has occurred in parallel to an overall qualitative shift in the environment towards asylum seekers. Dwyer (2005, p 636) argues that key principles relating to accessing national welfare rights with 'notions of need and entitlement' have become secondary to 'issues of claim and contribution'. For asylum seekers, this shift has become particularly acute with asylum legislation progressively changing entitlements for accessing financial services, accommodation and the entitlement to work. Burchardt (2004) charted a decade of declining entitlements up to the Nationality, Immigration and Asylum Act 2002 (see Table 6.1).

Table 6.1: Changing entitlements for asylum seekers

	1993 Act	1996 Act	1999 Act	2002 Act
Benefits				
Claim made 'at port'	90% IS + all other	90% IS + HB + CTB only	No benefits. Excluded from 1948 and 1989 Acts. Vouchers (value 70% IS) + dispersal	NASS cash support if applied 'as soon as reasonably practicable' and would otherwise be destitute (value 70% IS)
Claim made 'in-country'	90% IS + all other	No benefits. LA support through National Assistance Act 1948 and Children Act 1989 if otherwise destitute	As above	No benefits. NASS support only if denial would constitute human rights abuse
Housing	HB. LA housing. Restricted access to homelessness assistance	Excluded from waiting lists for LA housing	All rights to social housing removed. NASS accommodation arranged through compulsory dispersal	'At-port' applicants: induction centres followed by NASS dispersal 'In-country' applicants: NASS only if denial would constitute human rights abuse
Right to work	No restrictions	Not for first six months	Not for first six months	Not for duration of asylum claim

Notes: CTB = Council Tax Benefit; HB = Housing Benefit; IS = Income Support; LA = local authority.
Source: Burchardt (2004)

The Immigration and Asylum Act 1999 excluded asylum seekers from a number of mainstream benefits.[1] Due to the provision of separate support specifically for asylum seekers, they also do not qualify for several other benefits.[2] These tangible losses and incremental reductions of entitlements formally exclude asylum seekers from the rights and benefits available to those ordinarily resident within the UK.

This tightening of asylum legislation was a topic often reflected upon, with several direct comparisons made between the contemporary situation for asylum seekers and the way in which refugees were protected in the past. Asylum seekers survive in the UK without the permanent protection and associated rights of refugee status and this lack of legal status creates a major and discernable qualitative difference. A refugee who had arrived in the 1980s expressed this in clear terms: "When you look back in comparison to what other people have to do these days in order to seek protection, I was in a very privileged position. I think that if I was a young woman coming out of Iraq nowadays I wouldn't have a chance in hell".[3] This of course relates not only to UK policies but also to global dynamics of conflict and shifts in provision of UNHCR's 'durable solutions' (Crisp, 1999). However, this and other reflections highlighted the more restrictive entitlements and legislative framework presently encountered. This framework was confusing for RSPs and asylum seekers alike and was described with terms such as "harsh", "unfriendly" and "frustrating". Accessing good-quality legal and interpretation services was highlighted as essential as a direct result of this tighter legislation.

Temporary services

Letters from the Home Office detailed the 'temporary admission' of asylum seekers into the UK pending RSD. Letters from NASS replicated this, detailing reporting requirements – to police stations at set periods – and how accommodation was to be provided on a temporary basis. Letters relating to health and dental services also detailed the 'temporary registration' asylum seekers were able to make. Framing asylum seekers as temporary in this way was confusing: "They give you an appointment. Not your real doctor – it is temporary. First I got a temporary doctor. When will I get a real one?".[4] This asylum seeker had a letter from his

---

[1] Under section 115 of the Act: 'No person is entitled to income-based jobseeker's allowance ... or to – (a) attendance allowance, (b) severe disablement allowance, (c) invalid care allowance, (d) disability living allowance, (e) income support, (f) working families' tax credit, (g) disabled person's tax credit, (h) a social fund payment, (i) child benefit, (j) housing benefit, (k) council tax benefit'.

[2] Additional entitlements under the mainstream benefits system that asylum seekers are not entitled to include bereavement benefits, carer's allowances, Incapacity Benefit, Industrial Injuries Benefit, Maternity Allowance, Pension Credit, Retirement Pension, Statutory Adoption Pay, Statutory Maternity or Paternity Pay or Statutory Sick Pay (Refugee Council, 2004b).

[3] Interview with a female representative of an RCO, London, November 2002.

[4] Participant of a focus group, Leicester, July 2003.

GP regarding his registration as being temporary pending the outcome of his RSD. The question as to when he would obtain a 'real' doctor referred to when he would be able to be registered permanently. There was a consensus on this issue in other interviews with asylum seekers, refugees, RCOs as well as RSPs.

This temporary provision of services was not necessarily known by local residents who did not know that a negative asylum decision would involve loss of accommodation and other services: "The other people in their street do not realise this is just temporary – it will all be taken away from them when they get their decision".[5] The liminality of the dispersal system was clearly reinforced by this temporary access to services. Central policy retained a major impact on local-level access to services. This fragmentation of the refugee label into 'refugee' and 'asylum seeker' had often been effectively institutionalised with separate teams supporting these now distinct populations.

Access to services: identities, perceptions and status

If nationality, background, past socioeconomic status, education, socialisation, age, religion, sexuality, disability, 'race', ethnicity and other variables of asylum seekers are considered, it is clear that asylum seekers are as heterogeneous as the existing population of the UK. These intersections – or the 'intersectionality' (Mirza, 1997; Bhavnani et al, 2005) – of gender, 'race', class and other variables are essential ignored within the dispersal system, other than in cases of additional need. The compression of each combination of these identities into a one-dimensional label of 'asylum seeker' was highly problematic as provision of services for this population was an extremely complex and difficult task. Multiple identities meant that different services were necessary for different asylum seekers and their varieties of needs: "The person might be ready for employment or they might need mental health services. It depends on the person".[6] Whether the varieties of needs of this heterogeneous population were met was also dependent on resources provided within dispersal areas and this often depended on the perception of asylum seekers by local populations. National media coverage of asylum seekers had considerable impact on the ability to access to services at a local level:

> 'In [dispersal location], people who are at the very margins of society, have low income, have got high unemployment, they have got problems in their community – they see houses completely kitted out with all new stuff and then they see asylum seekers moving in, so they are up in arms that this has been provided, they are getting all this free. So you get the [name of national newspaper], a double-page spread about all this new stuff that has gone into these houses in [name of deprived area] and one of the asylum seekers has complained that

---

[5] Focus group with representatives of the voluntary sector, dispersal location, July 2003.
[6] Interview with a female representative of an RCO, London, June 2003.

he hasn't got a TV, which is a corruption of what was said, the paper doesn't report the following week that these houses had been broken into and boilers had been stripped, fridges had gone, and that was the poor deprived people of that estate, you know.'[7]

The provision of accommodation in mainly deprived areas with high unemployment and longstanding social exclusion made relationships between asylum seekers in this dispersal area and the "deprived" existing community tense. Coverage by a national newspaper had added to this tension. Negative media coverage was often identified as impacting on the perception of asylum seekers and, dangerously, the perception that they were not entitled to access certain services:

'There is a tremendous amount of awareness and good work going on. But when it comes down to the individual you have to deal with very often they have a low level of understanding and a narrow knowledge. Asylum seekers are entitled to services just as much as anybody else.... We have had hospitals ring here and say they are not entitled to access healthcare. Absolute nonsense! There is a lack of understanding. All this negative stuff that people hear. Regardless of whether someone is working in a certain capacity, they are still influenced by what they read and what they see on TV. And that does create problems.'

This same interviewee expressed how the new intensity and negativity in the asylum debate was qualitatively different to past arrivals of Kosovan refugees in the area, stressing how positive images in the media during the Kosovan crisis created goodwill locally and affected access to services:

'People were working through the night to get accommodation ready.... There was a lot of positive stuff in the media and that shaped how people were able to access services.... It has changed. Even though we had a lot of existing forums and people were aware, the method, the legalities, it is completely different. People don't seem to equate people that came from Kosovo with the people who come now for example from Iraq, Afghanistan or even European countries.'

This link to the negative media and the inferred impact on local goodwill towards refugees were a recurrent topic. The impact of this on how asylum seekers accessed services related to the general perception of asylum seekers, which had, as argued, its source in legislation and polemic images due to the deterrence context within which asylum policies were conceived.

Access to both health and educational services was also often referred to by representatives of agencies as being a part of a context of shortage of the general

---

[7] Focus group with representatives of the voluntary sector, dispersal location, July 2003.

decline in these services for the rest of the population of the UK. That there was a debate about whether or not asylum seekers should be able to access services was indicative of their social exclusion and 'outsider' status. Agencies assisting asylum seekers were engaging these existing mainstream services to create awareness of the needs and realities of asylum seekers.

Refugee-specific services in dispersal locations had to play 'catch-up'[8] rapidly upon the initial implementation of dispersal due to the speed at which the system was set up and mainstream services were reportedly taking more time to provide good-quality services. Representatives of RSPs and RCOs in London and the regions commented on how services followed dispersal rather than the other way around. Relocation during dispersal also had considerable impact on how asylum seekers accessed services.

Information provision

The quality of services for asylum seekers was an issue being addressed in dispersal locations. However, the main barrier to accessing services was identified once again as immigration status and the implications of this status in terms of the 'charity' approach of some organisations. Again linking the impact of a national policy to the local level, a representative of a RCO commented:

> 'Apart from all the access issues there is always an issue of having the same rights to access these services. Even though your welcoming pack is saying you can enrol with the local GP, as soon as you settle yourself down and go to your local GP they say, sorry we are full. And there is no next step from that. Because you don't have the same rights as others there is always a barrier to accessing services.'[9]

This issue of legal status apart, there was a difference of opinion about the quality, form and availability of information provided to asylum seekers. Generally, information was provided in written form. Outlining the difficulties with this type of written information, comments were made about how this did not take into account individuals with an oral history or visual learning background:

> 'There is no translated information. Even if there are information points they make it inaccessible for refugees.... When they arrive they get a pack full of organisations, some of them translated into different languages. They get the pack and then [the RSP] say OK you are fine, you have all the information. This pack is useful for me as a professional but the first day you arrive in London, even in your own language, if you have a housing issue go to this organisation, etc.

---

[8] Phrase used by several representatives of agencies in dispersal locations.
[9] Interview with female representative of RCO, London, June 2003.

It doesn't say the organisation actually has a person speaking your language. Impossible.'[10]

Factoring in considerations about the country of origin was largely absent with regard to these lists of organisations. If asylum seekers arrived from countries where services similar to those on offer did not exist, or if they were unaware of, or unaware of the right to access, services on offer these written lists were inadequate. The lack of childcare provision was a major barrier to accessing appropriate services. For the following RCO representative, the entire focus of providing written information was a wasted resource because it was not suitable for refugees who needed one-to-one assistance: "So giving them that pack does not do any good at all. Because the pack goes to the bin. You need somebody to go through one by one if they need to access anything".[11] This was reiterated by another RCO member who commented how asylum seekers would arrive in their office with these lists of telephone numbers and addresses, asking for them to call hostels or accommodation providers on their behalf. An asylum seeker commented on how the list alone was disregarded in favour of face-to-face advice: "They [RSP] told me to go the solicitor. They gave me a list of solicitors on the paper. I went to my cousin and he helped me find a good solicitor".[12]

The lists were clearly only the starting point to accessing services. Although translation of the lists and 'welcome packs' by some agencies was under way, it was clear that trusted family, friends and members of RCOs were sought out to assist in the process for those individuals not isolated during dispersal. Thus, while agencies contracted to the Home Office were fulfilling their contractual obligations to assist refugees accessing services, the way in which information was provided was not always suitable.

However difficult to generalise about services, certain issues were identified surrounding specific services and it was clear that asylum seekers placed priority on particular services largely due to the overarching context of deterrence and structures of the asylum and dispersal systems.

Legal services: the highest priority

Access to *good-quality* legal services (my emphasis) came out as the most important and essential element of claiming asylum in the UK and was a high priority for every interviewee. There was consensus among asylum seekers, refugees and representatives of RCOs and RSPs that the current RSD process was not reliable. Dispersed asylum seekers were forced to obtain good-quality legal advice due to this lack of quality in the RSD process.

---

[10] Interview with female representative of an RCO, London, June 2003.
[11] Interview with a female representative of an RCO, London, June 2003.
[12] Focus group participant, Leicester, July 2003.

Within dispersal areas there was a wide variety of quality in the legal representation available. Access to good-quality legal advice was arbitrary and the asylum process, from the initial interview through to any subsequent appeal stage, was again referred to as a "lottery"[13], dependent on the Home Office caseworker or subsequent appeal adjudicator. The importance, therefore, of good-quality legal advice in dispersal areas was extremely high and asylum seekers were fully prepared, once they had found a good solicitor, to retain their solicitors in the original city they found themselves in upon arrival in the UK and subsequently travelled long distances to access these services even though no provision was made for funding this travel. In one example, an asylum seeker described how she preferred to travel to her original solicitor in Birmingham each time rather than get a new solicitor in the new dispersal location: "My solicitor is in Birmingham because I was in Wolverhampton first and I don't want to change the solicitor because it causes a lot of problems. I travel every time".[14] This was not an isolated case and for this individual, who arrived in London, was dispersed to Wolverhampton, obtained a solicitor in Birmingham, attended screening interviews in Liverpool and had been relocated, the reason for not changing her solicitor revolved around trust. She had found a solicitor she trusted and that solicitor had already been able to ascertain details of her individual case history in the limited time allowed for solicitors for each asylum seeker.

A solicitor working in a dispersal city commented on how the balance of legal work had tipped from immigration to asylum work since the mid-1990s and that this was causing some resentment within longer-established black and minority ethnic communities:

> 'But asylum has taken over from immigration. As a result we sometimes have lots of queries from established [black and minority ethnic] communities. They say, "How about us?", "Why can't you make an appointment for us?". To some extent, a degree of hidden resentment has been created because of the meat that is created by the media – that asylum seekers come and take everything. Some of the established ones say, "Oh, it has become harder because of asylum seekers".'

Some 70% of all black and minority ethnic communities live in the 88 most deprived districts (ODPM, 2004, p 5) and dispersal was mainly to these same areas. That resentment from the 'established' black and minority ethnic communities was perceived was not, therefore, surprising. This solicitor also commented on how the sheer scale of asylum work being undertaken had an effect on their ability to campaign: "Also, our campaigning capacity has been reduced because of the sheer volume of casework. Anything I do now is in my spare time".

---

[13] Comment made by a solicitor during an asylum appeal case at Immigration Appellate Authority, Feltham, Middlesex, November 2004.
[14] Participant in a focus group, dispersal location, July 2003.

Restrictions on the number of hours they could spend on each case was also restrictive:

> 'At the moment, if we do more than 15 hours' work on a case we have to get permission. On average we do between 35 and 50 hours or more. We do far more than we have been claiming for. They are closing the fence around refugees from different angles.'

The introduction of tighter restrictions had not been matched with more resources. Nor had they been matched with higher quality in the decision-making process. This solicitor was, in fact, adamant that the quality of these decisions was much worse than a decade ago:

> 'I can assure you that the quality compared to ten years ago is *phenomenally bad* [solicitor's emphasis]. If you look at any decision made by the Home Office you can see they have just cut and paste from one file to another. They get names wrong, they get countries wrong, in one part of the decision it says you are to be removed to Iraq and in the next paragraph they are sending you to Turkey, then on the front page the nationality is Somali. What is this?'

Overall, asylum seekers lacked political trust in the RSD process and institutional trust in the Home Office or NASS. The need to remain with trusted solicitors, regardless of distances to be negotiated, centred around the need to retain, once found, good-quality legal advice.

Accommodation: a policing role for landlords

Tomlins et al (2002) noted that the housing careers of Vietnamese refugees were disadvantaged by the dispersal policy. They found that ethnicity played a greater influence on the location than tenure of housing and that ethnicity was a 'positive resource that Vietnamese households used to address the shortcoming of governmental and bureaucratic public policy', with the official dispersal policy being counteracted by secondary migration (2002, p 518).

During contemporary dispersal, monitoring of asylum seekers was carried out by accommodation providers. The monitoring and reporting role included in NASS contracts involved reporting to the Home Office any injury, accident, serious illness or death of individual asylum seekers. It also involved reporting violent or aggressive incidents that may have a negative effect on the reputation of the Home Office or individual accommodation provider. Accommodation providers were able to move asylum seekers out of properties if there was a dispute with local neighbours or agencies. A list of policing roles for the accommodation provider included suspecting asylum seekers of being engaged in criminal activities, living beyond their means, working for payment, fraud, allegations of sexual or physical abuse and theft of belongings. Any absences of more than a few days or persistent absences from the accommodation were also to be reported to the Home Office. By 2005, the management of minor antisocial and violent behaviour was recorded by accommodation providers and a record or incidents supplied to the Home Office and the local authority. This contractual obligation for accommodation providers to report an asylum seeker absent from their property was evidence of the control aspect of the NASS system although some housing providers were flexible in their interpretation of NASS rules: "[The subcontractor] should report if he [an asylum seeker] isn't in the house for three days. If they have some evidence that he is not in the house they should report that to NASS. In reality they don't in this case. But others may do". [15]

Another contractual obligation was to facilitate access to educational, health and other services for asylum seekers with the location of 'bedspaces' being close to post offices, local facilities and support groups. [16] The 'lottery' aspect of dispersal again appeared in relation to this, highlighting that the implementation of dispersal was characterised by a lack of consistency:

> 'Having fought their way through all the bureaucracy to get what they need they are moved on. It depends very much on who is their accommodation provider. It is very much a lottery as to who is your provider and whether they get assistance or they have to do it over again themselves.' [17]

For asylum seekers, accommodation was a high priority and accessing accommodation that was not shared and was in areas without high levels of deprivation had been actively sought out by a number of interviewees.

Factionalism not taken seriously during allocation of accommodation had, in one case, proved to be fatal. An unpublicised murder [18] of a male asylum seeker due to two differing nationalities sharing the same room in private accommodation illustrated how the concept of 'warring factions' being kept apart had not been considered:

> 'We have had trouble with the police for various reasons. We have had a murder – one asylum seeker has been arrested and accused of

---

[15] Interview with a representative of a voluntary organisation, dispersal location, November 2003.

[16] Interview with a male representative of a subcontractor to a PAP, dispersal location, June 2003.

[17] Focus group with representatives of the voluntary sector, dispersal location, July 2003.

[18] Details of the murder case did not reach even the local papers, dispersal location, June 2003.

murdering another asylum seeker. We have had stabbings and attempted stabbings between asylum seekers.'[19]

Little detail was provided of the murder during this interview but in a subsequent focus group a refugee recounted the specific details of how the murder had occurred over a religious dispute between two asylum seekers of different nationalities who were sharing the same room in private accommodation. It appeared that this dispute over religion had been the basis of each individual's claim for persecution and because this had not been considered they were placed in one bedroom. The individual recounting the details of this murder was extremely cautious, choosing words particularly carefully to describe events. Commenting on the perceived consequences and real implications for their family if they were to 'put pen to paper' about this murder for a local BME newspaper they asked: "What consequences would I have for writing about this?". This caution was due directly to their status as a refugee in the UK and the involvement of the police in this case. Being afraid of writing an article for a local paper again demonstrated the fear of repercussions and social exclusion of this individual.

Whereas in the past, refugees were considered too vulnerable to be at the mercy of private landlords, dispersal was largely based on the privatisation of accommodation provision through a selection process that was not transparent. Dispersal was not only led by accommodation, it was led mainly by cheap accommodation, much of which was privately owned: "All the accommodation is quite far away from the city where it is cheap, not central. Businesswise that makes sense".[20] Accommodation during dispersal became, over time, an exercise in cost control. A second wave of contracts five years into dispersal was largely awarded to accommodation providers who could provide cheap accommodation,[21] with the costs of signposting asylum seekers to services contained within these prices.

Translators and interpretation services: 'victims of translation'

Another high priority was access to *good-quality* translation and interpretation services in the specific dialects of the individual asylum seeker. The rapid development of interpretation services upon implementation of dispersal was another example of how services had to catch up with asylum seekers. Unsurprisingly, access to interpretation services throughout the entire process was considered by those unable to converse in English as a high priority.

For nationalities of asylum seekers arriving in small numbers, dispersal still involved sending individuals to different cities where often no interpretation

---

[19] Interview with male a representative of a subcontractor to a PAP, dispersal location, June 2003.

[20] Joint interview with representatives of the voluntary sector, dispersal location, June 2003.

[21] Conversation with a local authority representative, dispersal location, January 2004.

services were available. For example, as of March 2003 there was a total of 21 Burmese asylum seekers dispersed across the UK in 10 different dispersal locations. This provision of interpretation for smaller groups was commented on by an accommodation provider: "We have got the main languages but they do come from far afield –Vietnam, China. Sometimes we get caught out on languages".[22] Even when interpretation services were in place, dialects and the ability to trust interpreters were both barriers to access. One asylum seeker viewed himself as "a victim of translation".[23] This was because his application for asylum had been turned down on a point of credibility that related to a translation error in his initial interview. He had said that he was from the south of a particular town and the translator had mistranslated this to the south of the country. The translator in this case was Kurdish who spoke Arabic but did not speak the dialect of the Sudanese individual. It was clear that dialects were not properly catered for throughout the RSD and NASS process, with a solicitor in a dispersal location commenting: "*We have* confronted this issue many times. For example, in Farsi, they do use the same language but dialects are very different".[24]

The trust of interpreters was related closely to the issue of factionalism. A Kosovan asylum seeker discussed how he did not trust the interpreter provided to him by the RSP in his dispersal city: "The translator is from Kosovo. I have a problem with that. The place where I live, yes, he is from Kosovo".[25] The emphasis placed on not wanting to converse with this translator related directly to him not trusting him. The alternative practice of using the children of asylum seekers to act as interpreters was often related to this trust issue. Children interpreting at GP practices, and in other contexts where confidentiality was necessary, was considered to be prevalent.[26]

Health and dental services

Access to health services and interpretation was a clear problem. In one dispersal area, an asylum seeker discussed how he had been refused registration with the GP because he was at a hostel and had temporary status.[27] The power to define access to health services based on immigration was therefore clearly problematic. Johnson (2003) carried out research on how asylum seekers access health services during dispersal, also identifying how problems with interpretation impacted on accessing GPs as well as how relocation made registration with GPs difficult.

---

[22] Interview with a representative of a subcontractor to a PAP, dispersal location, June 2003.

[23] Interview with a male asylum seeker, Bristol, November 2003.

[24] Telephone conversation with a solicitor, dispersal location, November 2003.

[25] Focus group participant, dispersal location, August 2003.

[26] Access to a health workshop, Action for Refugee Women, International Women's Day, London, 6 March 2003.

[27] Joint interview with asylum seekers, Bristol, November 2003.

Another asylum seeker discussed how he was on a waiting list for a gallstone operation, the gallstone having been discovered through obtaining medical evidence of torture.[28] Because he had come to the end of the NASS system and was being evicted from NASS accommodation he did not know how he would be able to access medical support while homeless. While this interview was conducted prior to April 2004 when refused asylum seekers were no longer entitled to ongoing medical support, this individual was under the impression that not having an address meant that he would not be able to access any medical treatment. In another dispersal area this issue of continuity of care was also encountered earlier in the NASS system: "Ensuring continuity of care if they are on medication when they leave EA is difficult. Making sure they do not run out of medication before they have got set up in the dispersal area is hard to do".[29]

It was also the case that access to health services was problematic due to the closure of GP practices: "Access to health is a big problem because GPs' practices are closing down. There are some who will not take refugees and asylum seekers because they couldn't get an interpreter".[30] Health services required access to interpreters, and good-quality translation could make the difference between diagnosis and misdiagnosis. It was clear from both service providers and asylum seekers that access to interpretation was a problem during dispersal:

'NHS doctors are supposed to provide interpreters for asylum seekers when they make an appointment but apparently they don't usually do that so they are not following the law as they are supposed to.'[31]

'Even, when I was in [another dispersal city] I would talk with the doctor and he said he would offer me a translator. They give me appointment but he [the translator] was not there.'[32]

Because the services of GPs are arranged on a temporary basis, provision of good-quality interpretation services was made more difficult. This also applied to access to dental services, again provided on a temporary basis: "We arranged to see a doctor but there was no interpreter. We didn't speak any English. We couldn't explain to the doctor what was wrong. We didn't go to the dentist until it was an emergency".[33] The difficulty of accessing dentists also meant that some asylum seekers kept their registration with a dentist in the original city they

---

[28] Interview with an asylum seeker, dispersal location, November 2003.
[29] Focus group with representatives of the voluntary sector, dispersal location, July 2003.
[30] Focus group with representatives of the voluntary sector, dispersal location, July 2003.
[31] Interview with a representative of a subcontractor to a PAP, dispersal location, June 2003.
[32] Focus group participant, Leicester, July 2003.
[33] Focus group participant, Leicester, July 2003.

found themselves in prior to relocation: "I did not change my dentist because I prefer to travel each time. Because you must start again each time you move".[34]

One individual described how he had been in pain for three months because he was unable to access a dentist. He had not realised that a telephone number for a dentist had been included on the information sheet he was given two months earlier and was unable to call due to his lack of English. He had approached several agencies in an attempt to locate a dentist – his RSP, who had 'talked fast and gave him another piece of paper', solicitor and accommodation provider – all in vain until ultimately he located one through his ESOL (English for speakers of other languages) teacher.

Burnett and Peel (2001) have also discussed events during the 'refugee experience' such as massacres, detention, torture and rape in relation to the health of asylum seekers. The background of individuals and their particular health requirements were not fully catered for during the dispersal process. Physical health issues were sometimes dealt with but issues of depression stemming from the refugee experience were rarely considered upon the decision to disperse them. There is a long-established recognition that poverty is a primary cause of ill-health (Pantazis and Gordon, 1997, p 135). That dispersal did not take into account the physical health issues that asylum seekers arrive with before placing them into deprived areas was another aspect lost during its rapid implementation.

Different organisations were at various stages of understanding the health needs surrounding gender but there was some evidence that RSPs were adapting their services to incorporate the needs of women:

> 'Females from some countries are quite hesitant to go and see a male doctor so we try to arrange an appointment for them, at least a female nurse. If possible a female doctor but if not at least they are going to have a female person with them to make them more comfortable.... We noticed that a lot of female asylum seekers felt so lonely and deprived from services and the facilities that the city can offer. Because of that they felt quite scared to go out and quite vulnerable to go out on their own.'[35]

Issues such as women being isolated, lonely, scared and being threatened in dispersal locations were also highlighted and were related to their general wellbeing (Dumper, 2002).

Financial support: NASS

During interviews and focus groups it was clear that asylum seekers were disillusioned by NASS and the asylum system. The level of inefficiencies of NASS

---

[34] Focus group participant, Bristol, July 2003.
[35] Joint interview with representatives of the voluntary sector, dispersal location, June 2003.

have been well documented (Fekete, 2001; *The Guardian*, 2001). For example, a report from the Citizens Advice Bureau (CAB) (2002, p 1) set out the 'serious systematic problems with the standard of service provided' by NASS. These errors in administration remained evident in the present study with one asylum seeker recounting six errors being made in her case alone. Another female asylum seeker spoke of how she had been granted support but her children had been forgotten on the form and this had caused considerable confusion and difficulties. She had been left for two weeks with no money, with a computer omission in NASS being the cause of this. Another participant had also been told by NASS that she had a sister, with the inference being that this sister would be able to support her: "I was on the phone every day to NASS. Another person told me I had a sister on their computer and that they couldn't give me money. I said, 'You can't say I have a sister if I haven't!'".[36] The lack of continuity of caseworkers within NASS may well have been the reason for these mistakes. However, she ultimately had her case closed by NASS, without her knowledge, as a result of a documentation error.

Education: child and adult

Castles et al (2002, p 81) identified education and training as a gap in substantive research in relation to recent immigration and integration. This area requires considerable further investigation but several issues have emerged as a result of dispersal. Rutter mapped refugee education in the UK before dispersal began (1998) and, subsequently, detailed the effects that the NASS system was having on children's education and wellbeing (2003). These effects related to the long wait in emergency accommodation; inefficiencies of the processing of financial support by NASS; and poverty levels due to Income Support being below national levels. Rutter also found that school uniforms were beyond the budget of parents who were dispersed and that secondary migration to London was high.

Asylum seekers in the present study spoke about how education for children was a high priority but how relocation was a main cause of disruption when children were in school, in terms of the continuity of their education. They also spoke about problems with admissions, certification and the provision of uniform. In relation to the education of children it was clear that social exclusion occurred due to relocation, which would have future ramifications. As one asylum seeker, relocated from private accommodation in the West Midlands to accommodation held by the same company in the South West, commented:

> 'Sometimes they tell you, you have two weeks and you must move. If you have children this is trouble. They move you when they want. It is not good for me or for the children because my child, she missed her technology exam because it was the middle [of the term]. She had nearly finished her programme and since we came here she hasn't

---

[36] Focus group participant, dispersal location, June 2003.

gone to school. My son lost his highest-level exams – he only did the highest level in French, not technology because we couldn't find a school. If you say no they stop the money so you must.'[37]

The speed at which relocations occurred and the lack of continuity of education were clearly problematic. The syllabus in different areas of the country was also highlighted by this mother and others – with one mother deciding to keep her children in their original schools when she had been dispersed from Reading, which was not an official dispersal location, to Nottingham, which was.[38] Provision of financial support for purchase of school uniforms was not provided by NASS in these or other cases.

Admission to schools was also problematic. In one dispersal area, some schools had informally excluded refugee children through strict admissions criteria: "In terms of education some schools think they have enough languages and they have enough refugee children and they do not want any more. So there are barriers for the children who do not meet the criteria".[39]

Problems surrounding certification was also identified in relation to these barriers to accessing education for children: "There can be problems with getting children into school. They do not have their birth certificates to prove their age. They don't know what year they were born in. They can't prove if they were born before or after September for the school term".

In response to dispersal to Glasgow, units were established in schools in which specialist teachers support the English language development of newly arrived pupils becoming, over time, an integral part of the mainstream school (Smyth, 2005). Other areas have provided similar support.

For adults, admission clauses in further education colleges and universities meant that ESOL classes were often an option but vocational training and taking up degrees were not possible until 'home' status was obtained after a period of three years in the UK.[40] This exclusion directly due to legal status was one of the ways in which social exclusion was reinforced at a local level, adding to the liminality already being experienced due to the asylum and NASS systems. While such issues surrounding status were not specific to dispersal, the local perceptions of asylum seekers were influenced by these regulations. In another dispersal location, an interviewee of a further college commented on how these perceptions acted as an information barrier to education:

'I have seen that on the campus there are cases when students come to apply for a course and they need a bit of language support. They

---

[37] Participant in a focus group, dispersal location, July 2003.
[38] Female participant at an Action for Refugee Women conference, International Women's Day, London, March 2004.
[39] Focus group with female representatives of the voluntary sector, dispersal location July 2003.
[40] Questions on enrolment forms related to this status.

get sent to ESOL because someone feels, oh well, this person is not speaking English the way I think they should so I'll send him to ESOL. I have received a huge number of forms from students applying to do computing, healthcare and other courses. But someone does not understand and sends them in the wrong direction. The general idea is that if you are a refugee you need to go to ESOL. Not all departments, but some people do misunderstand.'[41]

This perception that asylum seekers should automatically be directed to ESOL classes rather than other vocational courses with language support was prevalent in government discourse about the educational requirements of asylum seekers. Some RCOs were providing classes for adult asylum seekers and refugees based on ESOL combined with information technology classes with transport and childcare costs provided.[42]

As well as these structural barriers to education, particular difficulties due to the financial limitations inherent in the NASS system were apparent. One participant explained how she needed two buses to get to ESOL classes but no travel expenses were paid by NASS or the college: "They should understand that some of us are away from the college. We have to change onto two buses to get here. My husband and I, it is double, we have to pay every day".

The location of accommodation in areas away from colleges was clearly an unresolved issue. The potential resulting trajectories towards social exclusion as a result of not being able to access further education were many. Compared to a refugee with nursing skills who arrived with very little English before the denial of permission to work and worked as an ancillary nurse in a maternity ward, carrying out basic tasks and learning relevant vocational English as she worked, these negative trajectories were clearly apparent. The relationship between past permanent status and rights as opposed to current temporary rights involves a more sophisticated and complex form of social exclusion. A former minister may already be literate and multilingual and the challenges of learning English may be much less than those faced by pre-literate individuals. The barriers to accessing education were therefore extremely variable.

Several interviewees commented on how the hardest things to learn in the UK were the idiosyncrasies, sense of humour and ironies of everyday life. These were not things that could be learned in a classroom but were essential for any form of 'integration' and employment was identified as the best route to this informal sense of inclusion. However, access to training for employment as well as employment advice for asylum seekers had essentially been removed from the equation in the implementation of dispersal due to the denial of permission of work. Carey-Wood et al (1995) argued that refugees learn to trust and rebuild

---

[41] Interview with a male representative of a further education college, dispersal location, July 2003.

[42] Interview with a male representative of an RCO, London, May 2003.

their lives through stable accommodation and, among other activities, gainful employment. However, these routes were not available to asylum seekers.

The lack of training for employment ran alongside a widespread confusion among employers about the legislation and regulations of migrants generally.[43] The formal exclusion of asylum seekers from employment meant that the social integrationist discourse of social exclusion that emphasises paid employment as a route to inclusion was not relevant. Asylum seekers did not gain work experience during the liminal stage and the absence of UK-based references for future employment had future ramifications.

Intangible barriers to accessing services

The intangible barriers to accessing services revolved around the histories and lives of asylum seekers and the way in which the dispersal system was experienced. Intangible barriers such as low self-confidence and low self-esteem of individuals were directly related to the more tangible barrier of language ability, as one refugee participant suggested:

> 'I think one of the big problems is language barrier. We can't communicate.... Even when we start to learn, in my case, there was no confidence. For years I was here, only a few years ago, we were running a campaign, with different people, I thought I had to say something so I spoke publicly. Before that, I was campaigning here and there, I was writing here and there, but I didn't have the confidence to speak in English.'[44]

This same individual stated that she had not 'opened her mouth' for two years upon arriving in the UK.[45] Low levels of self-esteem were an intangible barrier to inclusion and were often related to the deterrence context. In the words of one solicitor making a presentation to a women's network in a dispersal location, "These are difficult times and strength is needed to support each other. Everyday it is negative and this affects self-esteem. Each person has a personal story but people do not see that. People see only the negatives",[46]

The image of a refugee in the media and in the perceptions of the ordinarily resident population of the UK had, in the eyes of one mental health professional, major impacts on the mental health of individual asylum seekers. Her comments outlined the intangible links between headlines and mental health:

---

[43] Speaker at the conference 'From immigrants to new citizens: becoming a citizen in 21st century Britain, Sponsored by Learndirect and the Office of the Deputy Prime Minister, London, 18 November 2003.

[44] Focus group participant, dispersal location, July 2003.

[45] Focus group participant, dispersal location, July 2003.

[46] Presentation to a women's network, dispersal location, February 2003.

'Mental health takes a nosedive every time there is a negative headline. The collective perception that refugees are scroungers, or whatever, brings shame directly to an individual asylum seeker. And they internalise that. Now refugees in the media are "scum", they are the "worst of the worst". Nobody in their right mind would want to identify with that.'[47]

Given the negative perception of asylum seekers, some asylum seekers did not feel as though they had the right to access certain services due to their "life pending"[48] status. Another refugee made a direct link between such liminality and mental health by commenting that: "When I was only temporary I was naturally depressed about it. I didn't admit it but I was".[49]

The issue of self-esteem was also related to how socioeconomic status for many asylum seekers had declined rapidly upon reaching the UK. A representative of an RSL commented on this 'story not told':

'Doctors, teachers and lawyers who have had a high standard of living but are fleeing because of being a specific religion or ethnic group. They have come from a high standard of living to nothing. This takes their self-worth because they have to depend on people or the government for a small amount of money. No one looks at the positive contributions.'[50]

That asylum seekers turned to their own groups in these circumstances was not surprising. What was surprising was that details of how asylum seekers would even prefer to pay for services from their co-nationals rather than access free services were related to me on several occasions, particularly in relation to legal services. For example, one Burmese asylum seeker had a co-national write his antecedent history for him (for payment) rather than access this service for free through registered legal representatives.

The attitudes of frontline staff during access to mainstream services were informed by negative media coverage and the negative perception of asylum seekers that emanate from the legislative framework. For example, asylum seekers recounted encountering hostility from counter staff at post offices and other mainstream services providers.

Asylum seekers and refugees also considered that service providers did not understand needs fully because 'users' of the system were not involved in devising services:

---

[47] Telephone conversation with a mental health professional, February 2006.
[48] Speaker at the conference 'Hear my voice: refugee women's involvement in integration', Amnesty International Human Rights Centre, London, 15 June 2006.
[49] Interview with a refugee, dispersal location, July 2003.
[50] Joint interview with representatives of an RSL, dispersal location, October 2003.

'But another thing I tend to see is that the people themselves who assist refugees. They don't understand what people are going through – what refugees and asylum seekers are going through. They think they need something in the same way that the newspapers think.'[51]

Again this highlighted how perceptions and the image of asylum seekers had a major impact on access to services. The issue of this negative representation of asylum seekers was ever present. Comparisons were drawn to white people representing black people, men representing women and non-disabled people representing disabled people:

'They have representatives for black people, or women, or disabled people, all kinds of disadvantaged people, but not refugees. I have to say discrimination because I am a black woman, I am a refugee on top of that. So this is too much. You have to have a disabled person to help disabled people. If you want to help black people you have a black person to do that. If you want someone who works with refugees he needs to be a refugee. He understands more what a refugee or asylum seeker needs.'[52]

The focus of campaigns from the voluntary sector has, understandably, been on aspects of recent asylum legislation and on influencing the Home Office to make the dispersal process less inefficient. However, the RSP dual role of "pig in the middle"[53] between asylum seekers and the Home Office is a difficult one and did mean that certain issues were left off the agenda. This categorisation of being black, a woman and a refugee illustrated how issues surrounding status and discrimination were considered of equal importance to asylum seekers as campaigns to influence the dispersal system. A more participatory and beneficiary-based approach (Kaiser, 2002) would therefore incorporate more than advocacy surrounding the dispersal system and legislation.

RSPs approached their role from a perspective that incorporated the idea of a refugee experience. From this perspective, refugee-specific barriers to accessing services emanating out of the refugee experience were often emphasised, leading to a position where asylum seekers needed to be represented. RCOs and asylum seekers, on the other hand, tended to approach their role from a more structural perspective, emphasising their lack of rights in relation to others. One representative of an RCO commented on this tension:

---

[51] Interview with a representative of a further education college, dispersal location, July 2003.
[52] Focus group participant, dispersal location, July 2003.
[53] Focus group with representatives of the voluntary sector, dispersal location, July 2003.

'During that meeting I realised that the attitude was that refugees do not have enough capability to provide services to themselves or run their own group. There was a women's group there, much more politicised, much more aware of their own needs and more active than women's groups I work with here [in London]. But that organisation in [dispersal location] did not want to see them as capable of running their own thing. They wanted to push their own agenda. They had the attitude of seeing themselves as the dominant group, capable of making decisions on behalf of others. They could see no other way of doing things even though someone was in front of them saying, no, it is not the way you should do it.'[54]

This inability to hear what others had to say about what they wanted from the group had clearly been a frustration as each participant in this same meeting had different ideas about what their needs were and what the group should be set up to do. For the English-speaking group (made up of Iranian, Zimbabwean, Burundian and Columbian women) these needs were expressed as addressing social isolation and the need for an independent campaigning group whereas an Albanian-speaking group prioritised 'equality within the community' with longer-term settlement and rights issues and respect for women also identified. These more structural perspectives, emphasising issues around equality, were put forward by asylum seekers as barriers to accessing services.

Asylum seekers and refugees have been separated, to differing degrees, by service providers contracted to the Home Office by the way they provide services. Some had different teams for 'refugees' and 'asylum seekers', often due to the way in which funding was provided. This reification of differences (Lewis, H., 2005) between asylum seekers and refugees was another intangible barrier in that it reinforced the liminality imposed on asylum seekers by the asylum and dispersal systems. The barriers to accessing services were closely related to the issue of trust, both social and institutional.

Gaps in services in dispersal locations

The structure and speed at which dispersal was implemented did not enable gender issues to be fully thought through. There was little consideration of provision of female doctors, domestic violence or culturally specific services for gender-specific forms of persecution such as rape, 'honour' crimes or female genital mutilation. Issues emerging later, towards the end of the 2000s, included forced marriage and trafficking, with policy initiatives devised to address or 'combat' these. Engagement with, and the trust and cooperation of, so-called migrant communities who may have only recently arrived in the UK, is essential in addressing these issues.

---

[54] Interview with a female representative of an RCO, London, June 2003; discussion about meeting with female participants in a dispersal location, February 2003.

Individuals who had experienced interpersonal violence, like those who had been tortured prior to arrival, often experienced the asylum and dispersal systems without any opportunity to address the fragility of their existing capacity to trust.

These cross–cutting issues such as mental health, childcare and advocacy for rights were also often missing as they were not the responsibility of one agency. In a study by Ager et al (2002) into the mental health of socially isolated refugees in Edinburgh, it was found that the availability of familial social networks should be facilitated and wider co-ethnic linkages identified, particularly to 'bridge' support into host country customs and practices.

The issue of domestic violence was initially identified as a gap in services due to telephone calls being made to RCOs in London. This issue emerged from these grassroots organisations within refugee communities and was related to the declining socioeconomic status and dependent legal status of women. NASS did have a policy bulletin on domestic violence[55] but this was largely unknown to asylum seekers beyond the offices of RSPs.[56] The extremely limited access to culturally specific services for domestic violence or rape counselling was unsurprising given the high number of nationalities dispersed to each location. These high numbers made provision of culturally specific services difficult to identify as well as implement.

The issue of 'honour' crimes against female asylum seekers and refugees initially emerged from women's RCOs in London. It was argued by these London-based RCOs that the source of persecution often follows women to the UK because family members are the perpetrators of these crimes. Calls for awareness that legal practices in countries of origin surrounding protecting family honour were not relevant in a UK context were made. Asylum seekers living in 'closed social circles' were considered to have difficulties with the expectations of refugee communities in relation to this and other domestic violence issues.[57] Consciousness of 'honour' crimes has now become national due to the campaigning efforts of women within refugee communities.

Addressing the mental health of asylum seekers was a serious gap in the provision of services within dispersal locations. Mental health emerged as a major issue not catered for adequately during dispersal and, by the mid-2000s, geography was still a barrier to accessing these services: "Things like counselling for trauma are generally not available outside of London and the South East at the moment. Rather, the clients have moved first and services are now starting to catch up".[58]

---

[55] Policy Bulletin No.70.

[56] Speaker at the conference 'Hear my voice: refugee women's involvement in integration', Amnesty International Human Rights Centre, London, 15 June 2006.

[57] Speaker at the conference 'Hear my voice: refugee women's involvement in integration', Amnesty International Human Rights Centre, London, 15 June 2006.

[58] Interview with a representative of the Refugee Council, London, May 2003.

With mental health it was recognised that pathologising asylum seekers was something to be avoided.[59] This was a difficult issue as different groups conceptualise mental health in different ways and could take some time to emerge as practical issues of immediate survival were a priority upon arrival.[60] In dispersal areas, in order to access psychosocial support, an asylum seeker would need to access a suitable GP through their accommodation provider. This GP would need to be tolerant towards asylum seekers, have good interpretation services and recognise the need for such services. Payne (1997, p 159) has already argued that the relationship between poverty and deprivation results in poor mental health and, given the link between dispersal and deprivation outlined earlier as well as the temporary nature of registration with GPs, this route may well have proved difficult for many. An expansion of the Medical Foundation for the Victims of Torture into dispersal locations was also requested by some asylum seekers as it was perceived as being more political and interested in refugees than GPs.

The provision of inappropriate accommodation to asylum seekers and its link to poor mental health was evident. For two individuals in a dispersal area who had attended ESOL classes without having had a shower for one week due to lack of hot water in their hostel, the effect on their wellbeing was clear: "In the International Hotel everybody is going crazy!"[61]. Depression was also mentioned, with one asylum seeker commenting: "Dispersal is making them unstable and depressed".[62]

Addressing 'refugee experiences', a document produced as part of the campaigning work of the London-based Refugee Mental Health Action Group, stated:

> 'Social and economic deprivation, unemployment, homelessness, past and present trauma, racism, discrimination and isolation are major factors affecting the mental health of refugees. Addressing these issues within the specific social context of each person who is experiencing severe psychological distress is the key to the recovery process of that person.'[63]

Within this no distinction is drawn between trauma in the country of origin and the country of asylum, with circumstances surrounding trauma described in

---

[59] Speaker at the conference 'Rights and psychiatry in the UK: civil rights and mental health', Social Action for Health, London, 16 January 2003.
[60] Speaker at the 'Refugees and mental Health' conference, City & Hackney Primary Care Trust, Social Action for Health and Social Services, London, 8 October 2003.
[61] Focus group participant, Leicester, July 2003.
[62] Focus group participant, dispersal location, October 2003.
[63] 'Compulsory treatment is not treatment', Refugee Mental Health Action Group, Social Action for Health, London.

both the past and present. Again the more structural issues surrounding equality of rights and discriminatory practices were highlighted.

There was a real gap in knowledge and the provision of information about family reunification and a lack of basic information in relation to services around family tracing. There was very little knowledge of the Red Cross tracing service or the ways in which family reunification through the UNHCR could be obtained. On three different occasions, asylum seekers asked about how to arrange family reunification and on one occasion about how to trace family members. During the asylum and dispersal processes there was no facility for this due to the temporary status of admission. It was found that information about family reunification was difficult to find even for those wishing to begin the process in the country of origin to register their families with the UNHCR in anticipation of reunification sometime in the future. Policy implications of this include expanding the knowledge of the Red Cross tracing service and the UNHCR family reunification programme of which asylum seekers had no prior knowledge.

There was little knowledge of the only service available to appeal against refusal of NASS support – the Asylum Support Adjudicators – particularly in areas where there was no RSP presence. Some asylum seekers did not know to dial 999 in an emergency.

Gender was also often identified as a big issue in relation to accessing services, regardless of which nationality was being discussed, but gendered data was not publicly available from NASS. The dependent legal status of women on the main asylum applicant centred on power structures within the private sphere in the UK as well as gender roles imported from countries of origin. RCOs provided a more holistic service to women because they were able to cater for the particular nationality in relation to childcare requirements, the accessibility of venues, travel expenses, the timing of courses and support systems necessary. These different needs of women and approach were outlined by one RCO representative:

> 'We don't say this is the training and when you are finished our job is finished. The women come with different needs. Even during the training you have to provide advice on housing, advice on childcare, advice on parenting, different kinds of issues we have to fix up or refer them to appropriate services. It is not only our core activities of education and employment, we do so many things. This is service provision on a one-to-one basis.'[64]

Gaps in services were very evident during discussions with RCOs and their buffering role was one reason the dispersal process could continue.

Childcare came up time and time again as a major barrier to accessing services during interviews with asylum seekers, refugees and RCO representatives, during focus groups with asylum seekers, representatives of RCOs and RSPs, as well as

---

[64] Interview with a female representative of an RCO, London, May 2003.

being brought up by asylum seekers and refugees during conferences. Identified continually as a barrier, this issue cross-cut the entire process of access to services. In Leicester, one mother discussed this in terms of socialisation for her child. She was not aware of toddler groups so the park and the crèche at the further education college represented the only opportunities the child had to socialise with other children. This was not an isolated instance, with other interviewees also mentioning the need to find ways in which to socialise children:

> 'You need a crèche so that you can be involved in a class. The way to find out is by talking to people. They [the RSP] didn't help us with anything. But we are happy to come to college. We put him in the crèche so he is playing with other children for two hours. If it was not for him we would not come to English classes. He can have children to play with. It is a big problem for him to play with other children. We take him to the park but we cannot take him every day.'[65]

There were also problems identified with the areas in which women with children were placed and the local link between dispersal and deprivation. In one dispersal area, accommodation provided to women had not factored in socialisation of children or the safety of women: "There has been a problem with inappropriate accommodation given to women. Women with young children put in places where there are a lot of pubs and the women do not go out".[66]

Projects surrounding these gender issues were being established in dispersal areas, with women's development projects and 'routes to learning' projects being set up by Refugee Action and other agencies.[67] Social exclusion, therefore, had a gender aspect to it with understanding and responses to this varying considerably. However, the intangible barriers to accessing services and issues that emerged in dispersal locations also related to the lack of gender awareness during the planning stage of dispersal.

Conclusions

Tangible barriers to accessing services have been created through asylum legislation since the 1990s due to the linkage between service provision and immigration status. The material presented in this chapter illustrates how dispersal enforced a regime of temporary services meaning that social exclusion at a local level was an inherent part of a dispersed asylum seeker's experience. Similar issues emerging in different dispersal locations show how this local-level social exclusion was a result of government policy rather than local conditions. Dispersal did not cater

---

[65] Focus group participant, Leicester, July 2003.

[66] Focus group with female representatives of the voluntary sector, dispersal location, July 2003.

[67] Speaker at the conference 'Hear my voice: refugee women's involvement in integration', Amnesty International Human Rights Centre, London, 15 June 2006.

for the heterogeneity of asylum seekers' needs, partly due to the temporal focus on stages of the process within the UK rather than the broader issues relating to refugees generally.

The relationship between asylum seekers and their remaining rights and entitlements illustrated the weaknesses of the asylum and dispersal systems. The importance placed on *good-quality legal services* was a result of the asylum and NASS systems as well as the wider context of deterrence. It was often the case that solicitors were located in initial dispersal cities and asylum seekers preferred to travel to and from their offices when relocated. That asylum seekers did not receive travel expenses but still undertook these journeys at their own expense during a period of hardship indicated resistance to the difficulties imposed by dispersal. It also showed how institutional trust, once gained, was not easily relinquished. It also demonstrates how institutional trust can be restored if conditions are right.

Because of dispersal the privatisation of services for asylum seekers expanded considerably, grew faster and was able to be controlled more easily by NASS than any other sector. The policing of asylum seekers by private and public sector accommodation providers represents a further step in the shift towards a culture of suspicion and mistrust towards asylum seekers. This monitoring role has expanded the control functions of the Home Office to landlords, giving them powers over their tenants.

Another weakness of the asylum and dispersal systems was access to *good-quality translation and interpretation services* across the range of agencies offering services to asylum seekers, particularly in relation to dialects spoken. The continuity of healthcare and a lack of dental services also related to these interpretation services. The retention of dentists in different regions of the country was indicative of not being able to access services in dispersal cities due to imposed temporariness of an asylum seeker's presence. This willingness to travel to both legal and dental services indicated resistance to the policy-imposed liminality of the dispersal system.

Liminality was also resisted for children when parents chose to put children into crèches to enable socialisation. Disruption of education during relocation was an outcome of dispersal and there were clear examples of schools informally socially excluding refugee children through admissions criteria and certification issues.

The future social exclusion of those granted refugee status was formally and informally created due to the denial of permission to work during the asylum and dispersal processes.

Gender awareness has slowly evolved in the parallel system set up for dispersal. Issues have been being identified and campaigned for from within refugee communities and those working closest to asylum seekers. This resistance to homogeneity occurred partly as a result of an assertion by RCOs that an awareness of gender dimensions and multiple identities was necessary to tackle issues such as 'honour' crimes and domestic violence. Services surrounding gender-specific forms of persecution were largely absent when dispersal began and issues such as 'honour' crimes and domestic violence were again those that involved temporal conceptualisation beyond the focus on the administrative system post-arrival to the UK.

Gaps in services were invariably cross-cutting issues such as mental health and childcare, which were not the responsibility of a single agency and as such were indicative of a lack of overall coordination throughout the system.

Intangible barriers to accessing services revolved around legal status and media coverage that had the effect of reducing the self-esteem of individuals, forcing a retreat into communities where social trust could be accessed. The lack of user involvement in informing the policies of dispersal ran in parallel to the power structures ensuring social exclusion. Asylum seekers were compelled to access services through agencies by invoking the 'victimhood' facet of their identity, forcing them to go through extraordinary circumstances in the UK.

The inability to access permanent services and doubts about rights to access services negatively affects any sense of inclusion in the UK. Dispersal was about control and deterrence and accessing services that maintain asylum seekers in a state of liminality. In the next chapter 'belonging' is explored by viewing the trajectory of social networks asylum seekers create and maintain in order to move away from the NASS system. Attempts to reject the shame and stigma of the asylum seeker label are outlined along with the ways in which formal and informal social exclusion over time has been resisted. Calls for the socially constructed category of asylum seeker to be shaken off and for refugees to be seen as normal people will be explored.

SEVEN

Social networks and belonging

Introduction

> 'Most importantly, as a human, you are a social creature, so you have to have social networks in order to feel human. Because the immigration law already makes you dehuman anyway. So you have to have people around you to make you feel that you are still human even though the Home Office do not accept that.' [1]

> 'Refugees are forced to lay bare the scars of their victimhood even if they just want to find work and have a normal life.' [2]

> 'My life is like a jigsaw. Now I need to find new pieces.' [3]

This chapter explores the social networks of asylum seekers, particularly how these are created and maintained during the asylum and dispersal processes. To do this, Marx's (1990) continuum from total destruction to persistence of social networks over space and time is utilised. The quality of social networks is shown to be important and attention is paid to the more intangible benefits of these networks.

It is argued that, for those asylum seekers who have recourse to social networks, this is the most important way in which they create a sense of 'belonging' in the absence of political belonging. For those without this recourse, processes of 'remaking' belonging are viewed. It is suggested that gaining a sense of belonging involves a trajectory of different social networks that, over time, shift asylum seekers away from the stigma of the asylum seeker label. An inherent assumption within the dispersal policy that secondary migration is a negative outcome of dispersal is therefore challenged. The main uses of social networks are shown to be for survival, information (including gaining awareness of rights), advice, as an insurance against crisis situations such as threats of deportation as well as to feel human within a system regarded as dehumanising.

From this point a continuum between the concepts of liminality and belonging is suggested. This continuum draws on this and previous chapters that have described how legislation has tightened and restricted the rights and entitlements of asylum

---

[1]   Interview with a female representative of an RCO, London, June 2003.
[2]   Informal conversation with a representative of an RSP and funding organisation, London, November 2005.
[3]   Re-interview of a male refugee, Lincoln, May 2004.

seekers; how the structure, geography and process of the dispersal system have social excluded asylum seekers; and how tangible and intangible barriers to accessing services exist for asylum seekers. These multiple forms of social exclusion, plus the barriers to maintaining or creating social networks as a result of dispersal, highlight the liminality imposed by the asylum and dispersal systems. The 'one-size-fits-all' character of the dispersal system added an extra layer of liminality to the already difficult asylum process that asylum seekers negotiate.

It is argued that the asylum and dispersal systems are studies in liminality, or more precisely, 'policy-imposed liminality', and that these systems leave little room for the restoration of trust.

Asylum seekers resist policy-imposed liminality in several ways, particularly through recourse to pre-existing and creation of new social networks. These, and other forms of 'remaking' belonging, are shown to occur simultaneously to the policy-imposed liminality of the asylum and dispersal systems. Some of the strategies of resistance that asylum seekers adopt in order to cope with the imposition of this liminality are outlined, showing how these strategies entail avoiding engagement with 'officialdom'. It is suggested that resistance to liminality occurs through forms of belonging that are outside subsequent formal policy mechanisms to promote 'integration' upon receipt of a positive status determination and that through this resistance, asylum seekers begin to acquire a sense of belonging or inclusion.

Asylum seekers are thus simultaneously moving between being 'betwixt and between' and towards 'belonging', 'integrating' or being 'socially included'. On the one hand, the asylum and dispersal systems push them towards liminality while, on the other, asylum seekers simultaneously remake their own forms of belonging. It is suggested that many of the apparent ambiguities of the lives of asylum seekers in the UK relate to these simultaneous processes of forming belonging and being made to feel liminal.

The dispersal system leaves little room for political or institutional trust to be restored and hinders the restoration of social trust. An assumed link between social and political trust in theories of social capital is shown to be absent in relation to asylum seekers with experience of the asylum determination process and dispersal systems.

Dispersal and social networks

The wide variety of circumstances surrounding arrival in the UK meant that the disruption, existence and mobilisation of social networks were variable. The dispersal policy effectively denied the importance of all but immediate nuclear family social networks. For asylum seekers who did not arrive *en masse* and may therefore have been more likely to arrive without maintained networks during migration, recourse to social networks was already limited due to the form of migration. For those who had pre-existing social networks in the UK, recourse to these occurred despite the dispersal policy. For those without existing social networks in the UK, an extreme form of social exclusion was often the outcome of dispersal due to isolation imposed by the system. In both scenarios, the rapid creation, utilisation and mobilisation of social networks was often a matter of survival.

Understandings of the meaning of social networks were varied. Asylum seekers immediately recounted concrete examples of family, friends and acquaintances, either in the country of origin or in the UK. They also mentioned members of more 'imagined communities' (Anderson, 1991) such as co-nationals or members of a political party in the country of origin. Some of these more 'imagined' members had not been previously met but the presence of trusted friends in common or shared religious belief facilitated this network. Acquaintances were often people who had been met very briefly (in emergency accommodation, on the street or in the offices of RSPs) and considered trustworthy in their accounts of the negative and positive aspects of different dispersal cities. The concept of the 'strength of weak ties' (Granovetter, 1973, pp 1360-80) relates to these acquaintances and a shorthand term – 'brief encounters' – is used to describe these acquaintances. Koser and Pinkerton's (2002) definition of social networks incorporates this idea of weak ties, mentioning not only friends and family, but also 'agents' and other brief encounters influential during migration.

The transnational character of refugees is recognised in the literature on forced migration (Baker, 1990; Marx, 1990; Scott, 1991; Joly, 1996; Castles, 2003, 2005; Boswell and Crisp, 2004; Castles, 2005). Social networks of dispersed asylum seekers operated transnationally and it was not unusual for individual asylum seekers to have members of family in several different countries such as in Somalia, the United States (US) and other European countries. For one asylum seeker, his extended family in the US had contacted the agent who helped him arrive in the UK – someone described as a person "who brought me in and then he was gone".[4] He did not know anybody else in the UK and was keen to contact his family in Somalia. For asylum seekers, social networks were usually described as positive and important.

Representatives of RCOs discussed a range of individuals in the network including GPs, teachers and other daily contacts. A representative who had been in the country for a number of years commented at length on the characteristics of social networks: "First of all you leave everything behind. So you need to have a social network to get support, reduce the isolation and you have to try to feel that you are actually in a place that you can feel some familiarity".[5] This emphasis on inhabiting a place where some familiarity was felt was common. The other benefits of social networks were remarked on:

> 'Social networks enable you to transfer your skills. They also make you aware of your rights because you generally get information through

---

[4] Interview with an asylum seeker, Leicester, November 2003.
[5] Interview with a female representative of an RCO, London, June 2003.

your networks and can start seeking your rights. I am not talking about community organisations, I am talking about putting you in contact with your neighbours. And then with your advisors and local representatives – whoever is going to be involved in the process that you resettle here. They are all part of that social network. You need the right social network to be cared for, to be empowered. For example, I wouldn't take specialist medical care out of the social network, or your GP out of your social network. Every one of them has their responsibility of making you feel safe, comfortable and empowered. In terms of refugees, or people coming from other cultures, the social network includes everybody.' [6]

Vital support, the reduction of isolation, the provision of advice and the need to feel safe and comfortable were each facets considered important. This wider, inclusive and positive interpretation of the term 'social network' distinguished between contact with those with whom a sense of familiarity could be recreated and the professional services available to asylum seekers, but both were included in the interviewee's understanding of what social networks were.

Other RCO representatives included more negative and exploitative aspects of social networks such as 'gangmasters', relating this to the denial of the permission to work. Comments relating to exploitation of individuals revolved around how dispersal meant that paying back money to agents was impossible given the low levels of financial support provided during the process.

RSPs discussed how RCOs were often approached first for advice and information from their own 'communities': "Any relationship is based on trust and if you work with the client group in any way it is all based on trust. They usually go to someone who speaks their language first. They have to learn this is the way the system works".[7] Finding familiarity through language and seeking advice and information from RCOs when available enabled some trust to be reformed.

Staff members of RSPs who had been through the asylum process themselves often found themselves in difficult positions due to conflicting interests of 'professionalism' (Baycan, 2003a) and social networks. Because new arrivals did not necessarily distinguish between 'professional' and 'social' networks, notions of professionalism and boundaries were sometimes a cause of tension: "In order to be professional you have to act in a certain way and if the person is a social friend you have to act in a different way. In many cultures that gap does not exist. In my culture there is not that gap".[8] The logic behind the setting of professional boundaries was based around avoidance of burnout within a stressful and demanding environment. However, for another community development worker this dilemma was particularly acute. Keeping her distance from the community she

---

[6] Interview with a female representative of an RCO, London, June 2003.
[7] Focus group with female representatives of the voluntary sector, dispersal location, July 2003.
[8] Interview with a female representative of an RCO, London, June 2003.

was working with meant that members of this community had problems trusting her:"They do not trust me if I am apart from them. They do not understand why I should treat them differently to me".[9]

This creation of difference between the 'helpers' and the 'victims',[10] in her eyes, was disempowering and while she could understand the rationale behind such an approach, she found that it was not practical or useful for her own relationship with the community. Another refugee who had applied for a position as an interpreter with an RSP also heavily criticised this aspect of the training she was given for that role:

> 'It is not very good but I want you to know how they care for asylum seekers. We were training and they said you need to keep your professionalism dealing with asylum seekers. You can't make friends with them, you need to be professional, distance yourself like a tape recorder. If we find that you get related to them emotionally, we have to put you out of our place. Yup, this is the care they have. The one who comes with no friends, no family, if I get close to them it was a crime and they will put me out of there. What they do is act on behalf of NASS here and think of it as a job.'[11]

Thus, representatives of RSPs, who were at the frontline of advice for asylum seekers, were unable to make friends with them, effectively ruling them out of future social networks. It also meant that potential social trust that could have led to a greater trust in institutions was ruled out. This also applied to co-nationals with another representative of an RSP in a dispersal location discussing a particular nationality of community:"It felt very difficult. I didn't want to disperse any [nationality of asylum seekers] because they all had family and friends and community here".[12] For RSPs, social networks often did not include as broad a range as those discussed by RCO representatives, often due to the need for professionalism and maintaining boundaries between 'helpers' and 'victims'. As in the quote above, co-nationals were particularly difficult to disperse as a result of this.

As outlined in earlier chapters, agencies with less daily contact with asylum seekers were often those with more power and influence over the dispersal system. It was sometimes disturbing, therefore, that some of these agencies immediately associated the term 'social networks' in a more negative and criminalising way. For example, the ability to find illegal work, the ability to form 'gangs' quickly by mobile phone during 'unfortunate incidents' and 'confrontations' between groups in dispersal areas were discussed by one representative of a regional consortium:

---

[9] Discussion with a female refugee, Sheffield, January 2006.

[10] Discussion with a female refugee, Sheffield, January 2006.

[11] Focus group participant, dispersal location, July 2003.

[12] Joint interview with representatives of the voluntary sector, dispersal location, June 2003.

'They can call in reinforcements from other cities to join the fray ... and the police found people from a number of cities ... as a result of this late-night fight between two factions.... Inevitably, there are a lot of young single men who are largely quite mobile and they do have connections around the country. Many of them have got status but don't have anywhere to live and are literally moving around, living on people's floors.'[13]

This quote illustrates the more negative forms that social networks take and how mobility and maintenance of social networks was perceived to be a disadvantage. The social networks of asylum seekers were in this instance intrinsically linked to negative aspects of mobility, which is a broader feature of the containment and control of refugees (Crosby, 2006). That mobility was perceived as being negative even for those with status was indicative of this. Mobility, through social networks, from city to city to locate accommodation was not considered beneficial. Discussions like this and those surrounding ratios and concentrations of asylum seekers were divorced from the idea of social networks being a method of integration or inclusion.

Understanding of the term 'social networks' ranged from very concrete face-to-face friends, family and those who could be trusted to groups of mobile young men who could not be trusted. If Marx's (1990) continuum between the total destruction of refugees' social networks at one end and the persistence of social networks at the other end is used, this understanding of social networks is broadened. *En masse* arrivals are more likely to be at the latter end of this continuum due to some links being maintained during migration and others being created (1990, p 196). This continuum provides a useful framework for considering the social networks of dispersed asylum seekers.

Social networks destroyed or disrupted

'Refugees coming to live in the UK are devastated enough by leaving their homeland. The dispersal policy has negative impacts on asylum seekers' lives, such as depression caused by instability. They want to live among their own communities where they can get support emotionally and enjoy social activities.'[14]

Richmond's (1994b, p 19) discussion of primary and secondary ontological security relates to both the destruction of social networks before flight and disruption due to the dispersal system. As the refugee above points out, the instability around

---

[13] Interview with a representative of a regional consortium, dispersal location, January 2004.
[14] Comment written on an informed consent form by a female refugee, dispersal location, July 2003.

dispersal and lack of familiarity arising from being dispersed away from family and friends contribute to the intangible barriers of social exclusion. Before arriving in the UK, refugees will have had their ontological security threatened and the permanency of social worlds will have been called into question. The re-establishment of trust through normal routines is rarely enabled during dispersal and the asylum processes due to the overarching deterrence environment and negative portrayal of asylum seekers.

The total destruction or disruption of social networks from the country or origin often relates to distressing circumstances. One asylum seeker recounted how her four brothers, mother and niece had been killed in a massacre in an African country. She had retained contact with the existing members of her family by email. The effect of the destruction of familial social networks meant that support networks were absent in both the country of origin and subsequently the dispersal location. She had been sent to a dispersal city that had only one other family with the same nationality and, as such, found it difficult to socialise. Having children to care for meant that few opportunities to socialise were available and social isolation during dispersal was a factor for this and other mothers.[15]

The lottery of dispersal was an isolating experience for asylum seekers who did not have recourse to social and support networks within dispersal cities. Describing how a co-national had been dispersed and did not know who she could trust or who she could contact, David commented:

> 'I went to a girl from Zimbabwe, and she was living in a block of flats and she'd been in this block of flats three weeks and all she had was a sleeping bag, a blanket, a pillow and one chair. She had been there for three weeks. They are isolated as well. They don't have the back-up you see. None of that back-up.'[16]

That relationships formed during dispersal did "get split up fairly easily"[17] and was a common complaint. The lack of space for social networks during dispersal often meant that asylum seekers had nobody to share their individual histories with and this certainly created isolation. This was particularly the case with asylum seekers coming from countries that had a very small number of arrivals dispersed by NASS. An asylum seeker from Burma recounted her need to find somebody she would be able to relate to. She had spoken to many people who knew about the country she came from and about her basic circumstances but she had not found anybody who could relate to her individual history in the dispersal location and felt as though this had negated her (very active) past.

---

[15] Discussion during a seminar, 'Refugee women in Bristol', Refugee Action, Bristol, February 2003; discussion with a female asylum seeker, Bristol, November 2003.
[16] Joint interview with an asylum seeker and voluntary organisation employee, dispersal location, November 2003.
[17] Interview with a representative of an RSP, London, May 2003.

As Harrell-Bond (1986[18]) observed in *Imposing Aid*, her initial 'unrealistic and naïve faith in the power of the family system to buffer individuals undergoing stress' ultimately transformed into what she terms the 'over-socialized concept of man'. What she meant by this was that 'the demands of individual survival undermined social values' (1986), with the time it took for new supportive social units to establish themselves in refugee camps not being fully understood by aid agencies that designed delivery of material assistance around this presumption. This was similar to the assumption that all nationalities of asylum seekers would automatically be able to obtain support networks in their 'communities'. The assumption of support from co-nationals also relied on this over-socialised concept, which related to a sense of duty to accommodate fellow nationals. This duty, in circumstances where asylum seekers had no other forms of support, was rarely a sustainable alternative. As one caseworker commented, the duty did not provide suitable support or an alternative to provision of full support to asylum seekers:

> 'He says I'm going to accommodate you as long as you live here because it's my duty as a fellow country person to accommodate you. But after a month, there is someone living in your house, and they get fed up. They do. They get fed up and they say, "Well, just go to Refugee Action, do whatever you want, I really can't … stand it any more. I thought you were a nice person. You are not". [laughs] These things happen, we tell them from the very beginning. We say, "Well, are you sure?". They say, "Yeah, yeah, yeah that's fine". But they always, they can always come back and make "change of circumstances" and then apply for accommodation.'[19]

That the duty of co-nationals was ultimately inadequate was unsurprising if the over-socialised concept is considered in the light of the quality of relationships being tested during dispersal. Another Burmese refugee discussed how two co-nationals who had initially been dispersed to Newcastle and Sheffield were sleeping on his floor in London, not because he knew them well, but because they had been members of the same political organisation in their country of first asylum. He realised that this would need to be a temporary arrangement as it was not sustainable over the longer term. That 'imagined communities' (Anderson, 1991) like this were relied on as a safety net within a system specifically designed to support asylum seekers demonstrated its weaknesses.

---

[18] View at www.sussex.ac.uk/migration/1-3-7.html
[19] Joint interview with a representative of the voluntary sector, dispersal location, June 2003.

Social networks maintained

When possible, asylum seekers kept in touch with families in the country of origin by telephone and email. One asylum seeker who had left Iran in haste to avoid arrest knew that the friend he had been with at the time of his avoided arrest was still in prison and that his brother had been put in prison due directly to his departure from the country. Another Iranian male discussed at length his rapid departure and knowledge of the problems his family was encountering with the authorities due to his actions.

This contrasted to another asylum seeker from Somalia who could not contact his family because telephone lines were down: "I ring, I ring, it doesn't work".[20] For this individual who had family in three different continents, this was a major source of stress and his main priority was contacting family although he did not know how he could do this and what agencies could assist. Like many asylum seekers, he had no knowledge of the Red Cross tracing service. Maintaining transnational social networks was problematic given the lack of family reunification options for asylum seekers, even for husbands and wives. As one individual with refugee status commented: "I cannot bring my wife here because she does not have a passport – the Refugee Council and UNHCR told me that she has to have a passport".[21] Again, the lack of certification and documentation – a basic of the refugee experience – was presented as a barrier to family life.

The need to have some emotional support was a clear feature of the social networks of dispersed asylum seekers. Loss in the country of origin was often compounded by not being able to live close to friends or family within the UK, particularly when larger communities of co-nationals existed in other cities within the country. For example, one asylum seeker spoke about a number of people she knew based in Coventry whom another friend, dispersed to Manchester, was trying to contact: "She would be able to provide you with lots of information about the disadvantages of dispersal".[22] Her friend was unhappy about being dispersed to Manchester and had been placed in accommodation that she was particularly displeased with. Having lived very close to each other in the country of origin, dispersal to two different cities meant that the maintenance of social networks was, for this individual and others, carried out by email and telephone. Maintenance had changed from face-to-face contact to maintenance over distance. These distances crossed regions of the UK ,with friends being located in several different cities. The telephone, internet and email were also used to facilitate the maintenance of social networks with the country of origin. For those who had pre-existing networks in the UK, this aspect of the dispersal system was unduly punitive. However, they generally did have contact with these networks and some connection within the UK was available based initially on nationality but

---

[20] Focus group participant, dispersal location, July 2003.
[21] Interview with a refugee, 2006.
[22] Telephone interview with a previous interviewee, 2003.

later on socioeconomic background, gender and other facets of the identity of the individual.

The negative side of maintaining social networks closely related to gender, with asylum seekers living within close communities having issues surrounding the expectations of their gender roles in both the country of origin and the UK. Representatives of gender-based RCOs, individual female asylum seekers and grassroots campaigning organisations related issues such as 'honour' crimes, domestic violence and isolation within communities to these close social relations. This is an area that is under-researched although some of the issues around violence against women in South Asian communities are now being explored (Thiara and Gill, 2010). The issue of trust was closely related to this as invasion of privacy in the private realm of the home was identified as the greatest barrier to resolution of these.

The weaknesses of the dispersal system and the additional roles undertaken by RSPs were part of the reason why some asylum seekers were able to maintain social networks. This was framed as a direct result of the NASS system being unable to cope:

'We can't refuse this dispersal. We had to fill in people to go. But in a way we know clients face to face. We work with them. We have got them here and we know potentially who is going to travel and who isn't. So we know if someone really doesn't want to travel because they have got friends or family and then we don't put them on the list at all. We wait until we have got in-region dispersals around the area. Because the system doesn't cope.'[23]

The possibility for an RSP to argue for an asylum seeker to be dispersed close to their family was largely on the basis of particularly circumstances such as unique needs:

'NASS would say that you can make recommendations to try to get people to stay with their family or near their family and it has happened in certain circumstances, particularly for special needs or particular circumstances, you can actually argue to be dispersed to a certain areas.'[24]

In practice, however, this possibility was extremely limited and most asylum seekers therefore needed to maintain social networks over distance.

---

[23] Joint interview with a representative of the voluntary sector, dispersal location, June 2003.
[24] Interview with a representative of an RSP, London, May 2003.

Social networks created or developed

The dispersal system hindered the creation of social networks but those that were formed were dynamic and generally informal. There was a broad range of experiences of developing social networks, which related to the heterogeneity and aspirations of asylum seekers. The disruption of social networks in countries of origin meant that creation of new networks within the UK took on an added importance. There was also a strong gender dimension, with many women participants finding the creation of networks a difficult process due to childcare commitments.[25] In contrast, male participants were less likely to identify this as a problem, one of whom cited a pub specifically for minority ethnic groups where he was able to listen to music from his country of origin, which made him feel "at home".[26]

There was little evidence that social networks were created solely on the basis of nationality although some aspect of duty to co-nationals was clear on occasions and some nationalities demonstrated ties based around ideas of "brotherhood".[27] In other cases, co-nationals were not considered to be friends: "Other Iranians are not my friends, no!"[28]

As outlined earlier, shared accommodation sometimes brought out such conflicts and was particularly tense in one case of a Christian Iranian sharing with a Kurd from Iraq. The Iranian asylum seeker considered that the Kurdish asylum seeker was noisy and unaware of how to behave "unlike Iraqi Kurds".[29] It is well known that discrimination against Kurds occurs in both Iran and Iraq and, like factionalism, research into how discrimination in countries of origin translates into a UK context would be warranted. This sharing of one room was a microcosm of the difficulties occurring within the system. In those areas with several households designated for asylum seekers, the complexities inherent in the interplay of backgrounds and aspirations of individuals were clear.

The most important factor for asylum seekers was to find some connection with people in their locality. Religious organisations were an important venue for the creation of social networks. Several asylum seekers mentioned mosques and churches as a source of friendships and a useful point of contact and place where social trust could be established relatively easily:

---

[25] Interviews and focus groups, various dates; speaker at the conference 'Hear my voice: refugee women's involvement in integration', Amnesty International Human Rights Centre, London, 15 June 2006.

[26] Joint interview with an asylum seeker and a voluntary organisation employee, dispersal location, November 2003.

[27] Joint interview with two male Sudanese asylum seekers, dispersal location, October 2003.

[28] Interview with a male asylum seeker, dispersal location, November 2003.

[29] Interview with a male asylum seeker, dispersal location, November 2003.

> 'I have been talking to one person who was forced to move from London because of the dispersal policy and he was sent to Leeds. He was telling me he is very happy because he socialises with people, he goes to church. Especially for the Christian people, they go to church and from the church they socialise with people who are not refugees.'

The Home Office has an immovable policy position that integration should not begin until a positive asylum decision has been granted.[30] Socialising with people who were not asylum seekers was, however, a crucial element of resisting liminality and it was clear that the process of remaking 'belonging' began at this point rather than when a positive decision was obtained. This resistance to the Home Office position was invariably through social networks.

Another way in which asylum seekers found some connection was through further education and study. Building social networks through translating and interpretation for health visitors was another method identified for those dispersed prior to the denial of permission to work.[31] Thus, one of the characteristics of the networks created during dispersal was that they were informal and emphasis was placed on making friends beyond the 'refugee experience'. Another characteristic was that they created the basis for autonomy and independence. In every case, interviewees mentioned how they were seeking a normal existence that involved finding routes to independent living.

The role of RCOs in the creation of social networks was extremely complex and warrants further research. The high number of different nationalities dispersed to each location hindered the setting up of RCOs. In the classic 1918 study of Polish migrants conducted by Thomas and Znaniecki, it was estimated that between 200 and 300 individuals were required to form a critical mass for the emergence of an organic association. Inevitably for the nationalities with low numbers of asylum seekers this critical mass was not apparent in dispersal locations. Some of the smaller groups of less than 100 asylum seekers often found themselves accommodated in 10 different locations across England, Scotland and Wales and associations were subsequently impossible to form. For those with higher numbers, dispersal to more than 50 dispersal locations meant that this critical mass was also often not reached although some RCOs had emerged in the larger cities. For example, Ethiopian RCOs[32] were established in Birmingham, Liverpool, Manchester and Sheffield for the 481 Ethiopians living in 45 different locations across the UK. From the higher number of 3,295 Turkish asylum seekers accommodated in 63 different

---

[30] Jeremy Oppenheim, director of NASS, speaking at the conference 'Hear my voice: refugee women's involvement in integration', Amnesty International Human Rights Centre, London, 15 June 2006.

[31] Speaker at the conference 'Hear my voice: refugee women's involvement in integration', Amnesty International Human Rights Centre, London, 15 June 2006.

[32] With the assistance of the Ethiopian Community in Britain, London.

locations, RCOs were present in Glasgow, Hull, Liverpool and Manchester and[33] as of the end of March 2003 (Refugee Council, 2003b). That in numerical terms alone, RCOs could not be available in every dispersal location was problematic.

RCOs even if present were not necessarily contacted at the beginning of the process but were sometimes considered in the later stages as another method of creating social networks. Rituals of the exile experience were catered for in this way: "We also organise social occasions for Ethiopians in different situations, related to the Ethiopian holiday and things like that".[34] These rituals of exile surrounding, in this case, Ethiopian holidays were another way social networks were created. The changing role for London-based RCOs involved more outreach to dispersal areas than had previously been undertaken. The perception by some London-based organisations was that agencies in dispersal areas were not capable of assisting asylum seekers and therefore needed some sort of "developing".[35] This role was referred to as a 'parent' role by one representative:

'The parent community in London could not really give the necessary assistance and help outreach because of the limitations of manpower and funding. The alternative for those who are in dispersal in these places was for them to create their own social groups. We are encouraging them because it will enable us to give them any advice, either by telephone or by any one phone if we have a contact person, a contact point, instead of trying to cater for all.'[36]

Virtually no emphasis had been placed on empowering formal RCOs in London to assist in the development of RCOs in dispersal areas although in practice, this was happening. This was often informally and generally without extra resources being allocated towards this from official funding sources.

Of the complex array of agencies involved in the dispersal system and with the exception of public providers of education, it was mainly voluntary and faith-based organisations that had any impact on the creation and development of social networks of asylum seekers. However, the greatest impact was from the individual actions of asylum seekers identifying their own methods of creating and developing networks.

Social networks utilised or mobilised

The denial of the importance of social networks in the NASS system meant that creating networks quickly in dispersal locations often became a survival strategy. For example, upon threat of deportation, social networks became considerably

---

[33] With the assistance of Halkevi, London.
[34] Interview with a representative of an RCO, London, May 2003.
[35] Informal conversation with representatives of RSPs, dispersal locations, various dates.
[36] Interview with a representative of an RCO, London, May 2003.

and rapidly broader than friends and family. At this point, other acquaintances, representatives of RSPs, advocacy and charitable organisations, journalists, solicitors, doctors, other professionals working with refugees, Members of Parliament, a Baroness, QCs and others were temporarily mobilised.[37]

The main way in which social networks were utilised was for accommodation either at the end of the system when 'move-on' from NASS accommodation was necessary or prior to this as a result of opting out of the dispersal system altogether. They were also essential during the implementation of section 55 and had a major effect on buffering, countering or cushioning the negative aspects and inadequacies of the system:

> 'Social networks have got a very big role. So far, although the new legislation [section 55] really has a very big impact on too many people but *nobody* [interviewee emphasis] in this city has been left homeless. Maybe, we had individuals who have spent a night or two outside but that was it, until they met somebody from their community. The community networks work very well. The communities took people without knowing them. If they spoke the same language they said, "Well, I have a little space in my kitchen, bring a sleeping bag".'[38]

The conditions in which asylum seekers lived because of this were often poor, having to sleep on floors or not having regular meals depending on the capacities of the communities assisting. It was clear that section 55 made the role of community more important. That nobody was left homeless echoed the effect of new social security regulations introduced in 1996 when financial support for 'in-country' applicants was denied and local authorities became responsible for support if an asylum seeker would otherwise be 'destitute'.[39] As Reilly (1996, p 4) comments on this 1996 withdrawal, 'the number of cases that have been seen [by the agencies involved] ... are barely representative of the scale of the problem' and the reasons for the discrepancy in predicted numbers and those 'presenting' to refugee agencies were due to refugee communities 'bearing the greatest responsibility' with asylum seekers increasingly 'going "underground" ... afraid to report to official refugee agencies, local government bodies or even to their own community organisations for fear of deportation or detention' (1996, p 5).

The assumptions that 'communities' took on the support of those left destitute did not promote any longer-term solution or, like in the 1996 instance, a recognition of the unwillingness to approach official agencies for assistance (Reilly, 1996, p 5). The relationship between dispersal and deprivation has already been outlined. That communities assisting in this informal way would have been living

---

[37] List compiled following an attempt to release a Burmese individual from detention in 2005 when individuals were mobilised to take action on his behalf.
[38] Joint interview with representatives of the voluntary sector, dispersal location, June 2003.
[39] Through the National Assistance Act 1948 and the Children Act 1989.

in deprived conditions already was likely given this link. Placing social exclusion on top of social exclusion with up to 81 different nationalities in each dispersal location[40] must have meant that some asylum seekers were without support of community and these hidden consequences remain unresearched.

Social networks were also utilised to access services in dispersal areas. For one Iranian asylum seeker, his only source of information about how to access further education and legal services was cited as being friends.[41] Basic survival was also often a result of the creation of networks: "I only have £10 per week. I have no money. For clothes, stuff for shaving and washing, every time the pastor and his wife help me. To get all these things I need them".[42] Reliance on the church for this individual was therefore clearly a matter of survival. For those who depended on their communities, some sense of confidence was considered by many to be an additional benefit: "He said it is better if they are from the same community. Social networks are very important. This is about social contacts and social groups. They give you more confidence to act in the community".[43]

Information regarding countries of origin and awareness of rights was also gleaned through these community networks:

> '[translates question and answer] He said sometimes we have news in the community. If there is important news we get it from the community. He does not read so he has to get this by word of mouth. If there is something important that affects him, people will tell him.'[44]

This relates to what Griffiths et al (2005, p 201) found in relation to the current role for RCOs, which was described as 'essentially defensive' in that they were filling gaps in services, providing a basis for association and meeting essential needs. Given the circumstances in which they are currently operating and the lack of funding provided to RCOs, this 'defensive' role reflects a wider lack of emphasis on community development in dispersal areas.

A trajectory of social networks

That refugees engage in an active process of 'remaking' belonging is often ignored in studies of forced migration (Turton, 2003). The feeling about networks was clearly that they were essential for survival, information, confidence and insurance

---

[40] 81 was the highest number of different nationalities dispersed to one dispersal location (Newcastle) as at the end of March 2003.

[41] Interview with a male asylum seeker, Leicester, November 2003.

[42] Interview with a male asylum seeker, Leicester, November 2003.

[43] Translated response during an interview with an asylum seeker, dispersal location, November 2003.

[44] Translated response during an interview with an asylum seeker, dispersal location, November 2003.

against crisis situations. Some of these networks were clearly temporary pending future status determination, acquisition of language, future employment and other routes to independence. Social networks took on different forms dependent on the position within the asylum and dispersal systems. At the early stages, temporary networks and brief encounters facilitated survival and fulfilled the gap in the provision of basic information about rights and conditions in dispersal locations. Later, more permanent social networks were formed. During the early stages co-nationals were often mentioned: "We ended up associating in terms of countries for obvious reasons, we spoke the same language, we came from the same social background, we could understand each other". Later in the process, and after dispersal, this same individual commented on how he mixed with a similar 'strata' of people rather than just co-nationals. This 'strata' was based on his socioeconomic background and level of education. This individual from Zimbabwe had become close friends with a former surgeon from Iran. This former surgeon explained how he had been volunteering at a local hospital because he was not permitted to work. One of his duties had been to mop the floor of the surgeries and he was visibly distressed by this. A discussion ensued surrounding dignity, ending with the view that this particular voluntary work was too demeaning. The former surgeon kept looking at his fingertips, despairingly exclaiming: "These fingers can save lives and they ask me to mop the floor!".

It was clear that social trust had been created between asylum seekers of varying nationalities based on their educational level. Forms of social networks in other areas also shifted from being largely based on nationality to those based on other 'connections' such as class, educational level, gender, political affiliation and other variables. As these more diverse connections were identified over time during the dispersal system, asylum seekers essentially redirected themselves towards a form of 'belonging' based predominantly on social trust. A solicitor in a dispersal area commented on this diversity:

> 'If you put a group of asylum seekers together from different countries, what do they have in common? Except they are refugees. It is very difficult. With respect to my British friends and colleagues, sometimes they think that they can be grouped together. I said they can't. They are as much divided by class, gender and social background as you are. And then divided into different countries. I mean, I may not have any point of connection with someone else from [country of origin] except the language I use. Even that is questionable because they may be a minority group who use a different language. We would not enjoy the same things. There has to be political or social connections and they have to have time to find that.'[45]

---

[45] Interview with a solicitor, dispersal location, July 2003.

These routes to independence often involved moving to different cities and, as explored later, secondary migration could therefore be seen as a positive outcome of dispersal in that moving away from the negative experiences of the dispersal and asylum systems enabled belonging.

Shame, stigma and wanting to be normal

The trajectory of social networks was also related to the shame and stigma of the asylum seeker label. Shame and stigma were major themes emerging out of interviews as was the desire to remove the asylum seeker's label and live a normal life. In particular, stigma around legal status, rather than ethnic identity, was evident.

Having knowledge about the right to access services was one difficulty already explored. Another was the feeling of having the right to access services within deprived areas:

> 'You have got people living in the same street who are on social security who are they are at the bottom level of the economic ladder. They see all this new furniture suddenly going into this house, hotly pursued by a group of asylum seekers who are totally mystified as to where they are. Resentment starts to crop up. What we have done deliberately is say to the landlord you provide ... properties that are furnished, they are adequate, but it is mainly second-hand furniture. It blends much more into that neighbourhood. What we will be providing is what is typical of that particular area. We would not be doing anybody any favours if a furniture van suddenly draws up and suddenly a whole load of furniture goes in when Mrs Smith down the road is desperately trying to make ends meet.'[46]

Thus, to avoid resentment by a social excluded Mrs Smith, furniture for asylum seekers was second-hand and other services of accommodation providers geared to blend into the neighbourhood. In this context, asylum seekers experienced the feeling that their right to access to other services was constrained.

The desire to live in peace and have a normal life was succinctly put by one asylum seekers when he commented: "Somalia. No peace. No education. No normal. War".[47] This desire to be normal meant that, in some cases, aspects of personal histories, legal status and other issues that they felt brought 'shame' to them would be hidden or kept secret from friends or work colleagues:

> 'I have friends who are working in mainstream organisations and private companies and they don't talk about being a refugee. If

---

[46] Interview with a representative of a regional consortium, dispersal location, September 2003.
[47] Interview with an asylum seeker, dispersal location, November 2003.

they have to say something they just say they used to be married to somebody and that is why they are in the country. So, marrying a British person and having that status is more acceptable than being a refugee and having that status. This is a huge thing – you are sharing an office with a person and you cannot even talk about your very existence in the country.'[48]

Thus, the 'skeleton in the closet' was being a refugee and the stigma and shame attached to this status meant that personal histories were hidden. That 'strategies of invisibility' (Malkki, 1995b) existed at this personal level for refugees and asylum seekers in the UK was an indicator of the social exclusion experienced – in this case to an extent wherein individuals actively reinvent themselves to be socially included.

One direct appeal to get rid of the social constructed category of asylum seeker came from a Rwandan refugee at a conference organised by refugee women to celebrate International Women's Day. She called for the 'mask' to be taken off and for refugees to be seen as people and remember that: "She is a refugee today but she was somebody. I am calling for people to look behind the mask and see the person".[49] Issues of visibility and invisibility as well as the asylum seeker label were evident in other contexts. One organisation in the East Midlands had taken a group of asylum seekers to see a play about the life of asylum seekers, which, for one individual, was considered to be highly inappropriate in that it unnecessarily perpetuated the victimhood of his acquaintances.

Asylum seekers were also criminalised through association with the functions of the state that control crime. Throughout the process, asylum seekers were made to feel different from the existing population in a variety of ways. Legislation regulating asylum seekers and the lack of a normal existence, in the eyes of one asylum seeker, denied the possibility of being the same as others in the UK:

'To be a good citizen, means you have no problem with the police, you have no problems with the courts and you are a law-abiding person. But instead here we find ourselves like criminals everyday we get a letter from the court, from the police, we have to report, why you are late. You know, you are like a criminal. Like you are doing something wrong. I have never done anything wrong. I have always tried to be a good person. This always holds you back because you feel that you are not like the other people. You have a problem, you are restricted and you can't think for the longer term. You can't see physical pressure

---

[48] Interview with a female representative of an RCO, London, June 2003.
[49] Action for Refugee Women conference, International Women's Day, London, 5 March 2004.

on you but every time they tell you come to the court, come to the police, this also adds to your suffering.'[50]

The requirements to attend court and report at police stations meant that this individual and other interviewees felt guilty by association and therefore different from others. It was clear that this related to how different asylum seekers were made to feel:

> 'I want to get a job, I want to live like anybody else. I am not scared of death because I have seen lots of people dying in front of me and that became normal in my life. I do not want to come to the point that going to court is normal in my life.'[51]

This association with crime was taken one step further by another asylum seeker who did not know the word for court in English, calling it "the place you go if you kill someone".[52] Comments relating to stigma and shame from these individuals linked their experiences in the country of origin and the UK: from persecution in the country of origin to experiences in the UK of attending court as being their new 'normal' experience. A mother of four children who had attended court six times because of administrative errors was angry and had difficulty sleeping because of the stress involved.

Overall, the avoidance of shame and stigma was related by individuals as the way in which they felt they could have a normal life. Moving away from this shame and stigma was considered a high priority.

Secondary migration

Attempts to move away from this stigma and shame were evident. One way this manifested itself was by asylum seekers demonstrating a strong desire to move away from the NASS system and agencies involved in the process. New networks were generated to do this and sometimes this involved secondary migration. Policy makers often attach negative connotations to secondary migration, focusing on how this can be prevented. However, in many cases, secondary migration was a positive outcome, with the individual involved beginning a process of 'belonging' in the UK. Often it was the dispersal and asylum systems and associated stigmas that created the impulse for secondary migration. In some cases it was the problems surrounding 'move-on' from NASS accommodation that created this impulse. Secondary migration often revolved around reformulating and creating social networks. Secondary migration was often based on perceptions of safety

---

[50] Interview with an asylum seeker, dispersal location, November 2003.
[51] Interview with an asylum seeker, dispersal location, November 2003.
[52] Interview with an asylum seeker, dispersal location, November 2003.

and feeling comfortable. As one refugee said, "you identify where you belong" in the UK.

The nature of the dispersal and asylum systems involved making asylum seekers travel from place to place – to Croydon or Liverpool for screening, to police stations in different cities to report, to courts in different cities to appeal, to solicitors in different cities because of relocation and availability of good-quality legal services. These systems themselves created mobility of asylum seekers while simultaneously attempting to contain asylum seekers within their dispersal locations upon receipt of refugee status. Freedom of movement for asylum seekers was obviously severely compromised by compulsory dispersal

Do asylum seekers create 'social capital'?

In some theories of social capital, relationships of trust and reciprocity are paramount as is a link between social and political trust (Newton, 2006). In Putnam's (1993) concept of social capital, trust is a defining characteristic. Refugees mistrust and are mistrusted (Daniel and Knudsen, 1995) and others have argued that high levels of mistrust can be generated by the political economy of aid at a global level (Voutira and Harrell-Bond, 1995). Therefore, assuming trust as a starting point in refugee 'communities' is unreliable. Griffiths et al's (2005, p 8) initial 'positive orientation' to the concept of social capital reduced as their research progressed, with the concept ultimately conceived only as a useful metaphor for the benefits of participating in social networks.

The concept of 'social capital' became less useful as a way of describing social networks in the dispersal and asylum systems for several reasons relating to the characteristics of social networks in this system.

To begin with the argument by Rothstein and Kumlin (2005) that experiences with institutions influence social capital, it was clear that this system imposed liminality on asylum seekers and did not allow for the restoration of institutional trust. It was also clear that limits to the restoration of social trust were due to the compulsory character of dispersal and relocation throughout the system. Experiences with NASS and the Home Office were found to be largely negative and considerable suspicion and disbelief was shown towards asylum seekers from these organisations.

Weak ties (Granovetter, 1973; Coleman, 1988), or brief encounters, between asylum seekers were often the basis of social networks in the dispersal and asylum systems. The 'duty' of co-nationals to provide accommodation for distant family members or asylum seekers of the same nationality or clan may mean that individuals sleep on floors, shifting from friends to acquaintances if they are in receipt of SO support. One of the characteristics of this utilisation of social networks is that obtaining SO support is often about avoiding dispersal altogether, with floors and 'moving around the houses' considered preferential. There is a danger of presenting an overly positive image of social capital when describing how social networks are utilised in this way. Stemming from a very negative set of circumstances, this was about immediate survival rather than the creation of reciprocal arrangements and/or trust.

Being able to access information about rights, mobilisation of networks to campaign against deportation and individuals making themselves busy in order to avoid considerations of the destruction of their family networks are all reasons why recourse to social networks occurred during dispersal. Recourse to social networks was clearly a coping strategy because of the hostile context of deterrence. While social trust can be said to be generated in this way, institutional trust is not. Spaces for the restoration of trust are largely absent from the NASS system and in this sense, social capital is not such a useful idea.

Relations of power between the different agencies involved in the dispersal system, the broader deterrence context and hostile environment within which asylum seekers negotiate presented limitations to the formation of social capital. Structural limitations, competition for resources and the Home Office not having the obligation to accommodate friends or sometimes family in the same dispersal location clearly did not assist in the generation of social capital.

Dispersal of high numbers of different nationalities to a high number of cities was also not conducive to the generation of social capital. With up to 81 different nationalities dispersed to one city, the possibilities of swift creation of social capital were limited. Dispersal of an extremely heterogeneous population, although masked by the imposition of a one-dimensional label of asylum seeker, was also not conducive to the generation of social capital. Asylum seekers did not necessarily wish to associate with the label and found ways to set themselves apart from others – the 'refugee experience' that emphasises the similar experiences of victimhood of refugees was largely the construction of agencies in the process. Relocation during dispersal as well as the requirement to 'move on' once refugee status was obtained again hindered any form of social capital. In some cases, asylum seekers wanting to move away from the 'shame' of being an asylum seeker created the impulse for secondary migration.

The summation of these factors meant that coping strategy rather than social capital was a better description of the outcome of social networks during the dispersal and asylum systems.

Belonging: ghosts, shadows, masks and 'ordinary people'

As Malkki (1995b, p 8) has already suggested, whenever people are categorised, they categorise back: 'the Hutu refugees lived at some level within categories that were not of their own making, but they also subverted these categories, to create new ones'.

Whereas liminality has been used to describe refugees in camps in the development world, it was found that it is also relevant in describing the policy of contemporary compulsory dispersal and the asylum system individuals were moving through. For Hutu refugees living in towns, Malkki found that changes of identity were made to suit the particular situation they found themselves in.

This use of their situational identity incorporated the 'strategies of invisibility' outlined earlier. For Hutu refugees in camps, it was found that liminality was often viewed a rite of passage or temporary stage.

For asylum seekers in the dispersal system, it was found that elements of both of these situations were present. For this reason, a continuum between the concepts of liminality and belonging is suggested. This continuum draws on this and previous chapters that have described how legislation has tightened and restricted the rights and entitlements of asylum seekers; how the structure, geography and process of the dispersal system have social excluded asylum seekers; and how tangible and intangible barriers to accessing services exist for asylum seekers. On the one hand, these multiple forms of social exclusion, plus the barriers to maintaining or creating social networks as a result of dispersal, highlight the liminality imposed by the asylum and dispersal systems. On the other hand, asylum seekers resist policy-imposed liminality in several ways, particularly through recourse to pre-existing and creation of new social networks. These and other forms of 'remaking' belonging occur simultaneously to the policy-imposed liminality of the asylum and dispersal systems. Strategies of resistance that asylum seekers adopt to cope with the imposition of this liminality entail avoiding engagement with 'officialdom'. Resistance to liminality occurs through forms of belonging that are outside subsequent formal policy mechanisms to promote 'integration' upon receipt of a positive status determination and that through this resistance, asylum seekers begin to acquire a sense of belonging or inclusion. Asylum seekers are thus simultaneously moving between being 'betwixt and between' and towards 'belonging', 'integrating' or being 'socially included'.

Asylum seekers did, upon arrival in new cities, adopt 'strategies of invisibility' in an attempt to subvert and resist the centrally imposed label of asylum seeker. However, these attempts were often held back by the liminality imposed by the policy, distinctions and restrictions on their rights and entitlements as well as the imposition of 'difference' through reporting requirements and monitoring by accommodation providers. Thus, asylum seekers did seek to change their identities but were contained in the liminal space provided by their legal status. A quote from one refugee who had just gained legal status encompasses this: "When do I stop being a refugee? I define my own integration. I don't want you to do it for me or tell me what it is!"[53] This claiming of the term 'integration' as personal and not something others could provide for was subverted in its meaning, partly due to the emphasis given to this term by 'officialdom'. Belonging became something that had elements of resistance and subversion of labels at its core. Others writing about belonging have looked outside these personal definitions: 'Without political belonging the displaced have no rights, only charity' (Skultans, 2005).[54]

---

[53] Speaker from the floor at the conference 'From immigrants to new citizens: becoming a citizen in 21st century Britain', Sponsored by Learndirect and the Office of the Deputy Prime Minister, London, 18 November 2003.

[54] Notes from an oral presentation, attended by author.

As Skultans suggests, without political belonging there is only charity and asylum seekers in the asylum and dispersal systems were forced to invoke their victimhood in order to obtain financial support and access services. Adding to the complexity of this form of belonging, asylum seekers could be invoking their victimhood to gain access to services while simultaneously celebrating aspects of their culture and nationality. The ability to celebrate and be a victim at the same time demonstrates how the literature that oscillates between victimhood and celebration provides an inadequate image. This dependence on different social identities and 'situational identities' (Cohen and Kennedy, 2000, p 110) means that both the capabilities and vulnerabilities of asylum seekers need consideration. In the deterrence context of the UK, attempts to move away from the 'situational career' (de Voe, 1981) of being an asylum seeker and being framed as a client was an ever-present dimension. A part of this was individual asylum seekers emphasising their difference from other asylum seekers and in doing so, the heterogeneity of their experiences was clear. Different identities were drawn on as coping strategies, with inclusion occurring in those areas where asylum seekers felt a sense of welcome.

Social belonging for Castles (2003, p 20) involved multiple affiliations and it was clear that belonging in this study referred not only to the situation within the UK but also temporal and spatial expansion to include individual histories and circumstances within countries of origin. Asylum seekers and refugees interviewed demonstrated how these multiple affiliations meant that they simultaneously belonged in two countries at the same time. Diary entries for solicitors' appointments appeared next to the time the sun eclipsed the moon in Zimbabwe and declarations of refugees that they still belonged to their countries of origin demonstrated this. A shift from belonging to the country of origin to the UK was hampered by the policy-imposed liminality of the systems as well as the lengthy period spent waiting for status determination. During this time, belonging was sought through social networks that were initially nationality based but, as outlined earlier, were latterly based more on class, educational background and other individual facets of identity.

Belonging was not an aim of dispersal – in fact the reverse was true with an explicit deterrence element as outlined in earlier chapters. The immovable policy position of the Home Office that integration should only occur once a positive status decision has been granted was resisted by asylum seekers and particular forms of belonging have been an outcome of dispersal. It was clear that belonging was being remade through surroundings that provide familiarity.

Visibility was another aspect of belonging:

> 'We have a very big Somali community, they are very visible because of the way they dress. They have their own community group and people who can do things for them. There are other communities here. There is a French-speaking community, an Iranian community, an Iraqi community. People are trying to blend as much as they can.

Especially in a city like Leicester. It is multi-racial anyway. For me that is why it is easier to blend in.' [55]

That asylum seekers preferred and were more comfortable in multicultural cities was a clear indication that 'strategies of invisibility' (Malkki, 1995b), where asylum seekers could effectively hide from the stigma of the label, were operating. That asylum seekers were able to 'blend in' to these cities was countered by the raft of policy mechanisms to separate asylum seekers from the rest of the population. Parallel services set up especially for asylum seekers, the culture of disbelief at the Home Office and NASS, the NASS process, the hierarchical range of agencies involved and the link between dispersal and deprivation all socially excluded individuals in different ways. However, restoration of face-to-face social trust through social networks did begin despite these measures.

Asylum seekers were invisible to the populations of these larger cities but omnipresent during periods of threat. This ability to be everywhere and nowhere at the same time was a feature of the liminal period (Turner, 1967; Malkki, 1995b). As one refugee in this research commented: "They are like ghosts to their neighbours". Upon probing, what was meant by this was that asylum seekers were perceived as being simultaneously everywhere and nowhere, considered to be invisible and omnipresent and not considered to be like other ordinary people. This being outside the category of 'ordinary people' resonates with Turton's (2003) suggestion that forced migrants should be viewed as ordinary people who have been through extraordinary circumstances rather than focusing on their victimhood and/or behaviour. A Zimbabwean refugee who had just come out of the NASS system commented how: "In three years all I have done is be under NASS. I'm a shadow of what I was". [56]

Both these comments about ghosts and shadows demonstrated liminality and the perception of being socially excluded. The exclusion of asylum seekers from ordinary living patterns through exclusionary practices and the inability to restore normal routines during the dispersal process meant that they occupied liminal spaces. The Zimbabwean felt that having left Zimbabwe under considerable duress and not being accepted within the UK had stopped him from being a whole person. His subsequent description of how he had been made to feel excluded from the day he entered the NASS system left him with this 'shadow' description. For asylum seekers in the dispersal system, opting out of normal or ordinary living patterns was not voluntary – rather it was a requirement of the policy.

Asylum seekers were simultaneously invisible as individuals but visible as a group. The earlier reference to having a 'mask' taken off to reveal their real identities highlighted how asylum seekers in the system perceived their own loss of identity and perceived themselves as outside society in some way. These perceptions of

---

[55] Focus group with representatives of the voluntary sector, Leicester, July 2003.
[56] Joint interview with an asylum seeker and a voluntary organisation employee, Lincoln, November 2003.

being socially excluded from day one were strongly held. Belonging in this context took longer and was more directed towards refugee communities. Resistance to the discourse of victimhood and reference to the dynamic processes of survivors were created through this.

Social networks of refugees some 30 years ago within the UK were about resettlement, integration and inclusion and were made up of trade unions, student unions and academics. These networks addressed the political identity of refugees.[57] The qualitatively new context for asylum seekers did not address this political identity of asylum seekers.

The question as to whether the 'refugee experience' exists or whether it is just a compilation of the 'bits and pieces' of information of a person's individual life history that are presented in order to gain refugee status has already been addressed in the literature (Knudsen, 1995; Ager, 1999; Turton, 2003). The dangers of focusing on the trauma of the experience and 'pathologising' refugees and not balancing discourses of vulnerability with appreciation of the resilience of refugees has also been addressed (Ager, 1999; Harrell-Bond, 1999).

Within the UK, an 'asylum seeker experience' is sometimes actively constructed as a coping strategy by asylum seekers. This construction has to be seen in the context of the deterrence environment and resistance to policy-imposed liminality. Comments were made relating to this:

'You can never know what it is like.'[58]

'The English don't know.'[59]

'She has experience – she has been through it.'[60]

Each of these detail the 'border' that is constructed between asylum seekers and those who have not experienced forced migration. An asylum seeker expressed this in another way when commenting on the way in which he considered himself viewed by 'British people':

'People judge you according to their own scope and perspective. They have everything here, there is always water, they don't know about our life. They judge from their own scales. They don't look at our life there, how we have suffered there, what has happened to us. They can't do it, they can't because they haven't experienced it. Or

---

[57] Interview with a female representative of an RCO, London, November 2002.
[58] Participant in focus group, dispersal location, July 2003.
[59] Joint interview with asylum seekers, dispersal location, November 2003.
[60] Focus group participant, dispersal location, July 2003.

maybe they do know, they do understand, and they just don't want people to come here.'[61]

This constructed 'border' sometimes made it appear as though asylum seekers and refugees excluded themselves and placed themselves in a form of exile within the UK. However, the processes of social exclusion encountered upon arrival in the UK created this situation and the asylum and dispersal systems combined were the barrier to belonging.

An 'asylum seeker experience' exists but – and it is a big but – it is clearly an artificial imposition of policy and is used as a coping strategy for asylum seekers in a hostile deterrence environment.

Conclusions

As the quotes at the beginning of this chapter illustrate, in a deterrence environment asylum seekers found ways to make themselves feel 'human' and during dispersal social networks were utilised to retain a sense of being human within a dehumanising system. The uses of social networks also surrounded accessing information and advice about the asylum and NASS systems plus accessing services while within these systems. The reasons for mobilising social networks stemmed from negative circumstances relating to survival, access to information about rights and campaigning against deportation. As such, they were often a form of insurance against crisis situations. Survival and resistance to the liminality imposed by the asylum and dispersal systems were the most important motivations for the swift creation of networks. Recourse to social networks was the most important way in which policy-imposed liminality was resisted. While social trust was generated in this way, institutional trust was not. Spaces for the restoration of trust were largely absent from the system and in this sense, the concept of social capital stemming from negative circumstances was not such a useful idea and the utilisation of social networks was better described as a coping strategy.

The social networks of asylum seekers in the dispersal system were clearly based on dynamic and fluid relationships, be they strong or weak, positive or negative, which interconnected people globally, nationally and locally. Brief encounters with agents or acquaintances demonstrated the influence, strength and importance of weak ties during forced migration. Social networks destroyed and disrupted were not catered for by the dispersal policy, often resulting in social isolation. Social networks that had previously been comprised of face-to-face contacts with family, friends and acquaintances were maintained over distance by telephone and email. There was evidence of maintenance of social networks over considerable distances ranging from countries of origin to different cities across the UK. Social networks in the UK also comprised a broader range of service

---

[61] Interview with an asylum seeker, dispersal location, November 2003.

providers, professionals working with refugees and other agencies but institutional trust could not be assumed due, in part, to the conflicts of interest surrounding professionalism and boundaries. Members of an imagined community were also trusted by asylum seekers but to differing degrees.

The trajectory of social networks meant that, over time, asylum seekers moved away from the stigma and shame of the asylum and NASS systems and associated agencies. This sometimes involved secondary migration and such actions were found to be positive methods of forming a sense of belonging. Refugees engaged in an active process of remaking belonging and it was ultimately people rather than places that provided this belonging. The heterogeneity of asylum seekers became more and more apparent and any 'asylum seeker experience' was clearly a product of the parallel services set up for asylum seekers and a coping strategy due to the deterrence environment and requirement to resist the policy-imposed liminality of the asylum and NASS systems.

Asylum seekers have multiple identities and affiliations dependent on their country of origin, gender, age and political affiliations. These identities were often the reason for persecution in the first instance. The connection point to 'inclusion' or 'integration' for asylum seekers was not only based on nationality, but also socioeconomic background, gender and a multitude of other factors as diverse as the population of the UK. That asylum seekers were perceived themselves to be 'ghosts' and 'shadows' during dispersal, plus the call for people to take off their 'masks', highlighted how asylum seekers' quest for a normal and peaceful life was dependent on the image of asylum seekers and ways in which to shake off this label. Viewing the 'ordinary' person underneath these masks was one way to reject the socially constructed category of so-called 'asylum seeker'.

For belonging to occur beyond the narrow confines of social trust based on recourse to social networks, the image of asylum seekers would need to be made more positive and a welcome provided that allowed for restoration of institutional and political trust as well as social trust.

EIGHT

Conclusions

> We believe the current asylum system is based on the false premise that all asylum seekers are bogus.... This case raises serious questions about the way the UK asylum system operates in this country. Members of the public have a right to know if we have a fair asylum system or one which terrorises vulnerable people to the point they would kill themselves. (Robina Qureshi, Director of Positive Action in Housing, Glasgow, *The Guardian*, 9 March 2010)

On a Sunday morning in March 2010, the bodies of a family were found at the bottom of a 31-storey tower block in Glasgow. This family were asylum seekers who had just received a negative decision from the UKBA and were, at the time, accommodated by the YMCA in this tower block pending the outcome of their RSD process. Robina Qureshi's statement relating to these deaths confronted the daily realities of asylum seekers moving through this process and her press release detailed how it had become normal to find people in her office talking about ending their lives rather than face destitution or administrative removal.

Whatever the facts of this case will ultimately reveal, this fear of destitution, detention or administrative removal is real. The many layers of social exclusion experienced while waiting for a refugee status decision mean that lives are lived in limbo. Asylum seekers are mistrusted as a group and asylum policies are devised under an overarching framework of deterrence and mistrust. As Robina Qureshi argues, the way in which the asylum system operates is not perceived as fair, either by asylum seekers or by those ordinarily resident in the UK. Much has been written on the quality of the RSD process in the UK as well as the quality of country of origin information (eg NAO, 2004). Asylum seekers doubt the integrity of this process, often as a result of the disbelief they have encountered from the Home Office throughout their asylum process. As has been shown in earlier chapters, in many cases this feeling of being disbelieved is replicated during the dispersal process from NASS staff and agencies involved. The three members of the family in Glasgow were not believed and took their lives rather than be returned to their country of origin.

This book has investigated the contemporary compulsory dispersal and social exclusion of asylum seekers. The socially excluded are often characterised as living beyond a normal existence and being considered to be 'outside' mainstream society in some way (Levitas, 2000, p 358). Asylum seekers live 'outside' this mainstream society. They are socially excluded in the UK from the moment they arrive. Whether the current exclusion of asylum seekers is traced to divisions inherent in the historical formations of empire, post-Wall political exigencies to define borders or the increased focus on national security following 9/11, the result is the same. To be 'outside' society in some way, made visible as a group and put through a process of 'othering' serves only to perpetuate further mistrust of this group and further justify policies based on deterrence.

Dispersal of asylum seekers across the UK was seen as an example, to use the perjorative term, of 'burden-sharing'. In practice it became an example of burden-shifting, moving a socially constructed 'problem' from London and the South East of England to cities in England, Scotland, Wales and Northern Ireland, which, in the main, were sites of multiple deprivation. Burden-sharing is on the agendas of European states, as are the concepts of 'social exclusion' and 'social inclusion'. Developing countries already host the majority of the world's refugees. Greater cooperation from the traditional resettlement countries in sharing responsibility for refugees remains crucial and needs to go beyond making borders so impenetrable that only a tiny percentage of refugees are able to claim asylum in countries that have ratified international agreements and therefore have international obligations to refugees.

While this book documents only the dispersal system in the UK, European 'burden-sharing' or global 'responsibility-sharing' may face similar issues around implementation. Dispersal of asylum seekers across the UK is an example of how policies do not always translate well into practice when imposed on people. The views of refugees themselves are invariably left out of policy design, both globally and within the UK. Many have argued that for the global refugee regime to work effectively, the views, knowledge, experience and expertise of refugees need to be fully represented within these policies. This book demonstrates in microcosm how, when refugees' views and choices are left out of policy making and implementation of programmes, these policies do not work well. The knowledge and expertise of RCOs in the UK was not harnessed during dispersal and, as outlined in Chapter Three, RCOs took on a 'buffering' role during dispersal.

A key outcome of the dispersal policy is that asylum seekers are socially excluded in many ways as a result of the structure, geography and processes involved. Services that address the longer-term needs of asylum seekers remain patchy. Dispersal, along with the RSD process, are seen by asylum seekers to be the barriers to 'integration' or 'inclusion'. Given the deterrence environment in which asylum policies are made, this is not necessarily surprising. However, what impact this has on the longer-term personal 'integration' and sense of belonging in the UK, along with broader societal 'inclusion', is important for those who gain legal status. This and other aspects of the policy are outlined below.

Formal and informal social exclusion

The use of dichotomies such as 'exclusion' and 'inclusion' is always problematic. In the case of asylum seekers it invokes a distinction between 'members' and 'strangers' where a sense of belonging is based on membership and shared social capital of those ordinarily resident, which is counterposed by the extreme exclusion of new arrivals into the UK. This book has explored how the absence of political belonging means that other forms of belonging are sought out. In the face of this extreme exclusion, asylum seekers resist policy attempts to deny integration by creating their own forms of belonging.

A shift from a focus on poverty and its more structural causes to a discourse on social exclusion that focuses on the behaviour and distinctiveness of individuals has been discernable in government discourse over the past decades. As outlined in earlier, Levitas (1998, p 27) identified three discourses of social exclusion – the redistributionist discourse (RED), the moral underclass discourse (MUD) and the social integrationist discourse (SID). The RED framework is the most helpful in explaining the social exclusion of asylum seekers due to dispersal although the MUD framework was invoked by some agencies who focused on the behaviour of asylum seekers. It was clear that dispersal incorporated exclusionary mechanisms and the provision of only 70% of Income Support effectively excluded asylum seekers from ordinary living patterns. 'Failure to travel' to the dispersal areas was the most prominent way in which behaviour was described with the emphasis on the asylum seeker not conforming to the imposed constraints of the system. Asylum seekers were seen as distinct due to their circumstances. Asylum seekers were excluded from paid employment until a less temporary status was granted. This meant that they were not able to be included in what New Labour considered to be the primary route to inclusion – paid employment. The SID framework was therefore made redundant from the debate. Even for those who ultimately gained refugee status, Bloch (2004) has shown that refugees continue to experience lower rates of employment than their minority ethnic counterparts, taking on temporary and part-time work with poorer terms and conditions.

Multiple forms of social exclusion existed relating to the declining entitlements of asylum seekers as well as the structure, geography and process of the asylum and dispersal systems.

Social exclusion as a result of the structure and implementation of compulsory dispersal was examined in Chapters Three and Four. The dispersal policy was designed quickly, with little reference to academic studies or lessons learned from past experiences of dispersing recognised refugees, which showed how enforced dispersal policies were unsuccessful due to the agency and social networks of individuals. It was essentially a reactive policy, shaped by a small number of local authorities in London and the South East, which provided evidence that a national system for the dispersal of asylum seekers could solve a national 'problem'. The lack of planning and consultation during the design of the system led to an inefficient system that was ultimately implemented not by those who had designed it (civil servants in the Home Office) but by a range of agencies from the public, private and voluntary sectors. NASS was created to institutionalise redistribution with the support and service elements of its title ultimately becoming secondary to the ways in which it controlled and monitored asylum seekers. This policy, seen within the wider context of UK social policy design, has embraced market principles but has not placed a greater emphasis on user involvement.

In principle, if carried out on a voluntary basis, the idea of accommodating asylum seekers in areas outside London and the South East could be viable given the commitment of numerous organisations and individuals across the UK. However, in practice, the system that has evolved since 2000 is fraught with difficulties and conflicting agendas. Tensions were apparent from the beginning and the deficiencies in planning at the national level had great effect on implementation at the local level, with efforts to make dispersal more 'user friendly' at a local level constrained because of the centrally imposed categorisation of asylum seekers as a distinct group.

The separation of asylum seekers from mainstream service provision created a more visible group and entrenched the distinction, in the eyes of the resident population and service providers, between asylum seekers and refugees. This distinction was then institutionalised by the creation of NASS. The proliferation and conflicting roles of agencies involved meant power imbalances between organisations. The decision by the voluntary sector to take key roles during the implementation of dispersal and a new role for the private sector in provision of transportation and accommodation are key characteristics of contemporary compulsory dispersal.

A hierarchical structure for implementation of dispersal emerged with agencies at the top who were least likely to be involved with asylum seekers on a face-to-face basis having the most influence over the policy and those working locally with asylum seekers having the least. This emergent hierarchy was led by central government but the private sector largely operated outside local government structures. The voluntary sector was at the interface between asylum seekers and in-country deterrence and therefore inhabited the most visible and contested space within the system. The position of asylum seekers was outside this hierarchy and did not allow for adequate representation. RCOs were largely marginalised from the emergent structure.

Each organisation within this hierarchy sought to influence and control the process. The Home Office controlled the system and sought to control the asylum seekers within it. Local authorities sought to decentralise Home Office decision making, have some control over PAPs and, understandably, control the development of their cities in relation to the resources allocated to the provision of services to asylum seekers. PAPs sought to control the maintenance of their properties and, because of their monitoring and reporting obligations, control asylum seekers. RSPs wanted to control and influence the process and the evolution of the dispersal policy saw the abandonment of the cluster idea and shifted the way in which dispersal was implemented from individual to group dispersals. Redirection of asylum seekers to their own 'communities' for support was an unquestioned assumption, with the RCO role becoming one of 'buffering' dispersal. This was largely unrecognised and unfunded and very little emphasis was placed on using this channel to support subsequent integration strategies.

Chapter Four showed how the geography of dispersal was a reflection of the exclusionary policy context and, in particular, the availability of unpopular housing. There was a significant relationship between dispersal and deprivation. Areas used during compulsory dispersal, particularly at the outset, overlapped considerably with areas of multiple deprivation, with between 70 and 80% of dispersal areas located in the 88 most deprived local authority districts in England. Asylum seekers' experiences of dispersal also illustrated the link between dispersal and deprivation and the knowledge that accommodation allocated to them was largely located in deprived areas.

It was clear that larger cities and areas in London and the South East were popular with asylum seekers claiming SO support. This form of support illustrated a different pattern of settlement with the need to feel comfortable and invoke strategies of invisibility satisfied by moving to these larger cities. The number of locations of those in receipt of SO support was also higher than dispersal, showing how asylum seekers with social networks effectively dispersed themselves more widely than the institutional redistribution of the dispersal policy.

Compulsory dispersal resulted in social exclusion over time. In Chapter Five, the experiences of asylum seekers and process of social exclusion as a result of dispersal and the asylum system were explored. The dispersal system added an extra layer of liminality to the already difficult asylum process that asylum seekers negotiated. At each stage of the system a lack of control over the process, a lack of space for the restoration of different forms of trust and the inability to assume new identities other than that of asylum seeker were evident. Both formal and informal processes of social exclusion began at the point of arrival in the UK and continued throughout the dispersal process due to a lack of choice of dispersal location and type of accommodation.

In theory, dispersal imposed an equal distribution of deprivation on all forced migrants regardless of their socioeconomic backgrounds, country of origin, membership of a particular social group, political opinion, religion, gender, age or individual history. In practice, there was a wide variety of local conditions and standard of accommodation in dispersal locations. However, every destitute asylum seeker was dispersed without regard for the human resources and experiences they were potentially able to mobilise and this meant that individuals were effectively equalised and dehistoricised by dispersal. This dehistoricising of asylum seekers was replicated by agencies funded by the Home Office with the route to becoming a 'case' or a 'client' of NASS and the implementing agencies a dehumanising one. The situational identity of victimhood was invariably invoked to access the system, remaining entitlements and services.

Dispersal as a 'one-size-fits-all' policy demonstrated the consequences of Indra's (1999) examination of tensions in the theories of forced migration. The centre of gravity on the macro side has important consequences and what was lost in the focus on an administrative process was any attention to heterogeneity, resilience and capabilities of asylum seekers. The earlier stages of the refugee experience in countries of origin showed how this focus on an administrative process did not allow for an understanding of the prior experiences and subsequent needs of asylum seekers.

Exclusion and imposing liminality

Policy-imposed liminality was the primary lens for understanding how asylum seekers experienced social exclusion during dispersal. Liminality and (mis)trust were key concepts in understanding and illuminating the experiences of dispersed asylum seekers.

Compulsory dispersal led to multiple forms of social exclusion. Asylum seekers were disadvantaged due to declining entitlements; the structure, geography and process of dispersal; tangible and intangible barriers to accessing services; as well as barriers to maintaining or creating social networks. In combination, the policy of compulsory dispersal actively prevented asylum seekers from developing any sense of 'integration' or 'inclusion' within the UK by imposing temporary conditions and conditions on them. The in-country deterrence element of the system and asylum seekers being maintained at a standard of living below that of the rest of the population contributed to this.

The image of asylum seekers is of people wanting something, seeking something, not having the rights of others. Refugees, on the other hand, do have those rights and there are obligations for these to be provided, however negative the connotations surrounding the label. Addressing the entire 'refugee experience' from the period of threat in the country of origin showed how the rigid legal distinction between asylum seeker and refugee and connotations surrounding the semantics used in the dispersal and asylum systems were artificial. This also meant that the prevalent polemic categorisations, negative perceptions and inaccurate representations of asylum seekers were challenged.

As outlined in Chapters Three, Four and Six, asylum seekers mainly accessed temporary services through their accommodation providers due to contractual obligations to the Home Office for the provision of these services. This had several implications, not least of which was at the 'move-on' stage when those granted refugee status had to begin to renegotiate with mainstream agencies for support. For those given a negative RSD decision, dispersal meant that so-called 'failed asylum seekers' and 'hard cases' no longer received assistance in accessing services.

The power to define access to services based on complex hierarchies of centrally devised statuses was a form of social exclusion that could not be overcome at a regional or local level. Chapter Six focused on these declining rights of asylum seekers and the relationship to remaining entitlements. Dispersal enforced a regime of temporary services, meaning that social exclusion at a local level was an inherent part of a dispersed asylum seeker's experience. This temporary access to services, the lottery of accommodation type and location as well as relocation built into the system each contributed to this policy-imposed liminality. The individual histories of asylum seekers prior to reaching the UK were not catered for by agencies and not factoring in the basis and consequences of persecution meant that appropriate and adequate services were not always in place. Access to counselling, mental health professionals, assistance with family reunification and other emergent issues such as domestic violence were each services catching up in dispersal locations. Services surrounding gender-specific forms of persecution were largely absent when dispersal began and issues such as 'honour' crimes, female genital mutilation or trafficking were just not considered until later in the evolution of the system. Such gaps in services were invariably cross-cutting issues such as mental health and childcare, which were not the responsibility of a single agency and as such were indicative of a lack of overall coordination throughout the system.

Relocation during dispersal had considerable impact on how asylum seekers accessed services. Disruption of education during relocation was an outcome of dispersal and there were clear examples of schools informally socially excluding refugee children through admissions criteria and certification issues.

Asylum seekers were often not aware of their rights to equal access to services or, for some, did not wish to take up these rights because of the stigma and shame surrounding the image of asylum seekers. Asylum seekers were also compelled to access services through agencies by invoking the victimhood facet of their situational identity.

The qualitatively different environment in which asylum seekers were dispersed meant that access to good-quality legal services was a high priority. These legal services were not always in place in dispersal locations and retaining solicitors in initial dispersal locations was one way in which asylum seekers resisted liminality while acknowledging the temporariness of current dispersal locations. Another weakness was access to good-quality and trusted translation and interpretation services across the range of agencies offering services to asylum seekers.

Intangible barriers to accessing services revolved around status and media coverage and resulted in low self-esteem. The combination of discriminatory practices inherent in the dispersal and asylum systems and postcode discrimination in multiply deprived areas impacted greatly on the present and future social exclusion of asylum seekers.

Trust and mistrust

Daniel and Knudsen (1995, p 1) have argued that '[t]he refugee mistrusts and is mistrusted'. They suggest that the success of government policies pivots on a fulcrum of trust (1995, p 4) but recognise that restoration of trust in countries of asylum is often limited:

> In the best of all possible worlds, at the point of a refugee's reincorporation into a new culture and society, trust is reconstituted, if not restored. The real world, however, is not the best of all possible worlds.… Unlike life under 'ordinary' circumstances, or more correctly, under circumstances over which one exercises a certain measure of

control, in the life of a refugee, trust is overwhelmed by mistrust....'
(1995, pp 1-2)

The dispersal policy was formulated in an environment of mistrust towards asylum seekers and had an explicit deterrence element. In the past, quota refugees fleeing persecution arrived with secure status and their dispersal around the UK involved obtaining secure accommodation, employment and other routes to 'inclusion'. Contemporary compulsory dispersal of asylum seekers occurs without this secure status and implementation of the policy has led to an accommodation lottery based on 'bedspaces' and temporary access to services. Asylum seekers are denied paid employment and the exclusionary logic of the policy means that they encounter social exclusion in many forms. Contemporary dispersal of asylum seekers therefore operates in a qualitatively different environment from past instances of dispersal of refugees.

Different forms of trust – social, institutional, political and restorative – were distinguished in relation to the dispersal system. These disaggregated forms of trust also have broader relevance in debates surrounding social exclusion. Asylum seekers' experiences of institutions were seldom positive and did not provide space for the restoration of political or institutional trust. Socially excluded populations are also considered to mistrust neighbours, figures of authority, officialdom and services providers. Relationships of trust and reciprocity are also paramount in some theories of social capital (eg Putnam, 1993) as is a link between social and political trust (Newton, 2006). Mistrust is also important because community participation and user engagement depend on the ability to build political and institutional trust (Demos, 2003).

The dispersal system had implications for the restoration of each of these forms of trust because the foundations of future trust (or mistrust) were laid during this process. The empirical data provided has demonstrated that during dispersal asylum seekers were able to restore some social trust but very little trust in institutions or political processes was restored. The empirical material also highlights how dispersal-related punitive aspects of the asylum support system have a negative impact on the longer-term resettlement process or official 'integration' of those awarded refugee status. The view from asylum seekers within the system was that the Home Office in particular was an institution to be mistrusted for many years after the asylum determination and support processes had ended. The contradictions in Home Office's policy making effectively mean that the cohesion agenda, integration policy for refugees as well as initiatives that rely on gaining the trust of newly arrived populations run directly counter to asylum policy because of the lack of space for restoring trust.

Taken as a whole, these findings suggest that there is a need to address the issue of trust during the asylum support system. Separated, stigmatised and socially excluded, the institutionalisation of this mistrusted group away from mainstream services undermines any potential creation of space for trust that is an essential component of wider policy agendas. Overall, there was little space for asylum seekers to trust or be trusted – in particular, institutional and political trust was not restored. NASS replicated the culture of disbelief between the Home Office and asylum seekers and, consequently, 'officialdom' was something to be avoided.

Importantly, the link between social and political trust in theories of social capital was absent in relation to asylum seekers with experience of the asylum determination process and dispersal systems. Trust is a starting point and an essential component of community development, user engagement and community participation. This was neglected and under-resourced during the dispersal process due to the emphasis on maintaining asylum seekers in a liminal state pending status determination. The dispersal system and the management of asylum seekers run counter to the social cohesion agenda and subsequent emphasis on integration once refugee status is awarded.

When accessing services trust was important. In the case of legal services institutional trust, once gained, was not easily relinquished. The policing of asylum seekers by private and public sector accommodation providers represents a further step in the shift to a culture of suspicion and mistrust.

Between liminality and belonging

> [T]he experience of displacement is not only about the *loss* of a place ... it is also ... about the struggle to *make* a place in the world. (Turton, 2004, p 26)

A key finding was that asylum seekers did engage in an active process of remaking belonging by resisting the policy-imposed liminality of the dispersal and asylum systems. If a theoretical continuum between liminality and belonging is envisaged, the empirical data presented suggest that there are simultaneous processes occurring within this continuum. The cycle of displacement that asylum seekers are experiencing continues as a result of the dispersal policy while, at the same time, asylum seekers are beginning to emplace themselves and create their own belonging. Turton (2003) calls this '*dis*placement' and '*em*placement' wherein asylum seekers conduct a form of 'continuity maintenance' by seeking out the familiar and known.

Understanding that there are these dual processes ongoing along this continuum helps to explain the lives of asylum seekers and refugees as they negotiate new identities. Viewing these as simultaneous processes goes some way to explaining the often contradictory and seemingly ambiguous experiences of asylum seekers. Acknowledging that there are dual and ongoing processes that lead to either liminality (mainly through the policy response) or belonging (mainly through the actions of individuals) allows for a view that encompasses both vulnerabilities and capabilities.

Such resilience in the face of adversity and sense of inclusion through resistance to this policy-imposed liminality is the way in which asylum seekers begin to acquire a sense of belonging or inclusion in the UK. 'Integration' therefore occurs despite asylum policies and not because of them. Resisting policy-imposed liminality was evident throughout this study with 'failure to travel' being the main dispersal-specific form. Asylum seekers were not passive in this process and resisted, subverted and challenged this liminality with coping strategies, particularly through recourse to social networks. This resistance was invariably through routes that avoided direct confrontation with authority or official institutions. Chapter Seven illustrated how the most important way in which asylum seekers resisted policy-imposed liminality was through recourse to social networks.

The maintenance of social networks was hindered by the dispersal system because of the limitations of its design. However, for asylum seekers who had recourse to networks of relationships across the UK, this was the most important way in which they created a sense of 'belonging'. This involved a trajectory of different forms of social networks that, over time, shifted asylum seekers away from the stigma and shame of the asylum seeker label. For those who had not had their social networks destroyed *en route*, being able to maintain social networks was often a motivation for secondary migration, challenging the assumption that secondary migration was a negative outcome of dispersal. There was considerable evidence of maintenance of social networks over distances with these distances ranging from countries of origin to different cities across the UK.

For those who did not have this recourse and whose social networks had been destroyed *en route*, isolation was often the result of dispersal. When social networks had been destroyed in the countries of origin, further disruption due to dispersal could result in extreme accounts of exclusion.

The main uses of social networks were for accessing information for survival, information and advice as well as acting as an insurance against crisis situations such as deportation. Another crucial aspect was to allow individuals to feel human, which, in a deterrence environment, meant that during dispersal social networks were utilised to retain this sense of being human within what was widely perceived as being a dehumanising system. The uses of social networks also involved accessing information and advice about the asylum and dispersal systems plus accessing services while within these systems. Reasons for mobilising social networks stemmed from negative circumstances relating to survival, access to information about rights and campaigning against deportation. As such they were a form of insurance against crisis situations. Weak ties, or brief encounters with acquaintances, were a characteristic of these networks.

Overall, survival and resistance to the liminality imposed were the most important motivations for the swift creation or maintenance and mobilisation of networks. While social trust was generated in this way, institutional trust was not. Spaces for the restoration of trust were largely absent from the dispersal system and in this sense, the concept of social capital stemming from negative circumstances was not such a useful idea and the utilisation of social networks was better described as a coping strategy.

Refugees engaged in an active process of remaking belonging and it was ultimately people rather than places that provided this belonging. Asylum seekers constructed their experiences and identities to negotiate the systems imposed on them. The creation, or remaking, of social networks was not always based on nationality, with gender and other intersections of identity, individual connections or communities of interest allowing for 'inclusion' and 'belonging' to be created.

Remaining invisible as individuals but visible as a group, asylum seekers found their sense of belonging through social networks. The impulse for secondary migration was therefore a result of the negative aspects of the dispersal system as well as the positive benefits of social networks.

There is an immovable Home Office position that 'integration' should only commence once an asylum seeker obtains a positive RSD decision. The dispersal and asylum systems can be seen as conscious efforts to maintain asylum seekers in a liminal state pending this decision. Compulsory dispersal, initial and subsequent negative treatment, being unable to seek employment as well as the disbelief and mistrust of asylum seekers created by past legislation resulted in asylum seekers removing themselves where possible from the stigma and shame of the systems.

Chapter Seven discussed the impact of dispersal on the complex sense of 'belonging' felt by asylum seekers. Without political belonging, other forms of belonging are sought. Also without political belonging, a focus on victimhood and the need for charity is a result. Any aspiration an asylum seeker might have to live a normal, peaceful, independent existence is at odds with the asylum and dispersal systems. Separated, stigmatised and socially excluded, asylum seekers are made to proceed through a process that is characterised by waiting, being relocated, austere living conditions and having no control over the type or location of accommodation. Denying the opportunity to begin a process of resettlement and asylum seekers continue to go through extraordinary circumstances in the UK. The major stigma for asylum seekers relates more to their legal identity than their particular heritage or ethnic identity.

Arguably, it is the imposition of policy and legislation that distinguishes them from other migrants more than the experience of violence, flight and exile and other definitives of the so-called 'refugee experience'. It is not surprising that asylum seekers and refugees effectively hide from the stigma and shame imposed on them by their legal status. To become invisible becomes a priority and in that sense, dispersal to multicultural areas (which are also largely deprived areas) does contain some logic.

Asylum seekers had multiple identities and affiliations dependent on their country of origin, gender, age and political affiliations, with these identities often the reason for persecution in the first instance. The connection point to 'inclusion' for asylum seekers was not only based on nationality, but also socioeconomic background, gender and a multitude of other factors as diverse as the population of the UK. That asylum seekers were perceived themselves to be 'ghosts' and 'shadows' during dispersal, plus the call for people to take off their 'masks' highlighted how asylum seekers' quest for a normal and peaceful life was dependent on the image of asylum seekers and ways in which to shake off this label. Viewing the ordinary person underneath these masks was one way to reject the socially constructed category of asylum seekers.

It was clear that processes of belonging were occurring that were made through surroundings and social networks that provided familiarity. Liminality was resisted in large and small ways. Some resisted by, in official parlance, 'failing to travel', not getting on the coaches contracted by the Home Office to take them to their bedspaces in cities unknown to them. Others resisted more directly, by demonstrating, inflicting harm on themselves, stitching up their mouths in protest or conducting hunger strikes when conditions in their accommodation and as a result of the systems became intolerable. Many small everyday, yet active, forms of resistance occurred, invariably bypassing confrontation with authority.

Investigations into displacement as a period of transition from one status to another need to incorporate the positive and negative aspects. This study incorporated the capabilities and vulnerabilities of asylum seekers rather than the usual focus on vulnerabilities alone. This acknowledged that asylum seekers actively remake their belonging rather than focusing solely on losses encountered during the process of becoming a refugee.

The trajectory of asylum policy

The trajectory of asylum policy does not look promising. Election manifestos consistently highlight asylum and immigration as key areas for action and deterrence and calls for an independent asylum board have consistently been ignored over the years by political parties gaining power. The creation of such an independent board to oversee a fair and just asylum process would take the asylum issue out of the realms of politics.

Since commencement of this study the trajectory of asylum policy in the UK has increased the chances of liminality being experienced by asylum seekers. The government's recent strategy on asylum now means that even individuals granted refugee status may be reviewed after five years and, subject to conditions in their original countries, may lose their legal status if these countries are deemed safe. While at the time of writing these reviews had not occurred in practice, the threat of this potentially extends the period of liminality experienced beyond that described in this book and warrants further research.

Although the NASS system was considered controversial prior to its implementation by public, private and voluntary sector agencies, dispersal became regarded as less of a priority by campaign organisations than more immediate or harsher forms of deterrence such as destitution, deportation and detention. However, dispersal socially excluded asylum seekers over time by distinguishing their rights to welfare and services from other migrants. This was a slower, less visible and sometimes intangible process of social exclusion.

Separating asylum seekers from mainstream welfare provision laid the foundation for the tightening of access to other services and other entitlements in subsequent legislation. The use of accommodation in areas of multiple deprivation has also created structures of social exclusion on which subsequent policies, with the overarching aims of deterrence and control of asylum seekers, have been implemented. For example, refused asylum seekers are supported with accommodation and limited vouchers (known as section 4 or 'hard case' support) subject to their agreement to voluntary return to their countries of origin. This policy of destitution occurs in every dispersal location and the emphasis on provision of support based on return can only add to negative perceptions of asylum seekers. Accessing health services for those with a negative decision has also become more restrictive over time.

Proposals have been mooted to disperse children and young people and if this were ever to occur, lessons from the dispersal of adults as well as child protection and safeguarding standards would need thorough investigation prior to its implementation. That gaps in services remain for adult asylum seekers does not bode well for a similar system for children.

Additionally, a new Gateway programme for the resettlement of refugees with secure status is now in operation. However, the lack of planning, lack of consultation and inefficiencies of the asylum and NASS systems have left some local authorities across the countries reticent to participate in this scheme. During the period of this research, planning applications for accommodation centres were vehemently opposed by local residents, as were screening centres for asylum seekers in dispersal areas. Various forums have been set up across the UK to deal with anti-asylum seeker feelings of local populations. In this way, the mishandling of the dispersal of asylum seekers could be seen as having the unexpected outcome of reducing the number of areas in the UK where the local populations will give the go-ahead for the building of a new immigration centre, let alone populations of 'quota refugees' directly from protracted refugee situations in regions of origin.

Broader policy implications

Relating the findings of this research to the government's aims for dispersal was revealing. One aim was to redistribute costs away from London and the South East. Another aim of the policy was to deter new arrivals of asylum seekers and the policy was deliberately designed around the idea of deterrence. Provision of support outside the mainstream benefits system and exclusion from mainstream services was a conscious aspect of the design. Another aim was to avoid adding to problems of social exclusion and racial tension as well as the avoidance of secondary migration. There were several gaps between these aims and implementation. As outlined earlier, asylum seekers claiming SO support remain concentrated in London and the South East. Providing financial support outside the mainstream benefits system occurred and has resulted in the social exclusion of asylum seekers due to the institutionalisation of the distinction between 'asylum seeker' and 'refugee'. Placing asylum seekers in areas of high deprivation and existing social exclusion has not always meant that social exclusion and 'racial' tensions have been avoided. Squire (2009, pp 136-7) has argued that the inverse is probably true as dispersing new arrivals to areas that experience pressures on the provision of public services creates tensions and that dispersal, from the viewpoint of asylum seekers, might be interpreted as a 'divisive initiative that creates a hostile environment in which asylum seekers are vulnerable to physical attack'. The process of social exclusion that asylum seekers experience has been shown to result in policy-imposed liminality. Secondary migration, while difficult to quantify, also occurred with asylum seekers moving to larger cities where they feel comfortable, invisible and away from the stigma and shame of the NASS system.

Two main implications for future policy were identified, which related to liminality and (mis)trust. First, the compulsory character of dispersal was highly problematic. Second, separating asylum seekers from the mainstream benefits system and setting up parallel services for financial support were at the root of social exclusion.

The finding that there are several forms of social exclusion experienced by asylum seekers suggests that if debates around social exclusion are to be moved forward, a better understanding of the link between accommodating asylum seekers on a temporary basis and the requirement of other populations in multiply deprived areas needs to be developed. Policy for asylum seekers was managed by NASS and such a move would require a more joined-up approach from government agencies.

One route exists for refugees to be 'socially included', or have their concerns raised at a community level, and this is through Community Empowerment Networks of Local Strategic Partnerships (LSPs). These LSPs were devised as a result of the neighbourhood renewal agenda of the Labour government upon election. However, uptake of this opportunity by those in receipt of status was low due to lack of information provided to refugee community groups, legality and trust issues as well as the high political backlash that occurs when refugees are too high on the agenda.

Asylum seekers are a socially excluded group and their social exclusion begins prior to their arrival in the UK. Whether this current exclusion is traced back to the divisions inherent in the historical formations of empire, to political exigencies to defend borders following the fall of the Iron Curtain, or to the need for 'national security' post 9/11, the result is the same. To be 'outside' society in some way, made visible as a group and put through processess of 'othering' only serves to justify further mistrust of this group and to thereby perpetuate policies based on deterrence.

Bygones are not bygones for this population – persecution in countries of origin does mean that fair and just systems are necessary. Creating asylum policies under an overarching framework of deterrence will not enable this; instead they will increase the sense of liminality experienced and socially excluding people until they receive refugee status will have an indelible impact on their futures. Asylum seekers do resist such policy-imposed liminality as far as possible – they do remake their own 'belonging' and forms of 'inclusion' or 'integration'. These forms of belonging mainly lie outside any official or broader attempts to create community or social 'cohesion' and do not allow for trust to be restored in institutional or political processes of the UK. For belonging to occur beyond the narrow confines of social trust based on recourse to social networks, the image of asylum seekers would need to be made more positive and a welcome provided that allowed for restoration of institutional and political trust as well as social trust.

Bibliography

Africa Educational Trust (2002) *Refugees and Asylum Seekers in the Learning and Skills Council London North Area*, London: Learning and Skills Council.

Ager, A. (1999) 'Perspectives on the refugee experience', in A. Ager (ed) *Refugees: Perspectives on the Experience of Forced Migration*, London and New York, NY: Continuum.

Ager, A. (2002) 'Community contact and mental health amongst socially isolated refugees in Edinburgh', *Journal of Refugee Studies*, vol 15, no 1, pp 71-80.

Ager, A. and Strang, A. (2004) *Indicators of Integration: Final Report*, Home Office Development and Practice report 28, London: Home Office.

Ager, A. and Strang, A. (2008) 'Understanding integration: a conceptual framework', *Journal of Refugee Studies*, vol 21, no 2, pp 166-91.

Anderson, B. (1991) *Imagined Communities*, London: Verso.

Anderson, I. (2000) 'Housing and social exclusion: the changing debate', in Anderson, I. and Sim, D. (2000) *Social Exclusion and Housing: Context and Challenges*, London: Chartered Institute of Housing.

Anderson, I. and Sim, D. (2000) *Social Exclusion and Housing: Context and Challenges*, London: Chartered Institute of Housing.

Anderson, M.B. and Woodrow, P.J. (1989) *Rising from the Ashes: Development Strategies in Times of Disaster*, Boulder, CO: Westview Press.

Anie, A., Daniel, N., Tah, C. and Petruckevitch, A. (2005) *An Exploration of Factors Affecting the Successful Dispersal of Asylum Seekers*, Home Office Online Report 50/05, London: Home Office.

Asylum Aid (2002) *White Paper Response*, London: Asylum Aid, www. asylumsupportinfo/whitepaperreponses/asylumaid.htm

Audit Commission (2000a) *Another Country: Implementing Dispersal under the Immigration and Asylum Act 1999*, London: Audit Commission.

Audit Commission (2000b) *A New City: Supporting Asylum Seekers and Refugees in London*, London: Audit Commission.

Baker, R. (1990) 'The refugee experience: communication and stress, recollections of a refugee survivor', *Journal of Refugee Studies*, vol 3, no 1, pp 64-71.

Bascom, J. (1998) *Losing Place: Refugee Populations and Rural Transformations in East Africa*, New York, NY and Oxford: Berghahn Books.

Bauman, Z. (1992) *Intimations of Postmodernity*, London: Routledge.

Bauman, Z. (2000) *Liquid Modernity*, Cambridge: Cambridge University Press.

Bauman, Z. (2001) *Community: Seeking Safety in an Insecure World*, Cambridge: Polity Press.

Baycan, F. (2003a) 'Deconstructing "refugee women"', in *In-Exile*, September, London: Refugee Council.

Baycan, F. (2003b) 'Out of the loop: the disempowerment of refugee women in urban regeneration', MA Urban Regeneration, University of Westminster, London.

Becker, S. and Bryman, A. (2004) *Understanding Research for Social Policy and Practice: Themes, Methods and Approaches*, Bristol: The Policy Press.

Beirens, H., Hughes, N., Hek, R. and Spicer, N. (2007) 'Preventing social exclusion of refugee and asylum seeking children: building new networks', *Social Policy & Society*, vol 6, no 2, pp 219-29.

Beresford, P. (1996) 'Challenging the "them" and "us" of social policy research', in H. Dean (ed) *Ethics and Social Policy Research*, Luton: University of Luton Press.

Berkeley, R., Khan, O. and Ambikaipaker, M. (2006) *What's New about New Immigrants in Twenty-First Century Britain?*, York: Joseph Rowntree Foundation.

Berry, J.W. (1997) 'Immigration, acculturation and adaptation', *Applied Psychology: An International Review*, vol 46, no 1, pp 5-34.

Betts, A. (2004) 'International relations of the "new" extra-territorial approaches to refugee protection: explaining the policy initiatives of the UK government and UNHCR', Paper presented at the 2nd Annual Forced Migration Student Conference, University of Warwick, 15 March.

Bhavnani, R., Mirza, H.S. and Meetoo, V. (2005) *Tackling the Roots of Racism: Lessons for Success*, Bristol: The Policy Press.

Black, R. (2001) 'Fifty years of refugee studies: from theory to policy', *International Migration Review*, vol 35, no 1, pp 57-78.

Black, R. and Robinson, V. (eds) (1993) *Geography and Refugees: Patterns and Processes of Change*, London: Belhaven Press.

Blackwell, R.D. (1989) 'The disruption and reconstitution of family, network and community systems following torture, organised violence and exile', Paper presented at the Second International Conference of Centres, Institutions and Individuals Concerned with the Care of Victims of Organised Violence, Costa Rica, 27 November–2 December.

Blake, N. (2002) *Advice: In the Matter of the Human Rights Act 1998 and in the Matter of Refugee Action*, London: Winstanley Burgess Solicitors.

Blitz, B., Sales, R. and Marzano, L. (2005) 'Non-voluntary return? The politics of refugee return to Afghanistan', *Political Studies*, vol 53, pp 182-200.

Bloch, A. (1996) 'A survey of refugee resettlement: some theoretical and methodological issues', Paper presented at the British Sociological Association Annual Conference, University of Reading.

Bloch, A. (1997) 'Refugee migration and settlement: a case study of the London Borough of Newham', PhD thesis, Department of Social Policy and Politics, Goldsmiths College, University of London.

Bloch, A. (1999) 'Carrying out a survey of refugees: some methodological considerations and guidelines', *Journal of Refugee Studies*, vol 12, no 4, pp 367-83.

Bloch, A. (2004) 'Labour market participation and conditions of employment: a comparison of minority ethnic groups and refugees in Britain', *Sociological Research Online*, vol 9, no 2, www.socresonline.org.uk/9/2/bloch.html

Bloch, A. and Schuster, L. (2005) 'At the extremes of exclusion: deportation, detention and dispersal', *Ethnic and Racial Studies*, vol 28, no 3, pp 491-512.

Bloch, A. and Solomos, J. (2010) *Race and Ethnicity in the 21st Century*, Basingstoke: Palgrave Macmillan.

Blunkett, D. (2001) *Asylum, Migration and Citizenship – Home Secretary's Statement to the House of Commons: 29 October 2001*, London: Immigration & Nationality Directorate, Home Office, www.ind.homeoffice.gov.uk/news.asp?NewsId-101&SectionId=3

Boaz, A. and Solesbury, W. (2003) 'Reviewing the literature', Session during an ESRC Residential Summer School on Evidence Based Policy Research, Queen Mary, University of London, 16-20 June.

Boone, M.S. (1994) 'Thirty-year retrospective on the adjustment of Cuban refugee women', in L.A. Camino and R.M. Krulfeld (eds) *Reconstructing Lives, Recapturing Meaning: Refugee Identify, Gender and Culture Change*, Basel, Switzerland: Gordon & Breach Publishers.

Boswell, C. (2001) *Spreading the Costs of Asylum Seekers: A Critical Assessment of Dispersal Policies in Germany and the UK*, London: Anglo-German Foundation for the Study of Industrial Society.

Boswell, C. (2003) 'Burden-sharing in the European Union: lessons from the German and UK experience', *Journal of Refugee Studies*, vol 16, no 3, pp 316-35.

Boswell, C. and Crisp, J. (2004) *Poverty, International Migration and Asylum*. Policy Brief No 8, United Nations University, World Institiute for Development Economics Researcg (UNU-WIDER), Helsinki: Finland.

Bourdieu, P. (1967) *Reproduction*, London: Routledge.

Bourdieu, P. (1984) *Distinction: A Social Critique of the Judgement of Taste*, London: Routledge.

Bourdieu, P. (1986) 'The forms of capital', in J. Richardson (ed) *Handbook of Theory and Research for the Sociology of Education*, New York, NY: greenwood, pp 241-58.

Bourdieu, P. (1997) 'The forms of capital', in A.H. Halsey, H. Lauder, P. Brown and A. Stuart Wells (eds) *Education: Culture, Economy, Society*, Oxford: Oxford University Press.

Bousquet, G. (1987) 'Living in a state of limbo: a case study of Vietnamese refugees in Hong Kong camps', in S. Morgan and E. Colson (eds) *People in Upheaval*, New York, NY: Centre for Migration Studies.

Boyd, M. (1989) 'Family and personal networks in international migration: recent developments and new agendas', *International Migration Review*, vol 23, no 3, pp 638-72.

Boyle, P., Halfacree, K. and Robinson, V. (1998) *Exploring Contemporary Migration*, London: Longman.

Bracken, P.J., Giller, J.E. and Summerfield, D. (1995) 'Psychological responses to war and atrocity: the limitations of current concepts', *Social Science and Medicine*, vol 40, no 8, pp 1073-82.

Burchardt, T. (2004) 'Selective inclusion: asylum seekers and other marginalised groups', in J. Hills and K. Stewart (eds) *A More Equal Society? New Labour, Poverty, Inequality and Exclusion*, Bristol: The Policy Press.

Burchardt, T., Le Grand, J. and Piachaud, D. (2002a) 'Degrees of exclusion: developing a dynamic, multidimensional measure', in J. Hills, J. Le Grand and D. Piachaud (eds) *Understanding Social Exclusion*, Oxford: Oxford University Press.

Burchardt, T., Le Grand, J. and Piachaud, D. (2002b) 'Introduction', in J. Hills, J. Le Grand and D. Piachaud (eds) *Understanding Social Exclusion*, Oxford: Oxford University Press.

Burnett, A. and Peel, M. (2001a) 'Asylum seekers and refugees in Britain', *British Medical Journal*, vol 322, pp 485-8.

Burnett, A. and Peel, M. (2001b) 'Health needs of asylum seekers and refugees', *British Medical Journal*, vol 322, pp 544-7.

Buscher, D., Lester, E. and Coelho, P. (2005) *The Way Forward: Europe's Role in the Global Refugee Protection System – Guarding Refugee Protection Standards in Regions of Origin*, Brussels, Belgium: European Council on Refugees and Exiles (ECRE).

Calvar, J. (1999) 'Asylum seekers and refugees in the uk: the role of refugee community organisations and refugee agencies in the settlement process', PhD thesis, School of Social Sciences, Middlesex University.

Camino, L.A. and Krulfeld, R.M. (1994) *Reconstructing Lives, Recapturing Meaning: Refugee Identity, Gender and Culture Change*, Basel, Switzerland: Gordon & Breach Publishers.

Cantle, T. (2001) *Community Cohesion: A Report of the Independent Review Team*, London: Home Office.

Cantle, T. (2005) *Community Cohesion: A New Framework for Race and Diversity*, Basingstoke: Palgrave Macmillan.

Carey-Wood, J., Duke, K., Karn, V. and Marshall, T. (1995) *The Settlement of Refugee in Britain*, Home Office Research and Planning Unit report, London: HMSO.

Carter, M. and El-Hassan, A.A. (2003) *Between NASS and a Hard Place*, London: Housing Associations' Charitable Trust (HACT).

Castles, S. (2003) 'Towards a sociology of forced migration and social transformation', *Sociology*, vol 37, no 2, pp 13-34.

Castles, S. (2004) 'Why migration policies fail', *Ethnic and Racial Studies*, vol 27, no 2, pp 205-27.

Castles, S. (2005) 'Policy-driven research or research-driven policy? Challenges to, and dilemmas for, forced migration studies', Paper presented at the conference 'Seeking Refuge, Seeking Rights, Seeking a Future', Oxford Brookes University, Oxford, 13-14 May.

Castles, S. and Davidson, A. (2000) *Citizenship and Migration: Globalization and the Politics of Belonging*, Basingstoke: Palgrave.

Castles, S. and Loughna, S. (2004) 'Globalization, migration and asylum', in V. George and R.M. Page (eds) *Global Social Problems and Global Social Policy*, Cambridge: Polity Press.

Castles, S. and Miller, M.J. (2003) *The Age of Migration: International Population Movements in the Modern World*, Basingstoke: Palgrave Macmillan.

Castles, S., Crawley, H. and Loughna, S. (2003) *States of Conflict: Causes and Patterns of Forced Migration to the EU and Policy Responses*, London: IPPR.

Castles, S., Korac, M., Vasta, E. and Vertovec, V. (2002) *Integration: Mapping the Field*, Home Office Online Report 28/03, London: Home Office.

Chimni, B.S. (1998) 'The geopolitics of refugee studies: a view from the south', *Journal of Refugee* Studies, no 11, vol 4, pp 350-74.

Chimni, B.S. (1999) *From Resettlement to Involuntary Repatriation: Towards a Critical History of Durable Solutions to Refugee Problems*, New Issues in Refugee Research, Working Paper no 2, Geneva: Evaluation and Policy Analysis Unit, UNHCR.

Chimni, B.S. (2009) 'The birth of a "discipline": from refugee to forced migration studies', *Journal of Refugee Studies*, vol 22, no 1, pp 11-29.

Christie, K. and Kwok Bun, B. (1994) 'Refugees from Southeast Asia: a review essay', Paper presented at the 4th International Research and Advisory Panel Conference on Refugee and Forced Migration Studies, 5-9 January, Oxford.

Citizens Advice Bureau (2002) *Distant Voices*, London: CAB.

Cohen, R. (1994) *Frontiers of Identity: The British and Others*, Harlow, Essex: Longman.

Cohen, R. and Kennedy, P. (2000) *Global Sociology*, Basingstoke: Macmillan.

Cohen, S. (2002) 'The local state of immigration controls', *Critical Social Policy*, vol 22, no 3, pp 518-43.

Cohen, S. (2003) *No-One is Illegal: Asylum and Immigration Control Past and Present*, Stoke on Trent: Trentham.

Cohen, S., Humphries, B. and Mynott, E. (2002) *From Immigration Controls to Welfare Controls*, London and New York, NY: Routledge.

COIC (Commission on Integration and Cohesion) (2007) *Our Shared Future*, London: COIC.

Coleman, J.S. (1988) 'Social capital and the creation of human capital', *American Journal of Sociology*, vol 94, pp 95-121.

Colson, E. (1991) *Coping in Adversity*, Oxford: Refugee Studies Programme.

Colson, E. (2003) 'Forced migration and the anthropological response', *Journal of Refugee Studies*, vol 16, no 1, pp 1-18.

COMPAS (Centre on Migration, Policy and Society), Oxfam GB and the Refugee Studies Centre (2005) *A New Asylum Paradigm? Report on the One Day Workshop in Oxford on 14 June 2005*, Oxford: University of Oxford.

Connerton, P. (1989) *How Societies Remember*, Cambridge: Cambridge University Press.

Council of Europe (2005) *Report by Mr Alvaro Gil-Robles, Commissioner for Human Rights, on his Visit to the United Kingdom*, Strasburg: Office of the Commissioner for Human Rights.

Courtland Robinson, W. (1998) *Terms of Refuge: The Indochinese Exodus and the International Response*, London: Zed Books.

Craig, G. (2007) '"Cunning, unprincipled, loathsome": the racist tail wags the welfare dog', *Journal of Social Policy*, vol 36, no 4, pp 605-23.

Crisp, J. (1999) '*Who has Counted the Refugees?': UNHCR and the Politics of Numbers*, New Issues in Refugee Research, UNHCR Working Paper no 12, Geneva: Evaluation and Policy Analysis Unit, UNHCR.

Crisp, J. (2004a) *The Local Integration and Local Settlement of Refugees: A Conceptual and Historical Analysis*, New Issues in Refugee Research, Working Paper no 102, Geneva: Evaluation and Policy Analysis Unit, UNHCR.

Crisp, J. (2004b) *A New Asylum paradigm? Globalisation, Migration and the Uncertain Future of the International Refugee Regime*, UNHCR New Issues in Refugee Research Working Paper No 100, Geneva: UNHCR.

Crosby, A. (2006) *The Boundaries of Belonging: Reflections on Migration Policies into the 21st Century*, Inter Pares Occasional Paper no 7, Ottawa, Canada: InterPares.

Daniel, E.V. and Knudsen, J.C. (eds) (1995) *Mistrusting Refugees*, Berkeley, CA, Los Angeles, LA and London: University of California Press.

Dawson, A. (2001) *Mono-Cultural Communities and their Effect on Asylum/Immigration Seekers in Humberside*, London: Save the Children.

de Voe, D.M. (1981) 'Framing refugees as clients', *International Migration Review*, vol 15, pp 88-94.

Demos (2003) *Inside Out: Rethinking Inclusive Communities*, London: Demos.

Demuth, A. (2000) 'Some conceptual thoughts on migration research', in B. Agozino (ed) *Theoretical and Methodological Issues in Migration Research*, Aldershot: Ashgate.

DETR (Department of the Environment, Transport and the Regions) (1999) *Report by the Unpopular Housing Action Team*, London: DETR.

DETR (2000) *Indices of Deprivation 2000*, London: DETR.

Dona, G. (2010) 'Rethinking well-being: from contexts to processes', International *Journal of Migration, Health and Social Sciences*, vol 6, issue 2, pp 3-14.

Dona, G. and Berry, J.W. (1999) 'Refugee acculturation and re-acculturation', in Ager, A. (ed) *Refugees: Perspectives on the Experience of Forced Migration*, London and New York, NY: Continuum.

Douglas, M. (1966) *Purity and Danger*, London: Routledge & Kegan Paul.

Duke, K. (1996) 'Refugee communities in the UK: the role of the community group in the resettlement process', Paper presented at the British Sociological Association Annual Conference, University of Reading.

Duke, K. and Marshall, T. (1995) *Vietnamese Refugees since 1982*, Home Office Research Study 142, London: HMSO.

Dumper, H. (2002) *Is it Safe Here? Refugee Women's Experiences in the UK*, London: Refugee Action.

Dunar, B. (eds) (1998) *An End to Torture: Strategies for its Eradication*, London: Zed Books.

Dwyer, P. (2005) 'Governance, forced migration and welfare', *Social Policy & Administration*, vol 39, no 6, pp 622-39.

el Bushra, J. and Piza-Lopez, E. (1994) 'Gender, war and food', in J. Macrae and A. Zwi (eds) *War & Hunger: Rethinking International Responses to Complex Emergencies*, London: Zed Books.

Esterhuizen, L. (2004) *Doing Case Studies for the Refugee Sector: A DIY Handbook for Agencies and Practitioners*, London: ICAR.

Fekete, L. (2001) 'The emergence of xeno-racism', *Race & Class*, vol 43, no 2, pp 23-40.

Finch, N. (2001) 'The support and dispersal of asylum seekers', in J. Coker, J. Farbey, N. Finch and A. Stanley (eds) *Asylum Seekers: A Guide to Recent Legislation*, London: Immigration Law Practitioners' Association.

Finney, N. and Peach, E. (2004) *Attitudes towards Asylum Seekers, Refugees and Other Immigrants*, London: Commission for Racial Equality.

Finney, N. and Simpson, L. (2009) *'Sleepwalking to Segregation'?: Challenging Myths about Race and Migration*, Bristol: The Policy Press.

Fozzard, S. (1986) *The Closed Camps – As a Total Institution*, Seminar Paper, Oxford: Refugee Studies Programme.

Franklin, J. (ed) (2004) *Politics, Trust and Networks: Social Capital in Critical Perspective*, London: Families and Social Capital ESRC Research Group, London South Bank University.

Geddes, A. (2000) *Immigration and European Integration: Towards Fortress Europe?*, Manchester: Manchester University Press.

Gibney, M.J. (2001) *The State of Asylum: Democratization, Judicialization and Evolution of Refugee Policy in Europe*, New Issues in Refugee Research, Working Paper no 50, Geneva: Evaluation and Policy Analysis Unit, UNHCR.

GLA (Greater London Authority) (2004) *Destitution by Design: Withdrawl of Support from In-country Asylum Applicants*, London: GLA.

Glaser, B.G. and Strauss, A.L. (1968) *The Discovery of Grounded Theory*, London: Weidenfeld and Nicolson.

Gold, S.J. (1992) *Refugee Communities: A Comparative Field Study*, California: Sage.

Goodwin-Gill, G.S. (1996) *The Refugee in International Law*, Oxford: Clarendon Press.

Gordon, D. and Pantazis, C. (eds) (1997) *Breadline Britain in the 1990s*, Aldershot: Ashgate.

Gordon, D. and Townsend, P. (eds) (2000) *Breadline Europe: The Measurement of Poverty*, Bristol: The Policy Press.

Granovetter, M.S. (1973) 'The strength of weak ties', *American Journal of Sociology*, vol 78, no 6, pp 1360-80.

Griffiths, D., Sigona, N. and Zetter, R. (2005) *Refugee Community Organisations and Dispersal: Networks, Resources and Social Capital*, Bristol: The Policy Press.

Griffiths, D., Sigona, N. and Zetter, R. (2006) 'Integrative paradigms, marginal reality: refugee community organisations and dispersal in Britain', *Journal of Ethnic and Migration Studies*, vol 32, issue 5, pp 881-98.

Hale, S. (1993) 'The reception and resettlement of Vietnamese refugees in Britain', in V. Robinson (ed) *The International Refugee Crisis: British and Canadian Responses*, Basingstoke: Macmillan.

Hammar, T. (1993) 'The "Sweden-wide strategy" of refugee dispersal', in R. Black and V. Robinson (1993) *Geography and Refugees: Patterns and Processes of Change*, London: Belhaven Press.

Hammersley, M. and Atkinson, P. (1995) *Ethnography*, London and New York, NY: Routledge.

Hardin, R. (2006) *Trust*, Cambridge: Polity Press.

Harrell-Bond, B.E. (1986) *Imposing Aid: Emergency Assistance to Refugees*, Oxford: Oxford University Press.

Harrell-Bond, B.E. (1992) 'Counting the refugees', *Journal of Refugee Studies*, vol 5, no 3/4, pp 205-25.

Harrell-Bond, B.E. (1995) *Refugees and the International System: The Evolution of Solutions*, Oxford: Queen Elizabeth House.

Harrell-Bond, B.E. (1999) 'The experience of refugees as recipients of Aid', in A. Ager (ed) *Refugees: Perspectives on the Experience of Forced Migration*, London and New York, NY: Continuum.

Harrison, J. (2006) 'Boundary strategies: statecraft and imagined identities', PhD thesis, Department of Sociology, University of Leicester.

Harrison, M. and Phillips, D. (2010) 'Housing and neighbourhoods: a UK and European perspective', in A. Bloch and J. Solomos (eds) *Race and Ethnicity in the 21st Century*, Basingstoke: Palgrave Macmillan.

Hein, J. (1993) 'Refugees, immigrants and the state', *Annual Review of Sociology*, vol 19, pp 43-59.

Hills, J. and Stewart, K. (2004) *A More Equal Society? New Labour, Poverty, Inequality and Exclusion*, Bristol: The Policy Press.

Hills, J., Le Grand, J. and Piachaud, D. (eds) (2002) *Understanding Social Exclusion*, Oxford: Oxford University Press.

Hingorani, M. (2001) 'A right to life: the story of Ramin Khaleghi', *Race & Class*, vol 43, no 2, pp 105-31.

Hitchcox, L. (1987) 'Government and voluntary agencies in the resettlement of refugees in Europe', Conference Paper, Centre for Research in Ethnic Relations, University of Warwick.

Hitchcox, L. (1990) *Vietnamese Refugees in Southeast Asian Camps*, London: Macmillan.

Holmes, C. (1988) *John Bull's Island*, Basingstoke: Macmillan.

Holmes, C. (1991) *A Tolerant Country? Immigrants, Refugees and Minorities in Britain*, London and Boston, MA: Faber & Faber.

Home Office statistics, various dates.

Home Office (1998a) *Fairer, Faster and Firmer: A Modern Approach to Immigration and Asylum*, London: HMSO.

Home Office (1998b) *Getting it Right Together: Compact on Relations between Government and the Voluntary and Community Sector in England*, London: Home Office.

Home Office (1999) *Asylum Seekers' Support: An Information Document Setting Out Proposals for the New Support Scheme for Asylum Seekers in Genuine Need and Inviting Expressions of Interest from Potential Support Providers*, London: Immigration and Nationality Directorate.

Home Office (2001a) *Bridging the Information Gaps: A Conference of Research on Asylum and Immigration in the UK*, Report of proceedings, London: Home Office.

Home Office (2001b) *Secure Borders, Safe Haven: Integration with Diversity in Modern Britain*, London: HMSO.

Home Office (2001c) *Report of the Operational Reviews of the Voucher and Dispersal Schemes of the National Asylum Support Service*, London: Home Office.

Home Office (2005) *Controlling our Borders: Making Migration work for Britain – Five Year Strategy for Asylum and Immigration*, London: HMSO.

Hookham, M. (2004) 'Asylum fall figures rejected by charities', *Liverpool Echo*, 25 February.

House of Commons Home Affairs Select Committee (1985) *Refugees in Asylum, with Special Reference to the Vietnamese*, London: HMSO.

Human Rights Watch (2002) *Commentary on the United Kingdom Home Office White Paper: Secure Borders, Safe Haven*, www.asylumsupportinfo/whitepaperreponses/humanrightswatch.htm

Hynes, P. (2005a) 'Ethics and avoiding "harm" in research with refugees in the UK', Paper presented at the conference 'Displacement: Global Dynamics and Gendered Patterns', Centre for Women and Gender Research, University of Bergen, Norway, October.

Hynes, P. (2005b) 'Ethics, access and avoiding "harm" in research with refugees', Postgraduate 'Talking Head', Training Workshop for Postgraduates, King's College London, 23 June.

Hynes, P. (2006) *The Compulsory Dispersal of Asylum Seekers and Processes of Social Exclusion*, Summary of Findings, Swindon: Middlesex University and ESRC (English and translated into French, Arabic, Farsi, Kurdish and Somali).

Hynes, P. (2007) 'Dispersal of asylum seekers and processes of social exclusion in England', PhD thesis, Middlesex University.

Hynes, P. (2009) 'Contemporary compulsory dispersal and the absence of space for the restoration of trust', *Journal of Refugee Studies*, vol 22, no 1, pp 97–121.

Hynes, P. and Loughna, S. (2005) 'Did anybody ask the refugee? Rethinking durable solutions', Paper presented at the 9th International Conference of the International Association for the Study of Forced Migration (IASFM), Sao Paulo, Brazil, January.

Hynes, P. and Mon Thu, Y. (2008) 'To Sheffield with love', *Forced Migration Review*, no 30.

Hynes, P. and Sales, R. (2010) 'New communities: asylum seekers and dispersal', in J. Solomos and A. Bloch (eds) *Race and Ethnicity in the 21st Century*, Basingstoke: Palgrave Macmillan.

Hynes, T. (2002) 'It's easy to tell refugees don't vote', in *Refugee Women's News: Refugee Women & Protection*, London: Refugee Women's Association.

Hynes, T. (2003a) *The Issue of 'Trust' or 'Mistrust' in Research with Refugees: Choices Caveats and Considerations for Researchers*, New Issues in Refugee Research, Working Paper no 98, Geneva: Evaluation and Policy Analysis Unit, UNHCR.

Hynes, T. (2003b) 'Restricting access to the UK over the years', in *Refugee Women's News: Asylum in the UK – Out in the Cold?*, London: Refugee Women's Association.

Hynes, T. (2003c) 'Left out in the cold: the 8th of January', in *Refugee Women's News: Asylum in the UK – Out in the Cold?*, London: Refugee Women's Association.

Hynes, T. (2003d) 'Editorial introduction', in *Refugee Women's News: Against All Odds – Achievements & Refugees*, London: Refugee Women's Association.

ICAR (Information Centre about Asylum and Refugees) (2003) *Mapping the UK*, section on Leicester city, London: ICAR, www.icar.org.uk/?lid=1052

ICAR (2004) *A Rough Guide to Navigating Secondary Sources of Data and Information on Refugees and Asylum Seekers in the UK*, A guide produced for the 2nd Annual Postgraduate Conference on Forced Migration, Warwick University, 15 March, London: ICAR, www.icar.org.uk/publications

IND (Immigration & Nationality Directorate) (2003) *Section 55 (Late Claims) 2002 Act Guidance*, London: Home Office, www.ind.homeoffice.gov.uk/default.asp?PageId=3653

Indra, D.M. (1989) 'Ethnic human rights and feminist theory: gender implications for refugee studies and practice', *Journal of Refugee Studies*, vol 2, no 2, pp 221-42.

Indra, D.M. (1999) *Engendering Forced Migration: Theory and Practice*, New York, NY and Oxford: Berghahn Books.

Jacobsen, K. and Landau, L. (2003) *Researching Refugees: Some Methodological and Ethical Considerations in Social Science and Forced Migration*, New Issues in Refugee Research, Working Paper no 30, Geneva: Evaluation and Policy Analysis Unit, UNHCR.

JCWI (Joint Council for the Welfare of Immigrants), Refugee Council and Commission for Racial Equality (1998) *A Culture of Suspicion: The Impact of Internal Immigration Controls*, London: JCWI.

JCWI (2002) *Immigration, Nationality & Refugee Law Handbook*, London: JCWI.

Joly, D. (1996) *Haven or Hell? Asylum Policies and Refugees in Europe,* Basingstoke, MacMillan.

Johnson, M.R.D. (2003) *Asylum Seekers in Dispersal: Healthcare Issues*, Home Office Online Report 13/03, London: Home Office.

Joly, D. (1998) *Scapegoats and Social Actors: The Exclusion and Integration of Minorities in Western and Eastern Europe*, Basingstoke: Macmillan.

Jones, L. (2000) 'UK government policy and social exclusion: the experience of asylum seekers', MA dissertation, Department of Social Policy and Social Development, University of Manchester.

Jones, P. (1982) *Vietnamese Refugees*, Home Office Research and Planning Unit, Paper 13, London: HMSO.

Kaiser, T. (1999) 'Living in limbo: insecurity and the settlement of Sudanese refugees in Northern Uganda', DPhil thesis, Linacre College, University of Oxford.

Kaiser, T. (2002) *Participatory and Beneficiary-Based Approaches to the Evaluation of Humanitarian Programmes*, New Issues in Refugee Research, Working Paper no 51, Geneva: Evaluation and Policy Analysis Unit, UNHCR.

Kate, M.A. (2005) *The Provision of Protection to Asylum Seekers in Destination Countries*, New Issues in Refugee Research, Working Paper no 114, Geneva: Evaluation and Policy Analysis Unit, UNHCR.

Kay, D. (1987) *Chileans in Exile: Private Struggles, Public Lives*, Basingstoke: Macmillan.

Kaye, R. (1994) 'Setting the agenda: British refugee policy and the role of parties', Paper prepared for the 4th International Research and Advisory Panel Conference, Somerville College, Oxford, January.

Kelly, L. (2003) 'Bosnian refugees in Britain: questioning community', *Sociology*, vol 37, no 1, pp 35-49.

Kerrigan, S. (2005) 'Aliens Act 1905: 100 years of British immigration law', *In-Exile*, March, London: Refugee Council.

Khodyakov, D. (2007) 'Trust as a process: a three-dimensional approach', *Sociology*, vol 41, no 1, pp 115-32.

Kitts, H.J. (2005) 'Betwixt and between: refugees and stateless persons in limbo', *Refuge*, vol 22, no 2, pp 67-76.

Knudsen, J.C. (1995) 'When trust is on trial: negotiating refugee narratives', in E.V. Daniel and J.C. Knudsen (eds) *Mistrusting Refugees*, Berkeley, CA and London: University of California Press.

Korac, M. (2005) 'Creating solutions: the role of social networks and transnational links in shaping migration choices of forced migrants from the former Yugoslavia', Paper presented at the 9th International Conference of the International Association for the Study of Forced Migration (IASFM), Sao Paulo, Brazil, January.

Koser, K. (1997) 'Social networks and the asylum cycle: the case of Iranians in the Netherlands', *International Migration Review*, vol 31, no 3, pp 591-611.

Koser, K. and Lutz, H. (1998) *The New Migration in Europe: Social Constructions and Social Realities*, Basingstoke: Macmillan.

Koser, K. and Pinkerton, C. (2002) *The Social Networks of Asylum Seekers and the Dissemination of Information about Countries of Asylum*, London: Home Office.

Krulfeld, R.M. (1994) 'Methods in refugee research: two ethnographic approaches', in L.A. Camino and R.M. Krulfeld (eds) *Reconstructing Lives, Recapturing Meaning: Refugee Identify, Gender and Culture Change*, Basel, Switzerland: Gordon & Breach Publishers.

Kunz, E.F. (1973) 'The refugee in flight: kinetic models and forms of displacement', *International Migration Review*, vol 7, no 2, pp 125-46.

Kushner, T. and Knox, K. (1999) *Refugees in an Age of Genocide*, London: Frank Cass.

Kyambi, S. (2005) *Beyond Black and White: Mapping New Immigrant Communities*, London: IPPR.

Lakey, J. (1997) 'Neighbourhoods and housing', in T. Mahood, R. Berthoud, J. Lakey, J. Nazroo, P. Smith, S. Virdee and S. Beishon (eds) *Ethnic Minorities in Britain: Diversity and Disadvantage*, London: Policy Studies Institute.

Lam, T. and Martin, C. (1994) *Vietnamese in the UK: Fifteen Years of Settlement*, London: South Bank University.

Lammers, E. (2005) *Refugees, Asylum Seekers and Anthropologists: The Taboo on Giving*, Global Migration Perspectives, Working Paper no 29, Geneva: Global Commission on International Migration.

Leach, E.R. (1976) *Culture and Communication*, Cambridge: Cambridge University Press.

Lee, T.R. (1977) *Race and Residence: The Concentration and Dispersal of Immigrants in London*, Oxford: Clarendon Press.

Lemos, G. (2001) 'British benevolence?', *Inside Housing*, March.

Levitas, R. (1998) *The Inclusive Society? Social Exclusion and New Labour*, Basingstoke: Palgrave.

Levitas, R. (2000) 'What is social exclusion?', in D. Gordon and P. Townsend (eds) *Breadline Europe: The Measurement of Poverty*, Bristol: The Policy Press.

Levitas, R. (2006) 'The concept and measurement of social exclusion', in D. Gordon, R. Levitas and C. Pantazis (eds) *Poverty and Social Exclusion in Britain: The Millennium Survey*, Bristol: The Policy Press.

Lewis, H. (2005) 'Ethics and access in researching migrant populations', Postgraduate 'Talking Head', Training Workshop for Postgraduates, King's College London, 23 June.

Lewis, H. (2007a) *Destitution in Leeds: The Experiences of People Seeking Asylum and Supporting Agencies*, York: Joseph Rowntree Foundation.

Lewis, H. (2007b) 'Interrogating community: dispersed refugees in Leeds', Unpublished PhD thesis, University of Hull.

Lewis, H. (2010) 'Community moments: integration and transnationalism at "refugee" parties and events', *Journal of Refugee Studies*, vol 23, no 3, doi: 10.1093/jrs/feq037.

Lewis, H., Craig, G., Adamson, S. and Wilkinson, M. (2008) *Refugees, Asylum Seekers and Migrants in Yorkshire and Humber, 1999-2008*, Hull and Leeds: Centre for Research in Social Inclusion and Social Justice, University of Hull, and Yorkshire Futures.

Lewis, M. (2005) *Asylum: Understanding Public Attitudes*, London: IPPR.

Longo, A. and Sales, R. (2001) '"Faster, fairer, firmer": la politica migratoria in Gran Bretagna', *Studi Emigrazione*, vol 141, pp 131-47.

Lukes, S. and Hynes, P. (2008) *Insights into the SUNRISE Refugee Housing Experience*, London: Housing Associations Charitable Trust.

Lupton, R. and Power, A. (2002) 'Social exclusion and neighbourhoods', in J. Hills, J. Le Grand and D. Piachaud (eds) *Understanding Social Exclusion*, Oxford: Oxford University Press.

McNamara, D. (1990) 'The origins and effects of "humane deterrence" policies in Southeast Asia', in G. Loescher and L. Monahan (eds) *Refugees and International Relations*, Oxford: Clarendon Press.

Malkki, L. (1995a) 'Refugees and exile: from "refugee studies" to the national order of things', *Annual Review of Anthropology*, vol 24, pp 495-523.

Malkki, L. (1995b) *Purity and Exile*, Chicago, IL: University of Chicago Press.

Mamdani, M. (1993) 'The Ugandan Asian expulsion: twenty years after', *Journal of Refugee Studies*, vol 6, no 3, pp 260-74.

Marett, V. (1993) 'Resettlement of Ugandan Asians in Leicester', *Journal of Refugee Studies*, vol 6, no 3, pp 248-59.

Martin, J. and Singh, G. (2002) *Asian Leicester*, Stroud: Sutton Publishing.

Marx, E. (1990) 'The social world of refugees: a conceptual framework', *Journal of Refugee Studies*, vol 3, no 3, pp 189-203.

Massey, D. (1993) 'Politics and space/time', in M. Keith and S. Pile (eds) *Place and the Politics of Identity*, London: Routledge.

Mauss, M. (1954) *The Gift*, London: Routledge & Kegan Paul.

Mayor of London (2002) *Home Office White Paper Secure Borders, Safe Haven: Response on behalf of the Mayor of London*, London: Greater London Authority.

Mayor of London (2004) *Destitution by Design – Withdrawal of Support from In-Country Asylum Applicants: An Impact Assessment for London*, London: Greater London Authority.

Middleton, D. (2005) *Why Asylum Seekers Seek Refuge in Particular Destination Countries: An Exploration of Key Determinants*, Working Paper no 34, Geneva, Switzerland: Global Commission on International Migration.

Migrant Rights Network, various dates.

Miles, M.B. and Huberman, A.M. (1994) *Qualitative Data Analysis*, Thousand Oaks, CA: Sage Publications.

Mirza, H.S. (1997) *Black British Feminism: A Reader*, London: Routledge.

Mohan, J. (1999) *A United Kingdom? Economic, Social and Political Geographies*, London: Arnold.

Morris, L. (2002a) *Managing Migration: Civic Stratification and Migrant Rights*, London: Routledge.

Morris, L. (2002b) 'Britain's asylum and immigration regime: the shifting contours of rights', *Journal of Ethnic and Migration Studies*, vol 28, no 3, pp 409-25.

Morris, L. (ed) (2006) *Rights: Sociological Perspectives*, New York, NY: Routledge.

Morris, L. (2010) *Asylum, Welfare and the Cosmopolitan Ideal: A Sociology of Rights*, Oxford: Routledge-Cavendish.

Muecke, M.A. (1995) 'Trust abuse of trust, and mistrust among cambodian refugee women: a cultural interpretation', in E.V. Daniel and J.C. Knudsen (eds) *Mistrusting Refugees*, Berkeley, CA: University of California Press.

Muntarbhorn, V. (1990) *Refugee Problems and Developing Countries: Between Burden Sharing and Burden Shifting*, World Congress on Human Rights, New Delhi: School of International Studies, Jawaharlal Nehru University, India.

NACAB (National Association of Citizens Advice Bureau) (2002a) *Process Error: CAB Clients' Experience of the National Asylum Support Service*, London: CAB.

NACAB (2002b) *Distant Voices: CAB Clients' Experience of Continuing Problems with the National Asylum Support Service*, London: CAB.

NAO (National Audit Office) (2004) *Improving the Speed and Quality of Asylum Decisions*, Report by the Controller and Auditor General, London: The Stationery Office.

NCADC (National Coalition of Anti-Deportation Campaigns) various reports, various dates.

Newton, K. (2006) 'Social trust and politics', Paper presented at the ESRC Research Methods Festival, Oxford, 17-20 July.

Noll, G. (2003) 'Risky games? A theoretical approach to burden-sharing in the asylum field', *Journal of Refugee Studies*, vol 16, no 3, pp 236-52.

ODPM (Office of the Deputy Prime Minister) (2004) *Tackling Social Exclusion: Taking Stock and Looking to the Future*, London: Social Exclusion Unit.

Omidian, P.A. (1994) 'Life out of context: recording Afghan refugees' stories', in L.A. Camino and R.M. Krulfeld (eds) *Reconstructing Lives, Recapturing Meaning: Refugee Identity, Gender and Culture Change*, Basel, Switzerland: Gordon & Breach Publishers.

Pantazis, C. and Gordon, D. (1997) 'Poverty and health', in D. Gordon and C. Pantazis (eds) *Breadline Britain in the 1990s*, Aldershot: Ashgate.

Pantazis, C., Gordon, D. and Levitas, R. (2006) *Poverty and Social Exclusion in Britain: The Millennium Survey*, Bristol: The Policy Press.

Pasha, T. (2003) 'Support and benefits for asylum seekers: section 55 and human rights', Presentation at the conference 'Refugees, Asylum Seekers and Human Rights – the Balance Sheet So Far', Co-organised by the British Institute of Human Rights and JCWI, 11 November, King's College, London.

Payne, S. (1997) 'Poverty and mental health', in D. Gordon and C. Pantazis (eds) *Breadline Britain in the 1990s*, Aldershot: Ashgate.

Peach, C. (1996) 'Does Britain have ghettos?', *Transactions, Institute of British Geographers*, vol 21, no 1, pp 216-35.

Pearce, J.J., Hynes, P. and Bovarnick, S. (2009) *Breaking the Wall of Silence: Practitioner's Responses to the Trafficking of Children and Young People*, London: NSPCC Fresh Start and University of Bedfordshire.

Peckham, D., Wallace, E., Wilby, C. and Noble, J. (2004) *The Impact of Home Office Funded Services for Refugees: Findings from an Exploratory Survey of Clients*, Home Office Online Report 45/04, London: Home Office.

Peteet, J.M (1995) 'Transforming trust: dispossession and empowerment among palestinian refugees', in E.V. Daniel and J.C. Knudsen (eds) *Mistrusting Refugees*, Berkeley, CA: University of California Press.

Peutrell, R. (2003) 'Time to rekindle the spirit of activism', *New Start*, London.

Phillimore, J. and Goodson, L. (2006) 'Problem or opportunity? Asylum seekers, refugees, employment and social exclusion in deprived urban areas', *Urban Studies*, vol 43, no 10, pp 1715-36.

Pierson, J. (2002) *Tackling Social Exclusion*, London: Routledge and Community Care.

Putnam, R.D. (1993) *Making Democracy Work: Civic Traditions in Modern Italy*, Princeton, NJ: Princeton University Press.

Putnam, R.D. (2000) *Bowling Alone: The Collapse and Renewal of American Community*, New York, NY: Simon and Schuster.

Ramazanoglu, C. and Holland, J. (2002) *Feminist Methodology: Challenges and Choices*, London: Sage Publications.

Rapport, N. and Overing, J. (2000) *Social and Cultural Anthropology: The Key Concepts*, London and New York, NY: Routledge.

Reeskens, T. and Hooghe, M. (2008) 'Cross-cultural measurement equivalence of generalized trust: evidence from the European Social Survey 2002 and 2004, *Social Indicators Research*, vol 85, no 3, pp 515-32.

Refugee Action (1988) *Research into the Employment, Training and Educational Needs of Refugees from Vietnam in Leeds and Bradford*, Leeds: Manpower Services Commission and Refugee Action.

Refugee Action (1993) *The Unheard Community: A Look at the Housing Conditions and Needs of Refugees from Vietnam Living in London*, London: Community Development Foundation and Refugee Action.

Refugee Action (2003) *Section 55: Witness Statements*, London: Refugee Action, www.refugee-action.org.uk/

Refugee Council, statistics, various dates.

Refugee Council, *In-Exile*, various dates.

Refugee Council (1992) *Vietnamese Refugee Reception and Resettlement 1979-88*, London: Refugee Council.

Refugee Council (1998) *Briefing on the Government's Immigration & Asylum White Paper*, London: Refugee Council.

Refugee Council (1999) *Immigration & Asylum Act 1999: The New Support System for Asylum Seekers*, London: Refugee Council.

Refugee Council (1999) *Some Thoughts on Clusters*, London: Refugee Council.

Refugee Council (2000a) *The Immigration & Asylum Act 1999: What You Can Do Now...*, London: Refugee Council.

Refugee Council (2000b) *The Immigration & Asylum Act 1999*, London: Refugee Council.

Refugee Council (2001) *Refugee Council's Response to the New Asylum System Proposals*, London: Refugee Council, www.refugeecouncil.org.uk/infocentre/asylumpropos/proposals.htm

Refugee Council (2002a) *The Nationality, Immigration and Asylum Act 2002: Changes to the Asylum System in the UK*, London: Refugee Council.

Refugee Council (2002b) *Response to the Government's Consultation on the White Paper Safe Haven, Secure Borders*, London: Refugee Council, www.refugeecouncil.org.uk/infocentre/asylumprops/cons_response/regionalisation.htm

Refugee Council (2002c) *Government Announcement and Proposals since its White Paper on Asylum: A Summary*, London: Refugee Council.

Refugee Council (2002d) *Withdrawal of In-Country Asylum Support*, Briefing, London: Refugee Council.

Refugee Council (2002e) *Dispersal Statistics*, London: Refugee Council.

Refugee Council (2002f) *Asylum by Numbers: An Analysis of Available Asylum Data from 1985 to 2000*, London: Refugee Council.

Refugee Council (2003a) *Update: Withdrawal of In-country Asylum Support*, Briefing, London: Refugee Council.

Refugee Council (2003b) *Dispersal Statistics*, London: Refugee Council.

Refugee Council (2004a) *Section 55 – One Year On: The Real Impact of Denying Support to Destitute Asylum Applicants*, London: Refugee Council.

Refugee Council (2004b) *Overview of the NASS System*, Training notes, London: Refugee Council.

Refugee Council (2004c) *Hungry and Homeless: The Impact of the Withdrawal of State Support on Asylum Seekers, Refugee Communities and the Voluntary Sector*, London: Refugee Council.

Refugee Council and DH (Department of Health) (2003) *Caring for Dispersed Asylum Seekers: A Resource Pack*, London: Refugee Council.

Refugee Council et al (2003a) *Joint Statement on the Withdrawal of Asylum Support for In-country Applicants*, London: Refugee Council, Shelter, Amnesty International UK, Asylum Rights Campaign, CRISIS, JCORE, JCWI, Maternity Alliance, Medication Foundation for the Care of Victims of Torture, Migrant Helpline, Oxfam, Refugee Action and Refugee Arrivals Project.

Reilly, R. (1996) *Towards a Co-Ordinated Strategy: The Voluntary Sector Response to the Withdrawal of Social Security Benefits from Asylum Seekers*, London: Catholic Diocese of Westminster.

Reynell, J. (1989) *Political Pawns: Refugees on the Thai-Kampuchean Border*, Oxford: Oxfam.

Richmond, A.H. (1994a) 'Reactive migration: sociological perspectives on refugee movements', *The Journal of Refugee Studies*, vol 6, no 1, pp 7-24.

Richmond, A.H. (1994b) *Global Apartheid: Refugees, Racism and New World Order*, Oxford: Oxford University Press.

Richmond, A.H. (2002) 'Social exclusion: belonging and not belonging in the world system', *Refuge*, vol 21, no 1, pp 40-8.

Richmond, A.H. (2005) 'Citizenship, naturalization and asylum: the case of Britain', *Refuge*, vol 22, no 2, pp 59-66.

Robinson, D. and Reeve, K. (2006) *Experiences of New Immigration at the Neighbourhood Level*, York: Joseph Rowntree Foundation.

Robinson, V. (1986) *Transients, Settlers and Refugees: Asians in Britain*, Oxford: Clarendon Press.

Robinson, V. (1993a) 'Marching into the middle classes? The long-term resettlement of East African Asians in the UK', *Journal of Refugee Studies*, vol 6, no 3, pp 230-47.

Robinson, V. (1993b) 'North and south: resettling Vietnamese refugees in Australia and the UK', in R. Black and V. Robinson (eds) *Geography and Refugees: Patterns and Processes of Change*, London: Belhaven Press.

Robinson, V. (1998) 'The importance of information in the resettlement of refugees in the UK', *Journal of Refugee Studies*, vol 2, no 2, pp 146-59.

Robinson, V. (2002) '"Doing research" with refugees and asylum seekers', *Swansea Geographer*, vol 37, pp 61-7.

Robinson, V. (2003a) *Spreading the 'Burden'? A Review of Policies to Disperse Asylum Seekers and Refugees*, Bristol: The Policy Press.

Robinson, V. (2003b) 'An evidence base for future policy: reviewing UK resettlement policy', Presentation at the conference, 'Listening to the Evidence: The Future of UK Resettlement, London, 6 February.

Robinson, V. and Coleman, C. (2000) 'Lessons learned? A critical review of the government program to resettle Bosnian quota refugees in the United Kingdom', *International Migration Review*, vol 34, no 4, pp 1217-44.

Robinson, V. and Hale, S. (1989) *The Geography of Vietnamese Secondary Migration in the UK*, Coventry: ESRC Centre for Research in Ethnic Relations.

Rothstein, B. and Kumlin, S. (2005) *Making and Breaking Social capital: The Impact of Welfare State Institutions in Comparative Political Studies*, London: Sage.

Rutter, J. (1998) *Refugee Education: Mapping the Field*, Stoke-on-Trent: Trentham Books.

Rutter, J. (2003) *Working with Refugee Children*, York: Joseph Rowntree Foundation.

Sales, R. (2002) 'The deserving and the undeserving? Refugees, asylum seekers and welfare in Britain', *Critical Social Policy*, vol 22, no 3, pp 456-78.

Sales, R. (2005) 'Secure borders, safe havens: a contradiction in terms?', *Ethnic and Racial Studies*, vol 28, no 3, pp 445-62.

Sales, R. (2007) *Understanding Immigration and Refugee Policy: Contradictions and Continuities*, Bristol: The Policy Press.

Sales, R. and Hynes, P. (2004) *In and Against the State Again? The Voluntary Sector and Refugees in the UK*, London: Middlesex University.

Salford Housing and Urban Studies Unit (2004) *Ethical Guidelines Agreed by the Membership of the 2002-2004 ESRC Seminar Series on 'Eliciting the Views of Refugee People Seeking Asylum'*, Salford: University of Salford.

Sanderson, I. (2002) 'Making sense of "what works": evidence based policy making as instrumental rationality?', *Public Policy and Administration*, vol 17, no 3, pp 61-75.

Scholte, J.A. (2004) 'Defining globalization', Workshop on 'Dissecting Globalization', Venice International University, San Servolo, 21-22 July.

Schuster, L. (2003) *The Use and Abuse of Political Asylum in Britain and Germany*, London: Frank Cass.

Schuster, L. (2004) *The Exclusion of Asylum Seekers in Europe*, Working Paper no 1, Oxford: Centre on Migration, Policy and Society (COMPAS), University of Oxford.

Schuster, L. (2005a) 'A sledgehammer to crack a nut: deportation, detention and dispersal in Europe', *Social Policy and Administration*, vol 39, no 6, pp 606-21.

Schuster, L. (2005b) *The Realities of a New Asylum Paradigm*, Working Paper no 20, Oxford: Centre on Migration, Policy and Society (COMPAS), University of Oxford.

Scott, J. (1991) *Social Network Analysis: A Handbook*, London: Sage Publications.

Scott, J.C. (1985) *Weapons of the Weak: Everyday Forms of Peasant Resistance*, Yale, CT: Yale University Press.

Sen, A. (1992) *Inequality Reexamined*, Oxford: Clarendon Press.

Sen, A. (1999) *Development as Freedom*, Oxford: Oxford University Press.

Sen, A. (2006) *Identity and Violence: The Illusion of Destiny*, New York, NY: W.W. Norton.

Sepulveda, L. (2006) *Refugees, New Arrivals and Enterprise: Their Contribution and Constrains*, Draft report of early results prepared for Small Business Service, London: Department of Trade and Industry.

SEU (Social Exclusion Unit) (1999) *Report by the Unpopular Housing Action Team*, London: Department of the Environment, Transport and the Regions on behalf of the Office of the Deputy Prime Minister.

SEU (2001) *A New Commitment to Neighbourhood Renewal: National Strategy and Action Plan*, London: Cabinet Office.

SEU (2002) *Tackling Social Exclusion: Taking Stock and Looking to the Future – Emerging Findings*, London: SEU/Office of the Deputy Prime Minister.

Siisiäinen, M. (2000) 'Two concepts of social capital: Bourdieu vs. Putnam', Paper presented at the ISTR Fourth International Conference 'The Third Sector: For What and For Whom?', Trinity College, Dublin, Ireland, 5-8 July.

Sim, D. (2000) 'Housing inequalities and minority ethnic groups', in I. Anderson and D. Sim (eds) *Social Exclusion and Housing: Context and Challenges*, London: Chartered Institute of Housing.

Singh, G. (2003) 'Remembering and forgetting local history in Leicester', Paper prepared for the conference 'Immigration, History and Memory in Britain', De Montfort University, Leicester, September.

Skultans, V. (2005) 'Displacement and the intensification of culture: Latvian refugees in post-war Germany', Paper presented at the conference 'Displacement: Global Dynamics and Gendered Patterns', Centre for Women and Gender Research, University of Bergen, Norway, October.

Smith, L.T. (1999) *Decolonzing Methodologies: Research and Indigenous People*, London: Zed Books.

Smyth, G. (2005) 'Multilingual conferencing: one city's response to educating pupils from asylum seeking families', *Dve domovini*, vol 22, pp 21-8.

Solomos, J. (2003) *Race and Racism in Britain*, Basingstoke: Palgrave Macmillan.

Squire, V. (2009) *The Exclusionary Politics of Asylum*, Basingstoke: Palgrave Macmillan.

Srinivasan, S. (1994) 'An overview of research into refugee groups in Britain during the 1990s', Paper prepared for 4th International Research and Advisory Panel Conference, Somerville College, Oxford, January.

Stansfield, R. (2001) *Another Country, Another City*, Nottingham: Nottingham Asylum Seekers.

Stewart, E. (2004) 'Deficiencies in UK asylum data: practical and theoretical challenges', *Journal of Refugee Studies*, vol 17, no 1, pp 29-49.

Temple, B. (1997) 'Watch your tongue: issues in translation and cross-cultural research', *Sociology*, vol 31, no 3, pp 607-18.

Temple, B. (2002) 'Crossed wires: interpreters, translators and bilingual workers in cross-language research', *Qualitative Health Research*, vol 12, no 6, pp 844-54.

Temple, B. and Young, A. (2004) 'Qualitative research and translation dilemmas', *Qualitative Research*, vol 4, no 2, pp 161-78.

Temple, B. (2004) 'Ghost writers: using biographical methods across languages', in P. Chamberlayne, J. Bornat and U. Apitzsch (eds) *Biographical Methods and Professional Practice*, Bristol: The Policy Press.

Temple, B. and Moran, R. (2005) *Learning to Live Together*, Salford and York: University of Salford and Joseph Rowntree Foundation.

Temple, B. and Moran, R. (2006) *Doing Research with Refugees*, Bristol: The Policy Press.

The Guardian (2001) 'Welcome to Britain: a special investigation into asylum and immigration', June.

The Guardian (2003) 'Rape, hunger and homelessness', 1 November.

Thiara, R.K. and Gill, A.K. (2010) *Violence against Women in South Asian Communities: Issues for Policy and Practice*, London: Jessica Kingsley Publishers.

Thielemann, E.R. (2003a) 'Editorial introduction', *Journal of Refugee Studies*, vol 16, no 3, pp 225-35.

Thielemann, E.R. (2003b) 'Between interests and norms: explaining burden-sharing in the European Union', *Journal of Refugee Studies*, vol 16, no 3, pp 253-73.

Thomas, W.I. and Znaniecki, F. (1918) *The Polish Peasant in Europe and America*, Chicago, IL: Chicago University Press.

Thrift, N. (2006) 'Researching "place"', Conference presentation, ESRC Research Methods Festival, Oxford, 17-20 July.

Togeby, L. (2004) 'It depends ... how organisational participation affects political participation and social trust among second-generation immigrants in Denmark', *Journal of Ethnic and Migration Studies*, vol 30, no 3, pp 509-28.

Tomlins, R., Johnson, M.R.D. and Owen, D. (2002) 'The resource of ethnicity in the housing careers and preferences of the Vietnamese communities in London', *Housing Studies*, vol 17, no 3, pp 505-19.

Tonkiss, F. (2004) 'Trust and social capital, in J. Franklin (ed) *Politics, Trust and Networks: Social Capital in Critical Perspective*, London: South Bank University.

Tuitt, P. (1996) *False Images: The Law's Construction of the Refugee*, London: Pluto Press.

Turner, V. (1967) *The Forest of Symbols*, Ithaca, NY: Cornell University Press.

Turner, V. (1969) *The Ritual Process: Structure and Anti-Structure*, London: Routledge and Kegan Paul.

Turton, D. (2003) *Refugees, Forced Resettlers and 'Other Forced Migrants': Towards a Unitary Study of Forced Migration*, New Issues in Refugee Research, Working Paper no 94, Geneva, Switzerland: Evaluation and Policy Analysis Unit, UNHCR.

Turton, D. (2004) *The Meaning of Place in a World of Movement: Lessons from Long-Term Field Research in Southern Ethiopia*, Working Paper no 18, Oxford: Refugee Studies Centre, University of Oxford.

UNHCR (United Nations High Commissioner for Refugees) (1996) *Handbook on Voluntary Repatriation*, Geneva: International Protection.

UNHCR (2000) *The State of the World's Refugees: Fifty Years of Humanitarian Action*, Oxford: Oxford University Press.

UNHCR (2002) *Statistical Yearbook 2001: Refugees, Asylum Seekers and Other Persons of Concern – Trends in Displacement, Protection and Solutions*, Geneva: UNHCR.

van Gennep, A. (1960) *The Rites of Passage*, London: Routledge & Kegan Paul.

van Hear, N. (1993) 'Editorial Introduction to the Ugandan Asian Theme Papers', *Journal of Refugee Studies*, vol 6, no 3, pp 226-9.

van Hear, N. (1993) 'Mass expulsion of minorities: an overview', *Journal of Refugee Studies*, vol 6, no 3, pp 274-85.

van Hear, N. (2004) *I Went as Far as My Money Would Take Me: Conflict, Forced Migration and Class*, Working Paper no 6, Oxford: Centre on Migration, Policy and Society, University of Oxford.

Vertovec, S. (1999) 'Conceiving and researching transnationalism', *Ethnic and Racial Studies*, vol 22, no 2, pp 445-62.

Vertovec, S. (2006) *The Emergence of Super-Diversity in Britain*, Working Paper no 25, Oxford: Centre on Migration, Policy and Society (COMPAS), University of Oxford.

Voutira, E. and Harrell-Bond, B.E. (1995) 'In search of the locus of trust: the social world of the refugee camp', in E.V. Daniel and J.C. Knudsen (eds) *Mistrusting Refugees*, Berkeley, CA: University of California Press.

Waldron, S. (1987) 'Blaming the refugees', *Refugee Issues*, vol 3, no 3, pp 1-7.

Walton-Roberts, M. (2004) *Regional Immigration and Dispersal: Lessons from Small- and Medium-Sized Urban Centres in British Columbia*, Research on Immigration and Integration in the Metropolis, Working Paper no 04-03, Metropolis, Canada: Simon Fraser University and The University of British Columbia.

Ward, K. (2004) *Key Issues: UK Asylum Law and Process*, ICAR Navigation Guide, London: ICAR, www.icar.org.uk/res/nav/ng002/ng002-01.html

Willems, R. (2003) 'Embedding the refugee experience: forced migration and social networks in Dare es Salaam, Tanzania', PhD dissertation, University of Florida.

Wilson, R. (2001) *Dispersed: A Study of services for Asylum Seekers in West Yorkshire, December 1999 – March 2001*, York: Joseph Rowntree Foundation.

Woube, E. (2002) '"Driftback" to London', Conference presentation, London Refugee Housing Conference, HACT, Greater London Authority (GLA), London, 4 November.

Wren, K. (2007) 'Supporting asylum seekers and refugees in Glasgow: the role of multi-agency networks', *Journal of Refugee Studies*, vol 20, no 3, pp 391-413.

Wyatt, A. (2002) 'Evidence based policy making: the view from a centre', *Public Policy and Administration*, vol 17, no 3, pp 12-28.

Young, J. (1999) *The Exclusive Society*, London: Sage Publications.

Young, K. (2003) 'Rethinking "Evidence Based Policy"', Truncated version of a paper presented at the Social Policy Association conference, Middlesbrough, September.

Young, K., Ashby, D., Boaz, A. and Grayson, L. (2002) 'Social science and the evidence-based policy movement', *Social Policy & Society*, vol 1, no 3, pp 215-24.

Zetter, R. (1988) 'Refugees and refugees studies – a label and an agenda', *Journal of Refugee Studies*, vol 1, no 1, pp 1-6.

Zetter, R. (1999) 'International perspectives on refugee assistance', in Ager, A. (ed) *Refugees: Perspectives on the Experience of Forced Migration*, London and New York: Continuum.

Zetter, R. (2007) 'More labels, fewer refugees: remaking the refugee label in an era of globalization', *Journal of Refugee Studies*, vol 20, no 2, pp 172-92.

Zetter, R. and Pearl, M. (2000) 'The minority within the minority: refugee community organisations in the UK and the impact of restrictionism', *Journal of Ethnic and Migration Studies*, vol 26, no 4, pp 675-98.

Zetter, R., Griffiths, D., Ferretti, S. and Pearl, M. (2003) *An Assessment of the Impact of Asylum Policies in Europe 1990-2000*, Home Office Research Study 259, London: Home Office.

Zetter, R., Griffiths, D. and Sigona, N. (2005) 'Social capital or social exclusion? The impact of asylum seeker dispersal on UK refugee community organisations', *Community Development Journal*, vol 40, no 2, pp 169-81.

Zetter, R., Griffiths, D., Sigona, N., Flynn, D., Pasha, T. and Beynon, R. (2006) *Immigration, Social Cohesion and Social Capital: What are the Links?*, York: Joseph Rowntree Foundation.

Zetter, R., Pearl, M., Griffiths, D., Allender, P., Cairncross, L. and Robinson, V. (2002) *Dispersal: Facilitating Effectiveness and Efficiency – Final Report*, London: Home Office.

Zolberg, A. (1983) 'The Formation of New States as a Refugee Generating Process', *The Annals of the American Academy of Political and Social Science*, vol 467, no 1, pp 24-38.

Zolberg, A., Suhrke, A. and Aguayo, S. (1989) *Escape from Violence*, Oxford: Oxford University Press.

Index

Note: the letters *f*, *n* and *t* following page numbers denote information in figures, footnotes and tables respectively.